SHARED HOUSING
FOR THE
ELDERLY

Recent Titles in
Contributions to the Study of Aging

The Extreme Aged in America: A Portrait of an Expanding Population
Ira Rosenwaike, with the assistance of Barbara Logue

Old Age in a Bureaucratic Society: The Elderly, the Experts, and the State in
American History
David Van Tassel and Peter N. Stearns, editors

The Aged in Rural America
John A. Krout

Public Policy Opinion and the Elderly, 1952–1978
John E. Tropman

The Mirror of Time: Images of Aging and Dying
Joan M. Boyle and James E. Morriss

North American Elders: United States and Canadian Perspectives
Eloise Rathbone-McCuan and Betty Havens, editors

Hispanic Elderly in Transition: Theory, Research, Policy and Practice
Steven R. Applewhite, editor

Religion, Health, and Aging: A Review and Theoretical Integration
Harold George Koenig, Mona Smiley, and Jo Ann Ploch Gonzales

Philanthropy and Gerontology: The Role of American Foundations
Ann H. L. Sontz

Perceptions of Aging in Literature: A Cross-Cultural Study
Prisca von Dorotka Bagnell and Patricia Spencer Soper, editors

Residential Care for the Elderly: Critical Issues in Public Policy
Sharon A. Baggett

Senior Centers in America
John A. Krout

SHARED HOUSING
FOR THE
ELDERLY

Edited by
Dale J. Jaffe

CONTRIBUTIONS TO THE STUDY OF AGING, NUMBER 15

Erdman B. Palmore, *Series Adviser*

GREENWOOD PRESS
New York • Westport, Connecticut • London

Library of Congress Cataloging-in-Publication Data

Shared housing for the elderly / edited by Dale J. Jaffe.
    p.   cm.—(Contributions to the study of aging, ISSN
0732–085X ; no. 15)
    Bibliography: p.
    Includes index.
    ISBN 0–313–26284–5 (lib. bdg. : alk. paper)
    1. Aged—Housing—United States.   2. Shared housing—United
States.   I. Jaffe, Dale J.   II. Series.
HD7287.92.U54S46   1989
363.5′946—dc20   89–11938

British Library Cataloguing in Publication Data is available.

Library of Congress Catalog Card Number: 89–11938
ISBN: 0–313–26284–5
ISSN: 0732–085X

First published in 1989

Greenwood Press, Inc.
88 Post Road West, Westport, Connecticut 06881

Printed in the United States of America

The paper used in this book complies with the
Permanent Paper Standard issued by the National
Information Standards Organization (Z39.48–1984).

10 9 8 7 6 5 4 3 2 1

Contents

Part III: Case Studies

Tables and Figure

TABLES

FIGURE

Preface

There has been a great deal of interest in the concept of shared housing in the 1980s and tremendous growth in the number of shared housing programs in the United States. As those working in this area have struggled to keep existing programs alive and have advocated the expansion of this living arrangement, research and evaluation have become increasingly important and visible components of the shared housing movement. Although much of the earliest research took the form of program evaluations with the goal of answering some very concrete and practical questions posed by funding agencies and service providers, it was not long before academic researchers began to consider the homesharing form through more analytical and theoretical lenses. Until now, the products of these studies were mostly unpublished and difficult to access. Consequently, it seems timely and useful to bring together in one place a number of essays related to the homesharing phenomenon. All have been written expressly for this book.

Many of the contributors to this volume found themselves in each other's company at several professional meetings during the mid–1980s. Finally, in 1987, I decided that the time had come to attempt to organize a symposium devoted exclusively to the topic of shared housing at the Annual Meeting of the Gerontological Society of America in Washington, D.C. To my delight, all whom I approached accepted the invitation to present findings from their studies, and the idea for a published collection of papers emerged.

At that symposium, academics had the opportunity to meet shared housing practitioners including staff from the National Shared Housing Resource Center (NSHRC) in Philadelphia, a nonprofit agency devoted to information dissemination and technical assistance in the area of shared housing. This was an important event because it was the more formal contacts between the NSHRC and programs, practitioners, and researchers nationwide that permitted me to identify and include reports of research activities across the country that were not represented among our informal group at the symposium. Thus what follows represents the result of both formal and informal linkages among individual researchers, practitioners, and organizations in the burgeoning elderly shared housing network.

Given this background, the goals of the volume are twofold. First, I hope to encourage a more analytical treatment of the homesharing phenomenon in the future. Investigations of new phenomena are often initially descriptive, but after a certain amount of descriptive research has been accomplished, it is important for both theory construction and practice to make something more of the discreet descriptions. In this collection, we have attempted to do just that by looking for connections and relationships among different levels of analysis—the individuals involved in homesharing, the organizations that create homesharing matches, and the communities in which these organizations operate.

In providing a sampling of the first decade of research on shared housing, a second goal is to generate hypotheses and stimulate ideas for research and program development in the 1990s. The next wave of research will need to include larger scale comparative studies if the knowledge base in this area is to expand and be linked effectively with other substantive areas in the field of service delivery systems and, in particular, long-term care. We hope that future investigators will benefit from the information contained in the detailed case studies and regionwide perspectives offered in this book.

The contributors come from a wide range of backgrounds—both academic and nonacademic. Individuals holding faculty appointments in departments of sociology, psychology, social work, policy studies, urban planning, and gerontology are among the authors as are program founders, directors, and staff persons and private consultants and policy-makers. Many individual chapters are coauthored by individuals from different disciplines, and we hope that this multidisciplinary flavor is evident to all who read the book.

The publication of this book would not have been possible without the assistance and support of many individuals. Each of the 22 authors has his or her own group of significant others who helped make his or her contribution possible. I am confident in stating on behalf of the group as a whole, however, that we owe a collective debt of gratitude to the program staff people who responded to our questions and who opened the doors and records of their programs to us. Without this collaborative effort and partnership between researcher and practitioner, our knowledge would have been severely limited. We also must acknowledge the many homesharing participants who told us their stories about shared living and provided many of us with the grist for our theoretical mills. Finally, we express our gratitude to Erdman Palmore, editor of the series in which this book is published, for his support of the project from the very start, and to Loomis Mayer, editor of social and behavioral sciences at Greenwood Press, and his predecessor, Mary Sive, for their helpful suggestions and hard work on our behalf.

DALE J. JAFFE

Part I
INTRODUCTORY PERSPECTIVES

1

An Introduction to Elderly Shared Housing Research in the United States

Dale J. Jaffe

Although shared living arrangements between individuals unrelated by blood have existed in American society since the birth of the republic (Modell and Hareven, 1973), it is only in recent decades that such arrangements have been chosen by substantial numbers of older adults. In contrast to historically common types of shared living, such as adult-oriented forms of the past that involved a family's taking in a boarder to the economic benefit of each, a less commonly found type has recently emerged. In the more recent embodiment of this concept, an older adult who needs various forms of assistance to remain a relatively independent occupant of his or her home or who seeks companionship or assistance with living expenses (homeprovider) enters into a formally sanctioned exchange relationship. The home is, thereby, shared with an unrelated, usually younger, person who agrees to provide assistance or companionship in exchange for inexpensive living quarters (homeseeker).

The demography of shared living has been transformed by decades of broad social and economic change, and the growing awareness by formal social service bureaucracies during the 1970s that shared living could be a key component in community-based long-term care systems has added substantial impetus to the increase in the number of individuals who are involved in elderly shared housing arrangements and programs whose goal it is to recruit and match such individuals. The formal sanctioning of exchange through the involvement of an agency in the establishment of the arrangement distinguishes this form of shared housing, called agency-assisted shared housing (Schreter, 1986), from shared living arrangements in which an agency plays no role and the exchange is initiated and negotiated privately.

THE STUDY OF AGENCY-ASSISTED SHARED HOUSING

Perhaps the first study of elderly shared housing was conducted in Los Angeles County by Stephen McConnell and Carolyn Usher (1980). Based on interviews with 110 middle-aged and older homeowners, the investigators concluded that about one-third of the sample, or 34% of those interviewed, held a generally positive attitude toward the idea of homesharing. This finding was significant because it demonstrated the feasibility of the shared housing concept. By distinguishing between those who held positive and negative attitudes, McConnell and Usher were able to provide a basis for the initial marketing of shared housing programs nationwide. They found that those with positive attitudes were more likely to be living in large houses, reside in high crime areas, be black rather than white, be in the young-old as opposed to the old-old category, and generally be in a low-income group and in poor health. In addition, when supplemented with a sample of college students from three universities, data suggested that students were more positively inclined to live with older adults than older adults with students.

It was really with the publication of David Pritchard's analysis of the shared housing program of Mid-City Senior Enterprises in San Diego (1983) and Carol Schreter's study of shared housing in Kensington, Maryland (1984, 1986), that detailed treatments of agency-assisted shared housing appeared. Both offered in-depth analyses of the clients in their respective programs, looking for patterns in the types of individuals who were drawn to these particular shared housing arrangements. In addition, for the first time, both investigators considered data on match dissolution. This was a significant emphasis because it foreshadowed a major current research question by implicitly raising the question of what makes a good match.

As Pritchard and Schreter were publishing the results of their studies, the first comprehensive "how-to" manual was produced and disseminated by the National Shared Housing Resource Center in Philadelphia. Written by Leah Dobkin (1983), the manual described in great detail the nuts and bolts of establishing and running a homesharing program. Shortly thereafter, Sheila Peace and Charlotte Nusberg (1984) offered their synthesis of the existing knowledge on shared housing. Drawing from unpublished evaluations, the McConnell and Usher study, and information provided by the Shared Housing Resource Center, Peace and Nusberg offered a broad overview of typical program operations. The section on agency-assisted shared housing included discussions of organizational models, funding, staffing, and program functions (e.g., intake, matching, follow-up).

By 1983 several more intensive case studies of shared housing were underway. Most notable in terms of the eventual dissemination of results were the evaluation of Independent Living's Homeshare Program in Madison, Wisconsin, by Elizabeth Howe, Barbara Robins, and Dale Jaffe (1984); the evaluation of Project HOME in Burlington, Vermont, by Alfred Fengler and Nicholas Danigelis (1984); and the evaluation of Share-a-Home in Minneapolis/St. Paul, Minnesota, by Timothy Robinson, Richard Martin, and Martin Shafto (1983). All three evaluations had the financial backing of major foundations (Gulf + Western Foundation for Madison; Andrus Foundation for Burlington; McKnight Foundation for the Twin Cities), and this allowed for a depth of analysis that previously had not been feasible. With these research efforts, detailed organizational analyses of the structure and functioning of programs were coupled with intensive examinations of match characteristics and dynamics. When the Madison data were supplemented with additional national survey data, it became possible to look at elderly shared housing through a more analytical lens and specify a typology of shared housing programs (Jaffe and Howe, 1988) and a typology of homesharing matches (Jaffe and Howe, 1988; Jaffe, 1989; Howe and Jaffe in Chapter 8 in this volume). Furthermore, the elaboration of the match typology made it possible to improve program operations by providing a rationale for pairing specific case-management strategies and certain kinds of matches (Jaffe and Howe, in press).

The dissemination of this research and the continued growth of elderly shared housing services have, in turn, spawned a more recent wave of research. Some of it has a more applied flavor and deals with issues such as cost-effectiveness (Dobkin, 1985) and tailoring shared housing programs to the needs of particular population subgroups (Schreter and Turner, 1986). Other analyses have sought to test hypotheses or generate theories about programs and matches. Included in this volume are essays of both types. Before introducing the contents of this collection, however, let us consider some of the more salient issues that have emerged from nearly a decade of research on elderly shared housing.

THE THEME OF THE BOOK

If there is a major theme that one can identify after considering the research and practice literature on elderly shared housing, including that which is found in this book, it must be the contradiction between the enormous potential of shared housing as a partial antidote to a number of individual and social problems and the significant barriers to the growth and development of this living option in the United States.

Individuals are attracted to shared housing arrangements by the promise of an overall reduction of each person's individual housing expense. The cost of housing in most areas of the United States alone suggests that homesharing be an option that could meet the needs of many individuals within several subgroups of the society. The elderly and disabled, specifically, recognize the potential of shared housing as a vehicle for the provision of services or assistance that would enable them to remain in their communities even with varying degrees of functional impairment. For some, the security and companionship that shared housing offers is a sufficiently attractive feature to draw them into this type of arrangement. In sum, the need for inexpensive living, assistance with daily activities, and companionship that homesharing can address make it an option that has potential appeal to a broad segment of American society.

Not only can homesharing meet this array of needs, but it can do so in ways that are consistent with the current thrust of American social policy. It is virtually costless in terms of public dollars and represents a creative embodiment of the ideology of solving individual problems through the strengthening of individual, informal social support systems. In addition, the heavy emphasis on volunteer efforts that characterizes many agency-assisted homesharing programs fits in nicely with a broader public policy agenda of problem solving through private, voluntaristic means.

The most significant element inhibiting the growth of homesharing is an American value system that places a premium on privacy, autonomy, and self-sufficiency. For the most part, Americans do not want to live with individuals unrelated by blood, marriage, or romance, unless circumstances offer them little choice. As Jaffe has shown elsewhere (1989), in the case of elderly individuals who can no longer live by themselves at home, homesharing is viewed as the least objectionable option among a group of generally undesirable possibilities (i.e., having paid help at home at exorbitant cost, moving in with children, or going to nursing homes or retirement complexes). In general, people do not consider shared housing until circumstances or events provide a good deal of pressure for them to consider deviant alternatives.

Despite such barriers, and others described by Joyce Mantell and Mary Gildea in Chapter 2, shared housing has continued to grow in this country, and it is against this backdrop of opposing forces (needs versus barriers) that shared housing practitioners conduct their work, that homesharing participants attempt to get along, and that the study of shared housing has captured the imaginations and occupied the energies of an increasing number of investigators. Many of the chapters in this collection describe a reality that, to varying degrees, reflects just this tension.

THE SELF-FULFILLING PROPHECY IN SHARED HOUSING

Although the chapters in this book emphasize different aspects of the shared housing phenomenon, together they demonstrate the dynamics and products of a contradiction between needs and barriers. Presumably, because of a certain skepticism about the potential market for homesharing, given the American obsession with privacy and private property, potential sources of funding for homesharing programs to date have been cautious in making financial commitments. This hesitance, more than any other single factor, creates a self-fulfilling prophecy in which programs tend to remain small and unstable. As a result, they are often unable to do the work necessary to bring the vision of the homesharing concept to fruition.

What is the mechanism by which this self-fulfilling prophecy is fulfilled?

Because of limited funding, programs initially are small. They are often offshoots of existing social service programs and have few full-time members and small budgets; frequently, they are reliant on a bevy of volunteer workers to do much of the day-to-day work. The almost universal sentiment among program administrators regarding the inhibitory effect that charging fees to clients would produce reinforces the dependency of the program on one or a few limited sources of funding.

Starting out small puts a great deal of pressure on the paid staff of a homesharing program. Early success of the program is crucial in terms of keeping volunteers involved and committed, as Alfred Fengler and Nicholas Danigelis argue (Chapter 9), and for the effectiveness of the future marketing of the program, as Norma Maatta and her associates found in rural Pennsylvania (Chapter 4).

In practice, early success means having successful matches. Although there are many problems with equating match success with match longevity and interpersonal closeness (see Dale Jaffe and Christopher Wellin in Chapter 13), these characteristics are almost irresistible to the program staff as indicators of success. Concrete examples of warm, stable relationships keep volunteers excited about the homesharing concept and are used by staff to market the idea to potential clients who are uneasy about the prospect of living with a stranger. Unfortunately, given the context of scarce resources, the odds are that, early on at least, the program will have relatively few such success stories to relate.

The reason for this lack of success has to do with a role conflict that is exacerbated by the limited funding of programs and the time-consuming nature of effective matchmaking. The small staffs that administer homesharing programs find themselves torn between service activities, such as interviewing, matching, and follow-up, and administrative activities, such as fund raising and marketing. The dynamics of this struggle are perhaps best illustrated in Fengler and Danigelis's longitudinal study of Burlington's Project HOME. Essentially, both sets of activities are critical to the long-term viability of the program, and neither can be done as well as is desired given the typical level of funding of most programs. As Pritchard found in his survey of California homesharing program administrators, 68% of his respondents indicated that current levels of funding were insufficient to reach mandated goals.

At present, the technology of matchmaking is labor intense. Many contributors to this volume acknowledge the importance of having a large pool of applicants to draw from when trying to find a suitable partner for a homesharing client. The larger the pool, the greater the likelihood that the staff can find a partner with specific characteristics and, consequently, the more likely that clients will be satisfied initially with their housemates. Matchmaking, however, is time consuming when the pools of homeproviders and homeseekers are large. Applicants must be screened, home visits arranged, and files continuously updated and consulted when the staff seek to make a match with a particular client.

Ironically, large pools are rare in the early days of a program, but they are necessary to create successful matches, which, in turn, are the best marketing tools in the recruitment of new clients.

The data about matches themselves in the following chapters also show why matchmaking is such a time-consuming endeavor. Jon Pynoos and Arlyne June found that, in San Jose, client satisfaction is higher in matches with great amounts of exchange between homesharers than in matches with little exchange (see Chapter 10). Howe and Jaffe found that, in Madison, instrumental needs (i.e., needs for assistance with activities of daily living) are better met than expressive ones (e.g., companionship) (see Chapter 8). Jaffe and Wellin noted that, in Milwaukee, problems are more likely to occur in matches in which companionship is the main exchange commodity than when instrumental tasks are exchanged (see Chapter 13). Together, these findings suggest that successful matches may more often evolve in situations involving elderly clients who are somewhat frail and who, therefore, require assistance of various sorts than in situations in which companionship is the dominant need. Yet it is clear that matchmaking with frail clients requires significantly more staff time in establishing suitability, negotiating exchange agreements, and follow-up to minimize the potential of exploitation of one party by the other within the match.

Consider, too, Howe and Jaffe's contention (Chapter 8) that the greater the service needs of the client, the less likely that homesharing can be the only buffer to institutionalization, and one could conclude that the most successful matches may require even more staff time to link homesharing with other community-based services. Finally, the fact that most programs are intergenerational means that staff must invest time and effort in the recruitment of multiple types of homeseekers, adding to the already significant time demands of successful matchmaking. It appears that the very activities that increase the likelihood of successful matches and, thus, constitute the fuel for the successful institutionalization of a program are rendered problematic by the very limited funding base that characterizes its birth. In short, initial limited resources make growth and stability difficult and reinforce the original assumption among funding sources and gerontological experts alike that agency-assisted shared housing has limited appeal and is fraught with nearly insurmountable difficulties.

SOME KEYS TO SUCCESS

Some programs, however, do grow and actually become large. In their analysis of the Wichita program in Chapter 12, Janet Underwood and Connie Wulf argue that the keys to growth and stability include multiple sources of funding, integration of the homesharing program within an existing social service network, and support of local media. The media and existing referral networks of other diverse service professionals are crucial as resources in the recruitment of potential clients to homesharing programs.

A diversified funding base shields a program from the potentially disastrous effect of the fiscal retrenchment of one major contributor, and the best example of a diversified funding base for homesharing can be found in California. In Chapter 5 Pritchard outlines the structure of public and private funding in California. Federal money from the Department of Housing and Urban Development comes to California municipalities in the form of block grants, which are a common source of funding for homesharing programs. Other federal funds from the Administration on Aging are available through local Area Agencies on Aging. California, itself, funds homesharing programs through its Department of Housing and Community Development. In addition, there are private corporate funds, foundation grants, and individual donations that constitute the funding base of programs. State government, however, can go beyond a reactive role and can vigorously promote the shared housing concept. Statewide initiatives in both California and Michigan demonstrate the potential role of state government; in both cases, the state funds not only program operations but also a separate entity to provide technical assistance to fledgling programs.

Until a program is able to secure a diversified funding base and solidify its relations with other agencies and institutions in the area, it is clear, as in similar endeavors in which resources are scarce, that the personal charisma of program directors is extremely important in keeping the programs afloat. Hard work, dedication, and a strong ideological commitment to the concept of shared housing are crucial. It may also help, as Fengler and Danigelis suggest in Chapter 9, for the director to have a growth-oriented, entrepreneurial approach to the job.

SHARED HOUSING PROGRAMS AND MATCHES

The concrete reality in which the tension between needs and barriers is manifest and in which the self-fulfilling prophecy is operative is shaped by a number of factors that may have little to do with the nature and needs of aged individuals in American society. Not all agency-assisted shared housing programs are structured in the same way and not all individual homesharing match experiences are similar. Taken together, the chapters in this book suggest that it is primarily regional and local economic conditions, the structure of the existing social service delivery system, and the social demography of a community that explain a good deal of the diversity in both program structure and individual client experience. The regional or local housing market, for example, a factor that is clearly linked to the economic prosperity or decline of an area, influences the relative emphasis of the homesharing program. If housing costs are high and the availability of low-priced or moderately priced housing low, it is likely that a shared housing program will be shaped by the goal of solving a housing problem. Such was the case in Burlington, Vermont, where Fengler and Danigelis (Chapter 9) report a 10% vacancy rate, and in Orange County, California, where Thuras (Chapter 11) notes that the median cost of a home is greater than $170,000, the rental vacancy rate is 2.1% and the waiting lists for government subsidized housing are long. In turn, individuals who are matched for homesharing in such environments are likely to have lives that are relatively separate from each other since none of the exchange commodities involve assistance with everyday activities that would encourage frequent interaction.

In other areas where housing shortages are less severe or where there are large numbers of functionally impaired elderly living in the community, the shared housing program may assume a supportive home-care orientation in which homesharing is seen as a means of offering home-based assistance to those who might otherwise be at risk for institutionalization. Furthermore, supportive home-care matches are likely to produce closer social relationships than arrangements based solely on housing needs, since the provision of human assistance involves intimacy. In most cases, however, the survival of the organization requires that the program be an amalgam of the housing and supportive home-care models with an emphasis on one or the other, depending on the circumstances in the community.

The economic health of a community can also affect the financial viability of a shared housing program. Many sources of both public and private support for shared housing programs require a commitment of local matching funds. Certainly, the size of a community and the vitality of its economic base can influence the availability of local sources of support.

Perhaps because of initial skepticism in many communities about whether or not homesharing will attract large pools of homeproviders or homeseekers, homesharing programs are almost always piggy-backed onto existing programs or are elements of larger consortia of programs and agencies. The chapters in this book describe in some detail a variety of organizational sponsorships of homesharing programs. Depending on the nature of the existing service network and the particular sponsor or consortium of sponsors, a program is likely to assume a certain flavor and structure. The homesharing program in Burlington started as part of a Retired Seniors Volunteer Program (RSVP) and thus drew on a large number of volunteers to staff the shared housing component. The program in the city of California in Pennsylvania, as described by Maatta and her associates (Chapter 4), was administered through the town's senior center, a strategy designed to address the reluctance of seniors to participate by emphasizing the program's link to the most trusted elderly oriented institution in town. Programs in Milwaukee and Madison, Wisconsin, were established in large agencies providing a variety of services to the elderly. Although this might have led these programs to focus on the elderly exclusively, it became clear early in their histories that it was not possible to serve only the elderly and still survive, as Robins and Howe also discovered in their national survey of program administrators (see Chapter 3).

Related to the factors of economic climate and delivery-system structure in shaping homesharing programs and matches is the social demography of the community. The relative health of a local economy and the richness and ability of the existing service structure to deal with the problems of aging or of economic dislocation influences the demographic profile of individuals who seek homesharing. Thuras notes how in parts of Orange County, California, the immigration of refugees from Vietnam has affected the demography of the homeseeker pool (see Chapter 11). In San Jose, where economic forces have produced growth and development in some areas and stagnation in others, homeseekers are often underemployed or unemployed workers or displaced homemakers. In college towns with a white-collar flavor, such as Madison, Wisconsin, and Burlington, Vermont, homeseekers are usually students seeking inexpensive living arrangements. In sum, whereas all programs grapple with the tension between needs and barriers, the similarities or differences in the ways in which they define their goals and conduct their activities and, consequently, the ways in which the lives of their clients are affected are shaped by local economic, demographic, and organizational realities.

THE PLAN OF THE BOOK

The arguments made in this chapter reflect a modest synthesis of the contents of the chapters that follow. Space limitations make it impossible to delineate and discuss all of the themes and interesting propositions about homesharing that one could generate through a careful reading of the volume. Each reader, whether a practitioner, policy-maker, researcher, or elderly individual, is invited to read on and to consider the contents within the context of his or her own unique perspective.

The remaining chapters in this part on introductory perspectives attempt to locate the shared housing phenomenon in a broader context. Mantell and Gildea consider the history and growth of shared housing in the United States and the benefits of and barriers to further expansion (see Chapter 2). Robins and Howe conduct an empirical investigation into what factors predict the emergence of a shared housing program in a community (see Chapter 3). Maatta and her associates discuss the particular problems of homesharing in a rural context (see Chapter 4).

The next section on regionwide perspectives offers comprehensive analyses of statewide or provincewide networks of homesharing programs. They include Pritchard's analysis of California programs (Chapter 5), Melanie Hwalek and Elizabeth Longley's presentation of state-sponsored programs in Michigan (Chapter 6), and David Spence's discussion of several programs in Ontario, Canada (Chapter 7).

The final section includes six case studies of specific agency-assisted homesharing programs. They include Project HOME in Burlington, Vermont (Chapter 9); the Homeshare Program in Madison, Wisconsin (Chapter 8); Share-A-Home in Milwaukee, Wisconsin, (Chapter 13); Project Match, in San Jose, California (Chapter 10); two programs in Orange County, California (Chapter 11); and Share-A-Home in Wichita, Kansas (Chapter 12). In each case the authors have attempted to provide a sense of the community context within which these programs operate, a sense of the organizational structure and dynamics of homesharing programs, and a sense of patterns in the homesharing experiences of clients. Each case study, however, has its own unique emphasis or slant on the shared housing phenomenon. Together, they represent the broadest array to date of different examples of homesharing as a social form and partial solution to many current problems of elderly and young alike.

REFERENCES

Dobkin, Leah. *Shared Housing for Older People: A Planning Manual for Match-Up Programs*. Philadelphia: National Shared Housing Resource Center, 1983.

———. "Homesharing Programs: Are They Cost-Effective?" *Generations*, Spring 1985, pp. 50–51.

Fenger, Alfred, and Danigelis, Nicholas. *The Shared Home: Evaluation of a Concept and Its Implementation*. Final Report to Andrus Foundation, 1984.

Howe, Elizabeth; Robins, Barbara; and Jaffe, Dale. *Evaluation of Independent Living's Homeshare Program*. Madison Independent Living, 1984.

Jaffe, Dale. *Caring Strangers: The Sociology of Intergenerational Homesharing*. Greenwich, Conn. JAI Press, 1989.

Jaffe, Dale, and Howe, Elizabeth. "Agency-Assisted Shared Housing: The Nature of Programs and Matches." *The Gerontologist* 28 (1988):318–24.

———. "Case Management for Homesharing." *Journal of Gerontological Social Work*, in press.

McConnell, Stephen R., and Usher, Carolyn E. *Intergenerational House Sharing*. Los Angeles: Andrus Gerontology Center, University of Southern California, 1980.

Modell, John, and Hareven, Tamara. "Urbanization and the Malleable Household: An Examination of Boarding and Lodging in American Families." *Journal of Marriage and the Family*, August 1973, pp. 467–79.

Peace, Sheila, and Nusberg, Charlotte. *Shared Living: A Viable Alternative for the Elderly?* Washington, D.C.: International Federation on Aging, 1984.

Pritchard, David. "The Art of Matchmaking: A Case Study in Shared Housing." *The Gerontologist* 23 (1983):174–79.

Robinson, Timothy; Martin, Richard; and Shafto, Martin. *Share-a-Home: Final Report*. Minneapolis: The McKnight Foundation, 1983.

Schreter, Carol. "Residents of Shared Housing." *Social Thought*, Winter 1984, pp. 30–38.

———. "Advantages and Disadvantages of Shared Housing." *Journal of Housing for the Elderly* 3 (1986):121–38.

Schreter, Carol, and Turner, Lloyd. "Sharing and Subdividing Private Market Housing." *The Gerontologist* 26 (1986):181–86.

2

Elderly Shared Housing in the United States

Joyce Mantell and Mary Gildea

Shared Housing is a living arrangement in which two or more unrelated people share a home or apartment to their mutual advantage. Each person has a private bedroom and shares common areas such as the kitchen and the living, dining, and sitting rooms. Shared housing for the elderly has had a rich and significant role in our housing past and, if recent trends continue, will be an integral and growing part of housing options for older adults well into the future. Shared housing has enjoyed recent popularity because it is an affordable way of providing for the basic human needs of shelter, companionship, and independence.

HISTORY

From the time of the cave dwellers, many of society's members have housed themselves in shared situations. Shared housing was a commonplace and accepted practice at the turn of the century in America. Between 10% and 12% of the population shared homes in nineteenth-century American cities. In some areas, such as Boston, that figure approached 25%.

Many of these shared living arrangements were an outgrowth of the Industrial Revolution, which brought an influx of workers from rural areas to the cities, and of the surge of immigrants arriving since 1850. On the American frontier, in towns and on farms, shared housing was not only acceptable, it frequently was a necessity. Shared living was the only answer for many people, given their limited incomes and the scarcity of rental housing.

Homesharing was so prevalent in nineteenth-century America and on into the early twentieth century that social historians John Modell and Tamara Hareven described the family of that era in terms quite different from today's definition: "the 19th century American family was an accommodating and flexible institution, as had been its 17th and 18th century predecessors. Lodging was one major rubric under which its biologically defined limits were breached, by an instrumental relationship, based on economic and service exchange'' (Modell and Hareven, 1973:468).

Available data indicate that the need for shared housing was particularly acute at transitional periods in the life cycle. Homes tended to open up for homesharing when the families' own children were moving away or when a spouse had recently died. Couples in their forties and fifties and single homeowners often entered the homesharing market to supplement lost income, to gain companionship, or to obtain help with chores. People transplanted from farms to cities, newly arrived immigrants, and young, unmarried people formed the largest portion of seekers of shared arrangements. Many of these homeseekers were in transition between family life and adulthood, unmarried, or starting a new job and wanting independence from the constraints of family life. The need for affordable and transitional housing always has been relatively constant; yet the prevalence of shared housing dropped dramatically through the 1950s and 1960s.

What had caused the change? According to Modell and Hareven (1973), several factors—social, political, and economic—had combined over the years to make shared housing less acceptable and less widespread. By the 1920s homesharing came to be viewed as belonging somewhat to the ''underside'' of society, linked as it was to immigrants and the working poor. Some housing reformers of the time saw shared housing as contributing to overcrowded and unsafe conditions and sought to discourage it. At the same time, progressive moralists believed, however unjustifiably, that shared housing was a threat to the ''properly organized family,'' which they believed was in danger of disintegration in face of the rapid modernization of the period. In response to these social and moral pressures, the United States became the only country to define *family* narrowly along biological lines. This specific definition of *family* was then incorporated into local zoning laws, which effectively limited the use of property in many areas and erected legal barriers to shared housing that persist today. By defining a *shared home* as a multifamily unit, shared housing was pushed out of its traditional stronghold in ''single-family'' neighborhoods.

Another blow was dealt to shared housing in the 1920s when a housing boom put home ownership within reach for many people. The economic hardships of the Depression forced many people into shared arrangements, but with the coming of the New Deal and its social programs, people began to look to the government for social supports. After World War II housing came to be seen as the responsibility of the public sector. The housing boom in the 1950s, the Great Society of the 1960s, and increased federal involvement in housing all decreased the use of shared housing. Yet even as the role of government agencies expanded, other changes were occurring that have served as catalysts to focus attention on shared housing in the 1970s and 1980s.

Between 1970 and 1980 the U.S. Census Bureau reported that 670,000 Americans over the age of 65 were sharing living quarters with nonrelatives—a 35%

increase in that 10-year period (Richards, 1986). It is likely that the 1990 census data will uncover a similarly sizeable, if not even greater, increase. In 1987 alone, the shared housing programs that responded to a Shared Housing Resource Center study (response rate was 54%) assisted 16,000 individuals, 36% of whom were elderly. The expansion of the shared housing movement is helping to repopularize a once familiar type of housing for the first time in nearly half a century.

Shared housing in the 1980s is the same concept as its nineteenth-century counterpart, but it now exists within a more formalized framework. Beginning with Hartford's Project Homeshare in 1953, formal shared housing programs have sprung up around the country. In 1980 Gray Panther activist Maggie Kuhn convened a conference in Philadelphia to address intergenerational housing concerns. One conclusion of the conference was that there was a need for an organization that would provide support for shared housing programs throughout the country. Several months later, the Shared Housing Resource Center was established. The center set for itself the goal of promoting the development of shared housing through service to government agencies, shared housing programs, and consumers.

DEFINING THE SHARED HOUSING PROGRAM

There is now some form of shared housing service in 42 of the 50 states. Since 1980, there has been an 800% increase in the two most traditional types of programs—matchup and group shared residences. They operate in large and medium-sized urban areas, small towns, and suburban and rural communities. A closer look at the two most common forms of shared housing programs is an essential first step in any attempt to examine the depth, variety, and direction of the shared housing movement.

Group Shared Residence (GSR)

Also known as shared house, group home, congregate facility, share-a-home, shared living homes, sheltered housing, and enriched housing, most group shared residences are sponsored by nonprofit agencies that own or lease and manage one or more dwellings, shared by anywhere from 4 to 20 residents. Group shared residences generally operate in single-family structures in residential communities and exhibit few of the institutional characteristics of nursing, rooming, or boarding homes. The residence is a cooperative living arrangement whereby each resident has a private room and shares common living areas. Group residences vary in size, with the average building accommodating eight people. They range from charming Victorian mansions to modern facilities built expressly for shared housing. Although most are exclusively for the elderly, some are intergenerational, with students, displaced homemakers, and working couples living there as well. One of the most attractive features of a group shared residence is that residents have a measure of control over matters that affect them. Each person has a voice in decisions concerning the management and operations of the facility.

Matchup Programs

Also known as homesharing, shared living, shared housing, and housesharing programs, matchup programs are typically sponsored by public or private non-profit agencies. They recruit, screen, and "match" homeowners or apartment dwellers with suitable homesharers. Through the matching process of interviewing and screening, agencies facilitate two candidates coming together based on their needs, preferences, and interests. This type of shared housing arrangement is particularly attractive to the elderly since more than 70% of people over age 65 own their own homes. In a homesharing matchup, an elderly homeowner shares with one or more homeseekers who pay rent. Each has a private room and shares areas such as the living room, kitchen, and dining room. In many instances the homeseeker is a younger person who is willing to help the elderly person or couple with housekeeping, yard work, or shopping in exchange for room and board or reduced rent. In 1970 approximately 25 such programs existed, and today's figures reveal more than 200 (National Shared Housing Resource Center, 1988).

These programs are a grass-roots response to a growing housing crisis. With their recruiting, interviewing, and screening procedures, they are able to locate suitable housemates in today's complex housing market better than individuals are. Because of their community-based nature, these organizations are better positioned than state or federal agencies to respond to local needs and to implement innovative housing alternatives.

CURRENT PERSPECTIVES

A 1986 survey of Americans of age 55 and older revealed that 12–15% of those asked would consider homesharing with a nonrelative (American Association of Retired Persons, 1986). A similar survey in 1980 conducted by the National Council on Aging (NCOA) showed that only 7% of those older adults polled were interested in such an arrangement (Turner and Mangum, 1982). This increase, occurring over just a seven-year span, not only shows a general shift in attitudes, but it indicates that shared housing is a legitimate housing alternative that might well be chosen by Americans as they age.

A frequently cited reason for the reemergence of shared living is the increasing number of older Americans. The population of America has increased roughly threefold since 1900, and the age 65 and over population has risen eightfold. In 1986, 29,173 or 12.1% of all American citizens were over age 65, a 14.8% increase from 1980. It is expected that there will be 34.9 million older adults in America by the year 2000.

This growing population of older adults faces many problems, the most profound of which may be loneliness. A desire for independence and a reluctance to be uprooted from established connections of friends, churches, doctors, and family have resulted in a disturbing trend toward older people living alone. The Commonwealth Fund conducted a survey in 1986 entitled "Who Are the Elderly Living Alone?" The findings show that if growth continues at its current rate, by 1995 it can be expected that 40% of all people of age 65 and older will be living alone. Those older people living alone are twice as likely to be childless as are elderly people living with others. They are less likely to have a positive attitude and more frequently cite loneliness as a serious problem (Commonwealth Fund, 1986).

Many elderly persons also face a serious income problem. While the cost of health care, food, and housing is rising, the income of the elderly is often decreasing in buying power. At the same time, expenses of the elderly homeowner are increasing due to the increased health problems associated with aging, the need for hiring help with daily chores, and the need for major and minor home repairs associated with a house that itself is often aging.

Even in the face of these concerns elderly people have expressed a strong desire to live out their lives in their own homes. An American Association of Retired Persons (AARP) housing survey (1986) estimates that in households of people age 65 and older, 70% want to stay in their home. Because many older people own their homes and are choosing to remain in them throughout their lives, more attention must be paid to mechanisms that enable this population to "age in place."

INDIVIDUAL BENEFITS OF SHARED HOUSING

Not surprisingly, the reasons for homesharing given by homesharers in the 1980s closely parallel those from earlier in the century: additional income, companionship, security, and the need for services.

ADDITIONAL INCOME

"I am very interested in a housemate—since I own my home, the expense of only one is too great where two people could make our money go further."

"I thought that sharing my home might be a way of helping me to pay the bills while I get back on my feet."

Like their predecessors, today's homeproviders are seeking a stable source of additional income. A 1987 National Survey of Shared Housing Programs found that 50% of homeproviders had annual incomes between $5,000 and $10,000 and 88% had incomes below $15,000. The cost of upkeep on a home, in addition to utility, tax, and mortgage payments, is often difficult for people with limited means. Shared housing substantially reduces housing costs for homeproviders. This, in turn, increases disposable income and buying power.

Although the majority of all older Americans own their own homes, slightly fewer than 30% of older Americans are renters. They are often persons who sold their homes following the death of a spouse or whose children are leaving or who have lived alone most of their lives. They are faced with spiraling rents, condominium conversion, the limited availability of federally subsidized housing, and unsafe living conditions. Shared housing offers senior renters housing that is low cost, with rents that are, to a large extent, controlled.

The savings and income for people in a homesharing arrangement is difficult to ascertain because of variables such as rent, space allotted, and the condition of the housing. As an example, however, in Philadelphia the average annual savings for renters in homesharing situations is estimated at $1,500; for a homeowner, the additional income is closer to $2,200.

These estimates indicate the financial advantages of homesharing and do not address those benefits that cannot be assigned a monetary value. These are the intangibles that, in large part, determine the quality of the older person's life.

COMPANIONSHIP

"I think we're a very compatible match. The money isn't essential, though it helps. I did it mainly for the company. I really don't like living alone. I like being with people."

"I live with my daughter, her husband, and four children but would like to settle with someone my age but near to my family."

Shared housing meets the social and emotional support needs of the elderly through increased companionship without the loss of independence. Loneliness and isolation are more commonplace among today's elderly than they were in the early 1900s. There are similarities between the periods—homes are opened for homesharing following the death of a spouse or in the absence of dependents. The physical distance between parents and their children, however, is a relatively new phenomenon that has resulted in increased isolation for the elderly. At the same time, older people are not willing to sacrifice their independence by moving in with children. The ability of shared living to meet the needs for companionship and independence is an important reason for the increased interest in shared housing.

The intergenerational aspect of some shared housing arrangements adds another dimension to companionship. In addition to the informal and natural service exchange that arises in an intergenerational shared house, homesharers find it rewarding to live with persons from different generations. At the same time, shared housing acts to promote intergenerational cooperation and understanding. An 18-year-old student wrote in response to an article on homesharing that shared housing was "a wonderful idea! Older persons so often have so much to give and few to receive [sic]. Likewise young people can benefit from the wisdom of the experienced.''

SECURITY

''I have no one to guard my home so am unprotected from harm. This constant fear is always with us senior citizens if we live alone. I hope there is a roommate in my town to share my home.''

Shared housing provides psychological and physical security. Shared housing reduces stress often associated with living alone. Homesharers provide companionship and comfort to each other, knowing that someone will be available in case of an accident or illness. The alarming increase in crime, especially in larger cities and often in neighborhoods with high concentrations of elderly, also makes homesharing an attractive option. Indeed, another reason that homeproviders prefer intergenerational living is the sense of security that a younger, more physically able person contributes to a home.

SERVICES

''I have a large yard to mow, and I would like to get a nice gentleman age 65 to 70 years to help mow my grass in the summer. I have a small place in Florida where I go in the winter. I would like him to help drive to Florida.''

An increasing number of older Americans are entering into homesharing arrangements to secure help with tasks that they can no longer perform themselves or cannot afford to purchase. In what is referred to as a ''service-exchange match,'' there is a reduction in rent or a free room and occasionally a salary for services provided by either a homeowner or renter. Services can range from light housekeeping to the provision of meals and are clearly defined in a homesharing agreement. Service exchanges may well be the fastest growing component of the shared housing movement.

We find many older persons entering into homesharing arrangements not merely for financial reasons but for emotional and social ones as well. As one homesharer put it, ''It's just nice to come into the house and hear another human body moving about.''

SOCIAL BENEFITS OF SHARED HOUSING

Group shared residences may be the most cost-effective housing alternative to emerge in the past decade. Current information indicates that the average cost of developing a group residence unit is less than one-half of the cost of producing a HUD-subsidized 202 unit. Matchup programs are even more cost-effective.

The cost per match is roughly one-quarter of the HUD figure for producing a unit of housing. There are few, if any, housing programs in the country that provide shelter at these costs.

Furthermore, each shared housing match makes available a housing unit not previously on the market at a rent much lower than the community's market rents. This is accomplished without any state or local rent or construction subsidies. In addition, when the service-exchange component provides the older person with services that assist in activities of daily living, community resources are released to serve others. Formalized programs are just now beginning to keep records that document the cost-effectiveness of the matchup service for both the individual and the community.

Group shared residences and matchup programs are adaptable to a wide range of circumstances and can target a variety of specific special use populations. Shared housing can be modified to satisfy conditions in urban, suburban, and rural localities, and it can be adopted to the needs of the elderly, single-parent families, the homeless, and college students as well as a mix of these populations.

Shared housing can also be used as a strategy to address a variety of social issues such as displacement among low-income people and community and property stabilization. At the same time, shared housing promotes self-determination and independence and can reduce the demand for costly, formal supports such as nursing homes and other institutions. Furthermore, shared housing can be integrated into the neighborhood in an unobtrusive way.

FUTURE PERSPECTIVES

Shared living is enjoyed by many people today, and it meets a variety of society's needs in an efficient and effective manner. As the 1990s approach, a number of barriers exist that impede the development of shared housing and the growth of shared housing programs.

The barrier most frequently cited and discussed by shared housing programs is the lack of financial support. Most programs, which are nonprofit, are operating with one or two staff members and a core of volunteers. Precious staff time is often diverted from essential services to prepare grant proposals and applications. Funding is a particularly acute problem for programs offering matchup services because many serve a majority of clients whose average income is $10,000 and thus cannot derive sufficient income from service fees alone. Such programs must rely on other sources of income. Although some federal funds are available to homesharing programs, they are in short supply and competition for them is keen.

Adding to the problem of funding is the instability of the funding that does exist. Uncertainty about a program's funding weakens planning and adversely affects program operations. Although some states provide ongoing support to the same program year after year, others provide one-time startup funds only. The programs are then expected to raise steady funding elsewhere. Some states are considering three-year declining grants that would address the issue of organizational stability.

A second barrier to the growth of shared housing programs is that shared housing programs offer a continuum of services that are not often recognized by the traditional "bricks and mortar" funders and policy-makers. Programs are usually funded in relation to the number of "matches" and the average length of the match. A closer look at homesharing program activities reveals a broad range of services that includes housing counseling, a detailed screening process for homeseekers to insure the success of "matches," help with lease writing, and continuing support after the match has been made. To evaluate the value of a program only by the number of matches excludes an understanding of the range of services the program actually provides.

In addition, the length of a match varies greatly because matches meet a wide variety of needs on the part of the homesharers. Homesharers often choose a match as a transitional remedy in a time of severe need such as divorce, death in the family, career change, or relocation. In these short-term cases, shared housing is very successful despite the short length of the arrangement. To address the two issues of number and length of matches, more sophisticated evaluation criteria must be developed that take into account the full range of services provided by homesharing programs and the circumstances under which a match is developed. With more precise evaluative criteria, funding sources would have a tool to judge the effectiveness of a specific homesharing program.

A third barrier to shared housing is restrictive zoning regulations and building and fire codes. Presently, Cincinnati is the only city in the United States to have shared housing formally written into the zoning code. Audiences at public meetings are often hostile to the concept of shared housing because of bad experiences with boarding homes and other forms of group living. Public pressure often is a factor in the denial of zoning variances. Building codes do not recognize shared housing as a single family dwelling but designate it as a multifamily dwelling. This imposes restrictions such as external fire escapes, sprinklers, or fire doors, which increase development costs and discourage community group sponsorship.

Legal barriers pose a fourth obstacle for elderly interested in shared housing. Many elderly people are reluctant to enter a shared living arrangement for fear of being penalized by reduction of their income from Supplemental Security Income (SSI), food stamps, or fuel subsidies. Reductions occur because agencies often consider the income of all homesharers together rather than making the decision on an individual basis. Policies need to recognize and take into account the special circumstances of individuals in shared living arrangements for homesharing so that those who could benefit from shared housing are not forced to turn away. Encouraging public officials to look at housing options creatively will go a long way to improving the climate for shared housing.

Shared housing programs must emphasize educating policy-makers, funders, case workers, housing specialists, and the public about the benefits of shared housing and the special needs of shared housing programs to overcome these barriers to growth. A clear and uniform definition of shared housing must be developed and adhered to for shared housing to meet with greater public acceptance and for public policies and laws to be adopted or altered to reflect the realities of shared housing. To attain a clearer definition, programs should formalize methods of collecting data on their activities and should differentiate themselves from other forms of group living. With clear definitions and a clear sense of purpose, programs can and should begin to market the concept of shared housing.

CONCLUSIONS

The shared housing movement, in its more formalized role, currently has programs that are extremely successful. Coalitions of programs have developed in states such as New York, New Jersey, Texas, and Minnesota; a mid-America Coalition includes six states. Support through states and the aging network is very important to legitimize training time for staff and encourage exchange of information. There is a base of information increasingly being developed as researchers have begun to evaluate program operations and effects of this option on its participants. More and more, papers are being presented at professional conferences. Best practice models are currently available to assist programs as they plan for their community needs. It is encouraging to receive information requests from high school students preparing reports on shared housing issues. This documentation is critical in programs' efforts to secure a source of stable, ongoing funding. We are just beginning to develop in this area, however.

Although the reemergence of shared housing in the 1980s is primarily attributed to changing demographics and complexity of the needs of older Americans, one cannot overlook the impact that "formalizing" the movement has had on its growth and image. It is no small feat to overcome the stigma many older people have attached to "doubling-up" or to tinker with the American values of privacy and home ownership. Shared housing programs across the nation, both large and small, have been very successful in promoting the concept and educating consumers to the benefits of homesharing. They are carrying out their work creatively and meticulously, helping to chip away at the notion that shared housing is only for the "underside" of society. As this work continues, so will the expansion of the shared housing alternative with its sense of community and its emphasis on preserving the dignity and independence of the individual.

NOTE

The authors wish to offer special thanks to Claire Matthews, Diana Myers, and Sam Rhoads, whose involvement greatly enhanced the pages of this text. Furthermore, we wish to express our gratitude to the many shared housing programs whose commitment and dedication to the shared housing movement will be of lasting import.

REFERENCES

American Association of Retired Persons. *Understanding Senior Housing: An American Association of Retired Persons Survey of Consumers' Preferences, Concerns, and Needs*. Washington, D.C., 1986.

Commonwealth Fund. *Problems Facing Elderly Americans Living Alone*. New York, 1986.

Modell, John, and Hareven, Tamara K. "Urbanization and the Malleable Household: An Examination of Boarding and Lodging in American Families." *Journal of Marriage and the Family*, August 1973, pp. 467–79.

National Shared Housing Resource Center. *National Directory of Shared Housing Programs for Older Persons*. Philadelphia, 1988.

Richards, William. "Tired and Scared of Living Alone, More Elderly Try Sharing Homes." *Wall Street Journal*, 22 September 1986.

Turner, L., and Mangum, E. *Report on Housing Choices of Older Americans*. Washington, D.C.: National Council on the Aging, 1982.

3

Patterns of Homesharing in the United States

Barbara Robins and Elizabeth Howe

As people reach their later years, many of them need additional income or help with activities of daily living. There are many ways that these needs can be met, but one element that shapes the choices of many older people is their desire to "age in place" in their own homes. Because home ownership among the elderly is high—72% in 1986—there has been considerable interest in actually using this housing itself as a resource for meeting such needs. Home-equity conversion, for example, can be used to generate income that, in turn, could be used to pay for services provided in the home.

Homesharing is another such alternative. It involves the older person sharing their home with a nonrelative, either for rent or in exchange for services. Thus it offers an opportunity to deal with both the need for added income and the need for help with activities of daily life. Using data from the 1980 survey on Housing Choices of Older Americans, Carol Schreter and Lloyd Turner (1986) found that 2.5% of households in which at least one member was age 55 or older also included a nonrelative. In about one-third of these households, the older person shared the home with one other person, usually someone younger. In another one-third of the households, the older person shared the house with both a younger relative and an unrelated younger person.

Homesharing, or in older terminology "renting out rooms," was common in the nineteenth century and has survived on a smaller scale to this day. The difference now is that during the past 10 years or so, many formal programs have sprung up across the country to help older people find "roomers" or "live-ins." This chapter explores the nature of these programs: how many there are, where they are, what kinds of communities are likely to have homesharing programs, and what kinds of programs they are likely to be.

In brief, there are now about 169 programs in the continental United States primarily serving the elderly. They have increased rapidly in the past few years and now are found in 31 states and the District of Columbia. Some are primarily housing programs, whereas others are concerned primarily with helping the elderly with their service needs.

We expected that programs would be more likely to occur in communities with tight housing markets or ones with a substantial commitment to services for the elderly. Alternatively, we thought that these factors might shape the nature of a program once it was in existence. In fact, neither alternative seems to be the case. Programs occur in all kinds of communities, and the best predictors of the existence of a program are simply the size of the community, the percentage of its population over the age of 65, and the region of the country. Nor does the nature of a program seem to be a response to the nature of market demand for homesharing in a particular community.

If programs are not a response to an assessed community need, once a home-sharing program exists, its goals will be shaped in part by the need to adapt to the demand for homesharing in that particular community.

DATA AND METHODOLOGY

Several sources and types of data are used in this study. The description of all of the programs throughout the country is based on data on "matchup" programs from the *National Directory of Shared Housing Programs for Older People* (National Shared Housing Resource Center, 1983 and 1986).

To try to answer the question of what kind of communities are likely to have a homesharing program, we drew a random sample of 38 homesharing programs, stratified by region, from the 1983 *National Directory* and then compared the communities in which these 38 programs were located with a random sample of 38 other communities that did not have programs in 1983.

The community data are taken particularly from the 1980 Censuses of Population and Housing. In addition, we gathered information on programs serving the elderly in each community by counting programs listed under "Senior Citizens' Service Organizations" in the Yellow Pages of recent telephone directories. "Recent" here means directories primarily from 1985 and 1986 but including some from 1984 and 1987 as well.

Finally, to find out how homesharing programs are organized and run and how they adapt to their communities, we conducted telephone interviews with the directors of the 38 programs included in the community analysis. These 38 programs constituted a 36% sample of all homesharing programs in the United States as of 1983. The interviews were done in 1984 and used both closed and open-ended questions. Since the interviews were with program administrators, they focused primarily on how the programs operated. No systematic data were gathered on the nature and dynamics of homesharing matches themselves.

THE PREVALENCE OF HOMESHARING

In recent years homesharing has been increasing rapidly and spreading through-out the country. In 1983 there were 106 formal matchup programs in the continental United States. By 1986 there were 169. This represents an increase of 60% in three years. They seem initially to have developed particularly on the West and East coasts, with those two areas accounting for 85% of all programs in 1983. But as the idea has caught on, 46% of new programs sprang up in the Midwest and the Sunbelt, lowering the share of programs on both coasts to 70% by 1986.

The process of "catching on" has been significantly aided by networking among social service professionals and sometimes by funding, from HUD, from state agencies, and from several shared housing networks that serve as contact points for promoting shared housing. In this volume David Pritchard and Joelle Perkocha's analysis of shared housing in California (Chapter 5) details the efforts of the state to encourage shared housing through funding and technical assistance, as well as the networking taking place among programs themselves. This activity is particularly significant since California has far more programs—51 in 1986—than any other state. Texas, however, is a good example of the results of this kind of process on a smaller scale. In 1983 it had no programs, but due at least in part to an active State Department of Aging, by 1986 it had nine. In this analysis we focus primarily on community-level variables that might explain the existence of programs, but future work will also look at these deliberate efforts to stimulate homesharing activity.

It takes a moderate-size community to support a homesharing program. The mean size in 1986 was about 400,000. Only two programs are found in cities of less than 10,000 population, and about half (50% and 55% in 1983 and 1986, respectively) in cities smaller than 25,000 are in metropolitan areas. Over time, as homesharing has spread, communities smaller than 500,000 have come to be more represented, thereby decreasing the proportion of programs found in the largest cities.

Only 5% of communities have more than 1 program, and it seems to require at least 100,000, and more realistically about 400,000, population to sustain 2. But homesharing programs in larger cities often do not draw from the entire city, so in large cities like New York and Los Angeles, multiple programs coexist serving different areas. On a larger scale, some metropolitan areas—notably Washington, D.C., and Los Angeles are able to support as many as 7 and 14 programs, respectively.

Although the overall pattern nationally has been one of programmatic growth, programs do fail. The failure rate from 1983 to 1986 was 22% (23 of 106 programs). It is difficult to know whether or not this is high for new social programs in an environment where money is scarce. Three may simply have tried to operate in communities that were too small. Otherwise, from what we know, failure seems to reflect problems of small size and tenuous funding. We had some information on 10 of the failed programs, although only 5 were in our final sample. At least 4 had lost their funding, and 1 never had any. In 3 of the other cases the agency provided several programs, may have added homesharing with existing staff, and later decided to drop it.

Programs are sponsored by a fairly wide range of agencies, and here the difference between housing-oriented and service-oriented programs begins to emerge. In 1986, 39% were sponsored by organizations serving the elderly such as Area Agencies on Aging, the Grey Panthers, or a senior center. An additional 17% were sponsored by housing agencies such as housing authorities or housing opportunity agencies. General social service agencies such as Lutheran Social Services or a family service agency sponsored 31%. Over time the proportion of housing programs has remained fairly stable, but sponsorship by general social service agencies has gained at the expense of organizations specifically serving the elderly. This may indicate that as service-oriented homesharing has become more common, it has spread beyond the confines of agencies serving only the elderly.

Most programs are intended to serve the elderly, but by and large they cannot serve only the elderly and survive. Thus only 9% in 1986 served only senior citizens, down from 13% in 1983. Half are intergenerational, meaning that one member of the match, usually the homeprovider, must be elderly. Most of the rest serve people of all ages.

Here again, as one might expect, housing programs are somewhat different from others. Most housing-oriented programs do serve older people since they often have room to spare in their homes. No program sponsored by a housing agency, however, served only older people, compared with 9% for programs sponsored by senior organizations and 19% by general social service agencies. Conversely, all kinds of sponsors encourage intergenerational matches in which one homesharer is elderly, but housing-sponsored programs were the most likely (31%) to have no restrictions on the age composition of matches.

WHAT KIND OF COMMUNITIES DEVELOP
HOMESHARING PROGRAMS?

To explore the question of what kinds of communities develop homesharing programs we compared a sample of 38 communities with homesharing programs in 1983 to a sample of communities that did not have programs. The only restriction on the sample without programs was that the communities have at least 10,000 population, since it was evident that a minimum population size is necessary to support a program. Thus our dependent variable is the categorical variable of whether or not a community had a homesharing program.

We expected that several types of community characteristics might encourage or discourage the formation of a program. Two sets of variables were central to this analysis. One set was related to the nature of the housing market. We thought that "tight" housing markets with low vacancy rates, high rents, and high home

Table 3.1

Correlation Coefficients for Housing Market Variables (n = 76)

	vacancy rate	rent	home value
vacancy rate	--		
rent	-.2684 p=.01	--	
home value	-.3169 p=.003	.7005 p=.000	--
program*	.1515 p=.096	.0147 p=.450	-.1640 p=.078

* Program is coded 1= program, 2=no program.

values would tend to encourage homesharing. The second set of variables was related to the salience of the elderly in the community. We expected that the larger the proportion of older people in the community, the more programs there would be to serve them and the more likely it would be that homesharing would be part of that mix of programs.

In addition, several secondary hypotheses led us to include some additional independent variables. Two were thought of as conditions that might facilitate the emergence of homesharing—owner occupancy among the elderly and the proportion of the population between the ages of 18 and 24, a group that provides a pool of live-ins in some communities. Finally, it seemed important to include basic background variables such as the size of the community and region of the country.

As we will do here, we initially looked at relationships within each set of variables using Pearson correlation coefficients to see if they did actually constitute "sets" of related variables. Then, using multiple regression analysis, we looked at the relationship between these independent variables and the presence or absence of a homesharing program.

The results did not bear out our expectations that the housing market and organizational climate would explain the existence of programs. Instead, basic demographic variables such as the size of the community, the percentage of elderly, and the region seem to be better predictors of the presence of a program.

An initial examination of the correlations between the independent variables in each set and between them and a rough measure of the dependent variable does suggest the pattern we expected, though with some exceptions. Taking the nature of the housing market first, as Table 3.1 indicates, vacancy rates, rents, and home values were related to one another, and two of them were related to the existence of a program if the significance level is broadened to 0.10. Communities with lower vacancy rates have higher rents, and high rents are also associated with high home values. This suggests that in superheated housing

Table 3.2
Correlation Coefficients for Aging Programs (n = 76)

	percent > 65	aging organizations
percent > 65	--	
aging orgs	-.0934 p=.237	--
program*	-.1510 p=.097	-.2495 p=.026

* Program is coded 1=program, 2=no program.

markets, lack of vacancies and high rents predispose some renters to consider sharing whereas high home values and high property taxes might predispose older people with extra space in their homes to add to their incomes by renting a room.

Looking next, in Table 3.2, at variables related to services for the elderly, the relationships were not so orderly. Higher proportions of the elderly and the presence of more agencies serving them were both associated with the presence of homesharing programs. The proportion of people over age 65, however, is not significantly related to the number of senior organizations. In fact, the relationship is actually reversed. Instead, the existence of programs serving the elderly is more strongly related to population size (0.51 p = 0.000) and home values (0.23 p = 0.02), suggesting that it may be size and affluence rather than the presence of older residents that explains the richness of the service infrastructure.

Finally, the "facilitating" variables did not appear to contribute to the presence of a program. In fact, home ownership by the elderly was negatively correlated (0.29 p = 0.006). But as one might expect, larger population size was related to the existence of a homesharing program.

Although the correlation coefficients can begin to suggest patterns in the data, multiple regression analysis provides a way of looking at the explanatory power of the set of independent variables taken together. Since our dependent variable is the categorical variable of whether or not a program exists, we used logit regression analysis.

The analysis was simplified somewhat based on the results of the correlation matrix and some preliminary regression trials. Two variables, rent and the proportion of the population between ages 18 and 24, were excluded because they were repetitive and lacked explanatory power. The primary analysis included home value and vacancy rate for the housing market, the percentage of the population over age 65 for service orientation, and community population, region, and home ownership among the elderly. A second analysis was also done including organizations serving the elderly as well. Missing data for that variable,

Table 3.3
Multiple Regression—Homesharing Programs

Variables	T	Significance of T
Community Population	2.917	.0049
Percent > 65	1.700	.0940
Home Value	.426	.6710
Vacancy Rate	-.824	.4127
Owner Occupied > 65	-1.237	.2210
Region - 1	-1.780	.0797
2	-2.259	.0270
4	.148	.8810
Constant	1.478	.1440

R^2 .34
F = 4.228   Significance of F = .0004

however, reduce the number of cases from 74 to 60, and since it did not show aging organizations to be significant, that variable was dropped from the primary analysis.

The variables in the primary analysis explained 34% of the variation in the dependent variable (Table 3.3). The *F* statistic was 4.228, significant at the 0.0004 level. The variables that were most important for explaining the existence of homesharing programs, however, were not those related to the housing market or to existing services for the elderly. Neither vacancy rate nor home value were significant, nor, as we have seen, was the number of senior organizations. The best predictor of the existence of a program was city size, followed by the proportion of the population over age 65. Region, which compared the West with three other large census regions (Northeast, North Central, and South) showed that programs were significantly more likely to occur in the West than in the Midwest or South.

What does all of this mean? Our expectations that certain kinds of communities, especially those with tight housing markets or many services for the elderly, would be especially likely to have homesharing programs were certainly not borne out. This probably means that even by 1983 homesharing had become widely enough accepted, especially in the West and Northeast, that programs were to be found in all kinds of communities. This regional pattern may also have been partly a function of funding and encouragement by certain states.

In the years since 1983, programs have become even more widespread. This may well represent the operation of normal processes of innovation and diffusion, sometimes hurried along by governmental policy. We do not have data for a long enough time span to test this hypothesis systematically here, but our findings do indicate that homesharing began on the two coasts and in larger communities, and throughout the years it has spread inland and out to smaller places. Now, only increased community size and a larger proportion of elderly residents affect the occurrence of a program. With the further growth and geographical spread of programs in the years since 1983, this pattern may become even stronger.

A somewhat more speculative conclusion about how homesharing programs come to exist would be that it is not really broad market-demand factors that lead to the creation of homesharing programs. As suggested by other chapters in this volume, these programs are small and are often the creations of one person or an agency that may come to focus on the "need" for homesharing as a result of any of a variety of nonmarket influences—experience in another community, promotion by a state agency, the availability of funds, or the obvious need of some people already being served in other ways. Programs are set up and then the staff work hard to make them succeed. Regardless of what the larger market forces are, diligent work may be enough to keep a small program going.

ADAPTATION TO MARKETS

Although sheer determination may be enough to bring programs into existence and to make them work for a time, complete lack of responsiveness to such larger market forces could result in programs that remain small or even fail. The seven programs that went out of existence between 1983 and 1986 may have done so at least in part because they could not make enough matches. They were smaller in terms of the average number of matches, with 21 versus 54. At least one program director did not feel that the number of matches justified the expenditure on staff. They also had lower average match rates—that is, the proportion of applicants actually ending up in a match—with 13.3 versus 38.0 for all.

But does this small size and likelihood of failure have anything to do with market responsiveness? Our telephone survey found that three types of programs exist, and it is logical to ask whether they represent different responses, in terms of goals, recruitment strategies, and styles of operation, to different kinds of markets.[1]

Housing programs, which include 40% of all programs, are those in which live-ins in more than 60% of the matches paid rent. They are primarily concerned with increasing the supply of affordable housing by making use of underused space in houses belonging to older people (Lane and Feins, 1985). They deal largely with healthy, independent older people who want to rent out rooms for extra income. Their style of operation is often laissez-faire, bringing homesharers and homeseekers together but letting them make their own arrangements.

At the other extreme, 16% of the programs were primarily concerned with providing services to elderly people in need of help with activities of daily living. In these programs more than 70% of the homeseekers exchanged services for room and board and sometimes for a small salary in addition. All but one required at least one member of any match to be elderly, and most followed what might be called a "counseling" model for arranging matches. This involved checking references, working out a contract between the two sharers, and following up on matches once they had been arranged. This more elaborate approach is probably necessary when services are exchanged for room and board and when the older people involved are frail and sometimes not able to represent fully their own interests.

In between these two "pure" types of programs, the balance of 45% followed a mixed model, making both rent-paying and service-providing matches. Most followed a middle path in their style of making matches. Initial counseling and follow-up on matches, for example, were provided by most programs, but many only suggested the use of a contract.

This difference in clientele and operating style suggests that housing programs may be responses to communities with tight housing markets, whereas service programs may be more characteristic of communities with many elderly and rich networks of services for them. Indeed, the fact that housing-oriented programs are found in communities with significantly higher rents ($t = 2.45; p = 0.02$) and higher home values ($t = 1.84; p = 0.07$) suggests that this is the case.

To test this hypothesis further, a regression analysis was done using the independent variables used for the earlier analysis, relating to the nature of the housing market in the community, the service network for the elderly, and the community's demographic composition. This time, however, the dependent variable was the percentage of a program's matches in which the homeseeker paid rent. If a high proportion pay rent, the program is housing oriented; if a low proportion pay rent, it is service oriented.

The sample used here is only the 38 programs in our sample that had homesharing programs. The small size of this sample does increase somewhat the likelihood that results will not prove to be statistically significant. The nature of their programs—whether housing or service oriented—was determined from telephone interviews in 1984 with the project directors.

The results of the analysis do not bear out the hypothesis that programs respond to market demand factors in their communities. None of the correlations between the housing market variables and the percentage of homeseekers paying rent was significant. The only evidence in favor of the hypothesis was a weak relationship ($-0.23; p = 0.10$), which suggests that communities with many organizations for seniors may be more likely to have service-oriented homesharing programs.

The regression also provided no support for the idea that programs are responding to the nature of the housing market or to the demand for services by the elderly. The specific independent variables included in the analysis were community population, percentage over age 65, aging organizations, housing vacancy rate, home value, and region of the country. None of these variables was significantly related to the percentage of homeseekers paying rent. Nor was the set of variables as a whole a significant predictor of the dependent variable ($F = 1.26$, sig. $F = 0.31; R^2 = 0.31$).

Just as factors other than market demand bring homesharing programs into existence, so the form that a program takes does not seem to be a function of the nature of the community. This need not hold for all programs; some may be responding to market forces, but in the statistical analysis they clearly seem to be swamped by those that are not. This suggests that perhaps other factors such as requirements of funding agencies or the influence of model programs may determine whether programs focus on helping the independent elderly or on helping those in need of services. The large number of programs in California (one-third of the sample) may mean that policy in that particular state alone can affect the overall statistical results. Pritchard and Perkocha's discussion in this volume (Chapter 5) suggests that housing concerns have been dominant there, which may encourage the creation of housing-oriented programs even in communities without tight housing markets.

Responses to market demand may also be masked by the way in which we have defined homesharing programs. It is possible that some communities develop homesharing programs that serve only partial segments of a broader market. In Madison, Wisconsin, for example, the homesharing program is a service-oriented program serving frail elders, whereas independent seniors go to the university housing office (not considered a homesharing program here) to find renters to live in.

Thus the results of this analysis suggest that the issue of what forces shape the nature of homesharing programs is more complex than our initial hypothesis anticipated. Response to market demand may still be a factor, but even if it could be measured with complete accuracy, it is still probably not a dominant one. The influence of public policy may well play a more central role in shaping the nature of programs.

CONCLUSIONS

What do all of these findings mean for the organization and operation of homesharing programs? There is a good deal of enthusiasm "out there" about homesharing. There has been 60% growth in the number of programs throughout the country over a three-year period, actively encouraged by a number of state governments. Homesharing is an idea whose logic is hard to resist. It can provide income or services to the elderly and can help them manage in their own homes as they get older. Compared to more formal ways of meeting these needs, it is also very cheap at a time when money is scarce.

But the other side of homesharing must be accepted as well so that expectations do not become unrealistic. As Pritchard and Perkocha's survey of the California programs indicate, the truth is that people are reluctant to share. This means that many or most programs are likely to be small in terms of staff and matches, and will probably operate on a shoestring (Howe, 1985; Jaffe and Howe, 1988).

Our evidence suggests that neither the establishment of a program nor its operating style are particularly related to either housing market demand or measures of the demand for services for the elderly. It may well be that their existence and nature are shaped more by funding requirements, known program models, or preferences of program administrators.

If this is true, it suggests that program funders and administrators are doubly responsible for shaping programs that can succeed. How a program handles the process of matchmaking should depend on what kind of clients it is getting. A laissez-faire approach is appropriate for independent people trying to meet housing needs, but help with services may require a more counseling-oriented approach (Jaffe and Howe, in press).

Our analysis of what kinds of communities have homesharing suggests that no particular type of community is more suitable than another. On the other hand, because older people are often reluctant to share, it may well take a moderate-size community, perhaps in the 200,000 to 300,000 range, to support a homesharing program with 30 to 40 matches a year. We do not have any rule of thumb for this, but in our sample the average size of community with a program was 337,000 compared with 72,000 without; the average number of matches was 54. It does also seem that a higher proportion of elderly in the population helps to make a program succeed. But the bottom line is that one must work to make any homesharing program work, and a larger pool of possible sharers is an obvious advantage.

All of this suggests that the decision to start a homesharing program should be a little less ad hoc and more planned. Given the small budgets that most programs are likely to have, elaborate needs assessment and planning are probably unlikely, but the lack of any planning may lead to setting up programs that struggle along for a while and then fail. With realistic expectations and some advance planning, however, it should be possible to make the complete range of kinds of homesharing work in many communities.

NOTES

We would like to thank Faranak Seifolddini who played an active role in the preparation of this chapter.

1. These findings on different types of programs are substantially the same as those reported in Jaffe and Howe, 1988. The number of programs used here, however, is somewhat larger (38 versus 33 programs) because of the simple nature of the analysis.

REFERENCES

Howe, Elizabeth. "Homesharing for the Elderly." *Journal of Planning Education and Research* 4 (1985):185–94.

Jaffe, Dale, and Howe, Elizabeth. "Agency-Assisted Shared Housing: The Nature of Programs and Matches." *The Gerontologist* 28 (1988):318–24.

———. "Case Management for Homesharing." *Journal of Gerontological Social Work*, in press.

Lane, Terry Saunders, and Feins, Judith. "Are the Elderly Overhoused: Definitions of Space Utilization and Policy Implications." *The Gerontologist* 25 (1985):243–50.

National Shared Housing Resource Center. *National Directory of Shared Housing Programs for Older People*. Philadelphia, 1983 and 1986.
Schreter, Carol, and Turner, Lloyd. ''Sharing and Subdividing Private Market Housing.'' *The Gerontologist* 26 (1986):181–86.

4

Homesharing in a Rural Context

Norma Maatta, Karen Hornung, Mary Hart, and Karen Primm

Although homesharing is generally an urban phenomenon, Student Housing Alternative with Rural Elders (SHARE), located in the small town of California, Pennsylvania, has adapted the urban model to make shared housing a viable housing option for rural areas. SHARE developed from an acute need for alternative housing and a lack of supportive services for the rural elderly. Although it may follow some of the basic guidelines for urban homesharing, rural homesharing must be unique. Thus SHARE has had to be tailored to fit the demographic, economic, and social characteristics of the rural environment; to avoid being merely a transplanted urban model; and to provide an informal, personalized approach to service delivery.

Across the United States, rural elderly persons are more likely to be disadvantaged than their urban counterparts. Although they are more likely to own their own homes (approximately 83% compared with 65% for metropolitan areas), they also face more upkeep and home maintenance problems (Coward, 1985). They have minimal education (Bylund, 1985), subsist on low incomes generally below the poverty level (21% according to the 1980 census), have more personal and health problems (Coward, 1985), and derive less support from and have less interaction with their families (Youmanns, 1983). In addition, they have less access to public transportation (Krout, 1986), exist on nutritionally inadequate diets (Learner and Kivett, 1981), and have fewer and less varied social services (Taietz and Milton, 1979). The rural elderly of California, Pennsylvania, a small town of approximately 6,000 residents, located in the southwestern corner of the state at the upper reach of the Appalachian Plateau, are faced with the same problems besetting rural elderly nationwide.

California University of Pennsylvania, 1 of 14 universities in the state system of higher education, serves as the community's focal point. Its primary service area of Washington and Fayette counties has one of the highest concentrations of elderly in the nation. The two counties include 80,342 elderly, nearly 22% of the area's total population (*Pennsylvania Department of Labor and Industry*, 1987). In recent years, the economic base of the area has deteriorated. Primarily a steel manufacturing and mining region, the decline in production of these economic staples has left the area severely depressed. In the Primary Metropolitan Statistical Area, which includes Washington and Fayette counties, 96,000 persons over the age of 65 are labeled "economically disadvantaged" (*Pennsylvania Department of Labor and Industry*, 1986). Nearly 25% of these persons live alone.

The high jobless rate has precipitated an exodus of younger workers. With family support systems strained or depleted, the elderly are left with large houses to maintain on low incomes. Because the only other housing option in the California area is age-segregated housing for low-income elderly, a crucial need for alternative housing became evident. Like urban homesharing programs, rural shared housing is a means of meeting this need by providing the elderly financial assistance, help with household chores, home maintenance, and companionship.

The housing needs of the elderly in California, Pennsylvania are matched by the need for housing options for the more than 5,000 students in attendance at the university, only 30% of whom live on campus in the available dormitory space. As in other college communities, rents are often too high for the almost 70% of California students receiving some form of financial aid, and the number of adequate rental facilities accessible to campus is limited. Homesharing could provide benefits to students as well by offering lower rental fees in exchange for services, freedom from living in an age-segregated college environment, privacy, and the enrichment that the elderly's perspective on life can offer.

ISSUES IN RURAL HOMESHARING

These pools of elderly homeowners and college students, each with distinct housing needs, created a climate for an intergenerational shared housing project. Although the need existed, some fundamental problems with the concept remained because of the rural setting. According to the National Shared Housing Resource Center, "an essential for operating an effective match-up program is having a large enough pool of applicants (research has shown this number to be at least 60) so that one can match the specific requirements of any one client" (Dobkin, 1983). The majority of matchup programs serve communities that have populations of more than 300,000 (Dobkin, 1983). A major stumbling block for SHARE, therefore, was sheer numbers. Could large enough pools of homeowners and tenants be established?

Another problem not found in large urban areas was that public transportation within California and in the outlying areas is minimal. Although SHARE was designed to serve a 10-mile radius, bus service to outlying areas is so limited that unless students have their own transportation, a match too far from the central campus is problematic because neither local bus service nor taxi service is available.

A further obstacle to acceptance of homesharing in a rural area included the traditional values associated with the rural elderly. Some studies indicate a tendency for the rural elderly to understate needs (Auerbach, 1986), possibly because of their desire to be or to appear to be self-reliant and nondependent (Krout, 1986). Was it possible to overcome this tendency?

Additionally, urban areas are more likely to include elderly individuals who have had some contact with members of culturally diverse groups and who, therefore, might be more willing to accept minority students. California University has approximately 49 foreign and 226 minority students. In discussion with urban practitioners, the SHARE staff found that in urban areas, a more varied population of older people with a wider range of life experiences might be more willing to accept an innovative program in their community.

THE EMERGENCE OF SHARE

Despite the special characteristics of the rural elderly and the obstacles these characteristics presented, the Gerontology Department of California University of Pennsylvania and the California Senior Center, operated through the university's Gerontology Department, embarked on a collaborative effort to establish shared housing in a nonmetropolitan area. Early in 1987, a grant proposal was submitted to the Howard Heinz Endowment in Pittsburgh after a survey of students and elderly homeowners revealed a positive attitude toward homesharing (students, 70%; homeowners, 44%). The goal of an intergenerational shared housing project was not only to improve the quality of life for the elderly in southwestern Pennsylvania but also to provide a much-needed model for adoption by other small university or college towns. In July 1987 a two-year, $63,000 grant was awarded by the Howard Heinz Endowment with additional funding provided by California University. The major objectives were to pair 30 university students and 30 rural elders by June 1989 and to provide ongoing counseling, education, and support services to the participants. The project receives direction from two faculty members from the Gerontology Department. A full-time project coordinator/counselor is responsible for the day-to-day operations, with additional support provided by a part-time secretary and volunteers.

Because SHARE was born from the cooperation of two established entities with strong ties to the community, California University and the California Senior Center, the "match-up program and sponsor complemented each other's services" (Dobkin, 1983:18). The director of the Senior Center (trained in rural gerontology and a gerontology professor at the university) and the chairperson of the Gerontology Department have created in the community an atmosphere that has helped erode traditional negative attitudes toward social services by rural residents and produced strong citizen participation in the variety of services provided through the center.

The success of the California Senior Center is based on an overriding belief in the need for an informal, personalized approach to service delivery in rural areas and a sense of the community transcending traditional sociodemographic information (Bischoff, 1985). That the kinds of services offered and the sponsorship of delivery of services affect acceptance (Coward and Rathbone-McCaun, 1985) has been demonstrated in the California area. For these reasons, the staff has adopted R. T. Coward and G. R. Lee's theory of "ecologically sensitive intervention" (1985:122).

There are two basic reasons why ecologically sensitive intervention and informal service delivery is more important in rural areas than in urban areas. First, the rural elderly are much less likely to be aware of services. They are faced with greater isolation, poor health (Hayslip et al., 1980), greater geographic distances, large service areas, and poorer phone systems (Coward and Rathbone-McCuan, 1985). Past service utilization rates in rural communities suggest that current methods for informing the elderly are ineffective (Krout, 1986). Realizing that traditional publicity mechanisms such as television coverage and newspapers were nonexistent or limited (in the case of radio coverage), the staff of SHARE made it a policy to promote the program by nontraditional methods. Staff members are always highly visible in both church and community functions, like local parades and church luncheons. Presentations are also given for as many organizations as possible, regardless of the size of the group or the age range. By meeting with even a small group, the larger community is reached through word of mouth. With no mass media in rural areas, it is vital to publicize programs in a more personal way. Potential rural homesharers are also more likely to be aware of and become involved in the program because service delivery is mobile, making the staff accessible to rural elderly. All prospective homesharers, for example, are interviewed in the home. Unlike urban programs, applications are never mailed because face-to-face contact is essential in a rural community.

The second reason why informal service delivery is more needed in rural than urban programs is that there is strong resistance among the rural elderly to using formal services (Krout, 1986). E. J. Karcher and B. E. Karcher (1980) have noted that in rural communities there is a mistrust of government officials that serves as an obstacle to service delivery. This mistrust may be more prevalent among rural than urban elderly because of the rural values that emphasize cultural stability, gradual change, and the belief that ways of past living will endure into the future (Ansello, 1981). This suspiciousness of government and agency personnel has been lessened by the SHARE staff who realized that they must "establish their credentials as human beings before being accepted as credible service providers" (Scheidt, 1985:123). By becoming members in local churches, by frequenting local shops and banks, and by serving on community boards and committees, they are seen as concerned citizens and friends rather than bureaucrats. They have become "insiders" in the community and are seen as worthy of confidence and trust. Tested and proved to be effective in other center projects, the informal approach became the basis of and the reason for the success of SHARE, as is evident in the day-to-day program operation of marketing and matchmaking.

At the Senior Center, the cooperation among staff, center participants, community volunteers, and particularly university students has generated a change in elderly residents' attitudes toward students and vice versa. The "town-gown" relationship, always tenuous in California because of the high visibility of students, the noise and litter factors, and the proliferation of ill-kept landlord-owned apartments in residential neighborhoods, has intensified the xenophobia of this rural town. Through the efforts of the Gerontology Department, however, college students have engaged in Friendly Visiting, Meals-on-Wheels, center activities and programs, and, for gerontology majors, a hands-on practicum. The elderly have similarly participated in university functions. These improved relationships added to the feasibility of a shared housing program.

Like the provision of other services to the rural elderly, homesharing in a rural community differs from that in urban areas. Although SHARE seems to have broken all of the rules for a successful urban program—startup, orderly marketing, traditional follow-up, a large pool of clients—matches were made. We argue that the success of this program thus far has had to do with the fact that the California Senior Center has truly become the community focal point on aging. As such, any new program sponsored by the center has a good chance of receiving community support. In turn, we believe that much of the success of the center is related to the symbiotic relationship that exists between the center director and staff and the older people they serve. This relationship has promoted networking, for example, referrals from community members, senior center participants, neighbors, friends of potential participants, and ministers. SHARE has established an especially close rapport with the ministerial association in California, since the church plays an important role in the leisure activities of the rural elderly (Krout, 1986). Networking is also visible in the makeup of the SHARE Advisory Board, which includes representatives from the ministry, the legal profession, the university administration and faculty, prominent citizens, and staff from the Senior Center. This informal, personalized approach to service delivery had of necessity to be different from the more formal style of urban areas (Osgood, 1977) and was crucial in the initial development of program operations and marketing generally and in the development of SHARE specifically.

Since the Heinz grant was awarded in late July and the new semester began in September, it was necessary to advertise the program quickly. Traditional homesharing startup time and marketing methods were not feasible. Flyers announcing SHARE were attached to bulletin boards and included in packets for new students attending the late summer orientation program. Immediate inquiries from students and parents, however, presented a problem, since at that time there was no pool of elderly homeowners. Thus it was necessary to develop another marketing plan for older homeowners. Marketing for homeowners during the first few months was informal, as SHARE staff began talking to senior center participants who appeared to be likely candidates. Even without a slide show, brochures, or posters, senior citizens were immediately recruited.

MATCHMAKING

Tenant and homeowner application forms, modeled after those developed by The National Shared Housing Resource Center, were used to screen clients, along with interviews and postinterview evaluations by the program coordinator and the director of the Senior Center. Setting high selection standards may be another feature of SHARE that sets it apart from other homesharing programs. Student clients who appeared to seek only inexpensive housing without any interest in the elderly were considered unsuitable and were immediately rejected. Whether or not this judgmental approach excluded students who might have proved to be good tenants or whose attitudes about the elderly might have changed is unknown. The approach was justified as a reasonable means of eliminating potential problem matches. Because of the informal mode of communication (the "grapevine") found in rural communities, it was essential that the initial matches be successful for the program to endure. The credibility of the project, particularly with elderly homeowners, had to be established early in the project and maintained throughout its duration. Thus few chances could be taken in the arrangement of the initial matches.

The matchmaking process itself used the personalized approach necessary in a rural area. The participation of a student's family in the process was the rule rather than the exception, so parents, brothers, and sisters often accompanied the student and program coordinator to meet the homeowner and to gauge both the housing environment and the character and personality of the elder. Such encounters between student, family, homeowner, and program coordinator are a unique feature of SHARE. This one-to-one approach continues in the provision to program participants of ongoing counseling regarding housing options as well as information and referral services on financial assistance, health services, transportation, and so on. Follow-up counseling in rural areas can be as formal as home visits but is often as simple as the center director's casually talking to a homesharer at the local church or at the supermarket.

The key to marketing SHARE was and primarily continues to be word-of-mouth advertising. By September, however, more orthodox marketing techniques were developed, such as advertising through the senior center newsletter, church bulletins, and newspaper articles. Marketing was successful in that by September 10 matches had been made; by June 1988, there were 20. To widen the pool of homeowners, an outreach program was begun in September for outlying areas. A slide show and appropriate narrative were designed for use by the program coordinator at meetings of the American Association of Retired Persons; civic, church, business, and professional groups; and women's organizations.

THE CLIENTS

Reasons given by participants for engaging in homesharing varied. As in urban areas, students in this initial phase of the program were motivated by finances, a need for privacy, a desire for a homelike setting, and companionship. Unlike urban areas, however, where the main reason for homesharing among older homeowners is financial aid (Schreter, 1986), SHARE's older participants stated that the primary and overwhelming motivation was companionship, a wish to escape isolation and loneliness. Perhaps the greater lack of opportunity for socialization and the limited transportation in the area account for this motivation. It is astonishing that in this economically depressed area financial assistance was not a major factor. It was, in fact, difficult to convince some homeowners to charge enough rent to cover the rising cost of utilities or to contract for an exchange of services. Rents ranged from a mere $25 to $200 per month, with an average of only $75. Service exchanges included light housekeeping, yardwork and shoveling snow, running errands, caring for pets, and cooking. Most matches were contracted on a semester-to-semester basis, with some lasting only one semester and others indefinitely.

Student tenants, 12 women and 7 men, ranged in age from 18 to 47. Five were freshmen, 2 sophomores, 6 juniors, and 6 graduate students. Three were married and homesharing only during the school week. Students who had transportation were placed up to eight miles from campus. Some students had meal tickets at the university dining hall. Others had kitchen privileges and ate dinner with the homeowner or had meals included with the rent. It appears at this point in the project that the typical student homeseeker is an older, serious student who is family oriented and has often had previous positive relationships with older people.

Homeowners ranged in age from 57 to 97 with an average age of 82. They included 12 women, 4 men, and 3 married couples. Two homeowners were single; the others, widowed or divorced. Seven lived in California; the rest, in outlying small towns. Only 6 had any form of transportation. The typical homeowner is widowed, lives alone, has an affinity for young people, or is looking for companionship after the death of a spouse.

CONCLUSION

The rural intergenerational homesharing project at California, then, differs from urban programs. Most fundamentally, the approach is more informal. Although informality may be part of service delivery in urban areas, urban observers of our operations have noted that the sense of communication between the staff of SHARE and the California community is vastly different from that in urban areas; rural practitioners, for example, are often involved in many aspects of participants' lives and provide informal counseling to these individuals. Second, families of both homeowners and students are involved in the entire homesharing process. Third, homesharers are dealing with "trusted friends" rather than mere agency personnel, because the SHARE staff has adopted Coward and Lee's theory of "ecologically sensitive intervention." Finally, strong, ongoing community involvement (networking) is a vital component of SHARE.

From the staff point of view, participation in rural shared housing has prompted awareness of several policy issues:

1. Rural homesharing is a viable housing alternative that is especially important in nonmetropolitan areas because of the severe lack of housing options.

2. An increase in rural homesharing options will further the current trend toward in-home supportive services rather than institutionalization.

3. Ongoing funding in a rural area is more difficult to obtain because of the relatively meager economic base. Churches and social service agencies in rural communities do not have the finances to contribute to long-term support.

4. Matchmaking in rural areas is less cost-effective than in urban locations. The amount of funds allocated for new programs in rural communities, however, should not depend on the utilization rates of previous programs (Osgood, 1977).

5. The pairing of elders and young people in the same unit challenges the assumption that elders prefer age-segregated housing.

SHARE has been in operation for only a short time. Undoubtedly, as SHARE continues to develop, changes will occur in some areas. There are a number of unanswered questions about rural shared housing that can be answered only after additional years of experience.

1. Are typically aged freshmen too young for homesharing? Since they are in the process of divorcing themselves from parental authority, is homesharing with an elderly homeowner workable?

2. Will the elderly who participate in the program continue to be involved? Will they seek new matches when previous ones terminate?

3. Will students or homeowners be more likely to break a contract?

4. Will students' attitudes toward the elderly be changed through homesharing and vice versa?

5. Are homesharing participants less lonely than nonhomesharers? Does loneliness diminish during the match and intensify after its terminating?

6. Can a small town or rural area support an intergenerational housing program?

7. What is the profile of a successful rural homesharer?

8. Will the attitudes of older people in the general population change toward homesharing because of SHARE?

Although these questions remain to be answered, what is immediately obvious to SHARE staff is that any intergenerational homesharing program in a rural area cannot be just a "scaled-down version of big city programs" (Coward and

Lee, 1985). It must meet the needs of the rural elderly with an informal approach directly suited to their needs, traditions, values, and spirit of independence.

REFERENCES

Ansello, E. F. "Antecedent Principles in Rural Gerontology Education." In *Toward Mental Health of the Rural Elderly*, edited by P. Kim and C. Wilson. Landover, Md.: University Press of America, 1981.

Auerbach, A. J. "The Elderly in Rural Areas: Differences in Urban Areas and Implications for Practice." In *The Aged in Rural America*, edited by J. A. Krout. Westport, Conn.: Greenwood Press, 1986.

Bischoff, H. G. W. "Rural Settings: A New Frontier." In *The Elderly in Rural Society*, edited by R. T. Coward and G. R. Lee. New York: Springer Press, 1985.

Bureau of the Census. *Census Report, 1980*. Washington, D.C.: U.S. Government Printing Office, 1980.

Bylund, R. A. "Rural Housing: Perspective for the Aged." In *The Elderly in Rural Society*, edited by R. T. Coward and G. R. Lee. New York: Springer Press, 1985.

Bylund, R. A., LeRay, N. L., and Crawford, C. O. "Housing Quality of the Elderly: A Rural-Urban Comparison." *Journal of Minority Aging* 4 (1979):14–24.

Coward, R. T. "Delivering Social Services in Small Towns and Rural Communities." In *The Aged in Rural America*, edited by J. A. Krout. Westport, Conn.: Greenwood Press, 1977.

Coward, R. T., and Lee, G. R., *The Elderly in Rural Society*. New York: Springer Press, 1985.

Coward, R. T., and Rathbone-McCuan, E. "Delivering Health and Human Services to the Elderly in Rural Society." In *The Elderly in Rural Society*, edited by R. T. Coward and G. R. Lee. New York: Springer Press, 1985.

Dobkin, Leah. *Shared Housing for Older People: A Planning Manual for Match-Up Programs*. Philadelphia: National Shared Housing Resource Center, 1983.

Hayslip, B., Ritter, M., Altman, R., and McDonnell, G. "Home Care Services and the Rural Elderly." *The Gerontologist* 20 (1980):192–99.

Karcher, E. J., and Karcher, B. E. "Education and Religion: Potential Partners in Service to the Rural Elderly." *Educational Gerontology: International Quarterly* 5 (1980):409–21.

Krout, J. A. *The Aged in Rural America*. Westport, Conn.: Greenwood Press, 1986.

Learner, R. M., and Kivett, V. R. "Discriminates of Perceived Dietary Adequacy among the Rural Elderly." *Geriatrics* 78 (1981):330–37.

Osgood, Mary H. "Rural and Urban Attitudes towards Welfare." *Social Work* 22 (1977):41–47.

Pennsylvania Department of Labor and Industry. Office of Employment Security, Labor Market Analyst. *Annual Planning Information Report*, 1986 and 1987.

Scheidt, Rick J. "The Mental Health of the Aged in Rural Environments." In *The Elderly in Rural Society*, edited by R. T. Coward and G. R. Lee. New York: Springer Press, 1985.

Schreter, C. A. "Advantages and Disadvantages of Shared Housing." *Journal of Housing for the Elderly* 3 (1986):121–38.

Taietz, P., and Milton, S. "Rural-Urban Differences in the Structure of Services for the

Elderly in Upstate New York Counties.'' *Journal of Gerontology* 34 (1979):429–37.

Youmanns, E. G. *Aging Patterns in a Rural and an Urban Area of Kentucky*. Agricultural Equipment Station Bulletin Number 681. Lexington, Kentucky, 1963.

Part II
REGIONWIDE
PERSPECTIVES

5

Shared Housing in California: A Regional Perspective

David C. Pritchard and Joelle Perkocha

Affordable housing is one of the cornerstones of an effective long-term-care delivery system for the elderly. The housing problems of this population are critical in many locations due to a number of adverse market conditions, such as insufficient public funds to meet the need for rent subsidies and construction of low-income housing, conversion of apartments to condominiums, and indiscriminate rent increases, all of which affect opportunities for the elderly to obtain appropriate and affordable housing. Steadily increasing rents have an especially insidious effect on substantial numbers of older persons who are below or just above the poverty level and whose fixed incomes fail to keep pace with the increase in the cost of living. Because of the priority elderly individuals give to safe, familiar, and comfortable living arrangements, many will reduce spending for other basic necessities significantly in order to remain in rental housing that has become overpriced or in owned homes whose upkeep is costly. To address this problem, the concept of shared housing offers one alternative solution to the housing dilemma of the elderly.

To develop a greater understanding of how shared housing has been developing as a resource for the elderly, the case of California is presented as a large regional area representing perhaps the largest concentration of homesharing programs in one state in the country. To describe the shared housing activity as comprehensively as possible, data and information were gathered from several sources. Documents were obtained and officials interviewed from the California Departments of Aging and of Housing and Community Development. A formal survey was conducted of all identified shared housing projects throughout the state. Additional information was provided by the Human Investment Project of San Mateo, California, the agency responsible for technical assistance to shared housing programs in the state. Numerous informal interviews with shared housing program staff occurred at conferences and other professional meetings. The result of these contacts and data-collection techniques is a broadly based description of the status of shared housing in California.

OVERVIEW

Shared housing in California has been an organized phenomenon since 1978 when Project Match in Santa Clara County was initiated with Community Employment and Training Act (CETA) funds. Alternative Living for the Aging, another major homesharing program, was established during the same year in Los Angeles. Both programs have grown and flourished and, as role models, have provided guidance to many shared housing programs throughout the state. In 1986, 51 programs were operational in California (California Department of Aging, 1986). The heavily populated urban areas have witnessed the greatest growth in numbers and types of programs, but the rural areas, despite smaller populations to draw on, have also demonstrated that shared housing is a reasonable alternative to high housing costs. Although the current research is focused on the 51 identified programs, there is evidence that there are additional, informal shared housing programs in California operating on an ad hoc basis through senior centers, churches, and other organizations.

Eighty-six percent of the shared housing programs are organized with nonprofit status. Seven are considered public entities, either operated as programs by the cities or by Public Housing Authorities. Recent changes in Housing Authority regulations have made it possible for two people to use their Section 8 Certificates (federal housing rental subsidies) in a shared housing situation. Because of this change, some Housing Authorities are choosing to implement their own shared housing programs, and others are contracting with established programs to provide the counseling component seen as necessary to promoting successful shared living arrangements.

Staffing levels for the 51 programs ranged from situations involving one paid staff and a part-time volunteer to a full-time equivalent staff of eight. Program budgets ranged from a low of $7,000 for a part-time program to well over a quarter of a million dollars annually, depending upon the types and kinds of related housing services offered. During 1986 these programs processed 24,780 applications for shared housing and were able to place 6,912 individuals in matching arrangements.

More than 85% of the programs served an intergenerational population and often included special outreach to the disabled. Only 15% of the programs served seniors exclusively. Several programs in the major metropolitan markets around the state offered the one-on-one matchup program and augmented this service with the ''group share'' concept. In a group share or Lease-a-Home situation, the nonprofit agency leased a vacant home from a private landlord and filled it with shared housing applicants. This offered all of the usual benefits of homesharing with the additional advantages of being able to accommodate each sharer's personal furniture, an important feature not usually available in most traditional shared housing situations. An outgrowth of the group share concept was Co-housing, which was based on a Scandinavian model of community living. Co-housing, through a group process, brings together potential sharers who "self-select" their housemates and then move into homes large enough to accommodate the needs of three to five adults. To enrich further this variety of homesharing options, some developers in California have been experimenting with new apartment buildings designed for shared living.

FUNDING SUPPORT

Financial support has been a central issue and concern in any consideration of the viability and effectiveness of shared housing. Funding for shared housing programs has derived from both the public and private sectors. A great deal of the public monies identified for shared housing programs originated at the federal level and has been channeled to the state and ultimately the local level. Many shared housing programs have received funds through a variety of public and private sources. To illustrate, a typical shared housing program in California may first have received funds from the local city's Community Development Block Grant (CDBG) program, which has been part of the federal Housing and Urban Development Department's revenue-sharing efforts. The same program may also have received support from the local Area Agency on Aging, whose funds also originated in Washington through the Administration on Aging. A third source of funding may have been the California Department of Housing and Community Development's (HCD) Senior Citizen Shared Housing Program (SCSHP). Finally, this mix of program funding may have been augmented by monies from the private sector through corporate, foundation, or individual support. Despite the range of potential funding sources, most shared housing projects in California struggle to obtain a level of funding that is adequate to support an effective program with sufficient professional staff.

Approximately 30 senior citizen shared housing programs throughout the state have been funded since 1981 by the California Department of HCD to focus on the housing needs of older adults. These grants have ranged in size from $6,400 to $86,000 for a two-year period. The SCSHP has been increasing in size since its inception and has been funded through the California Housing Trust Fund. The Trust Fund itself received state revenues generated by off-shore oil production. This source of income to the trust is due to expire in January 1989 unless extended by the state legislature. Even if the "sunset" date is extended, there is some question as to whether the Housing Trust Fund will continue to be funded by Tidelands Oil Revenues or whether another funding source will have to be identified. The SCSHP is not automatically funded each year by the state. Such funding requires action by the state administration and is subject to yearly legislative review.

A new source of funding for many programs, particularly those in the San

Francisco bay area, has derived from local Redevelopment Agencies. As prescribed by state law, each city has the right to establish its own Redevelopment Agency. Specific objectives of these agencies included the creation or expansion of a tax base, the provision of employment opportunities, an increase in the supply of low- and moderate-income housing, and an improvement of the social, economic, and psychological environment. Specifically, the redevelopment law required that 20% of the taxes generated to the agency be used for purposes of increasing and improving the supply of low- and moderate-income housing. Serendipitously, a shared housing program is uniquely situated to help the redevelopment agency meet its 20% "set aside" goals for low- and moderate-income housing. Shared housing clients who are homeowners are able to provide affordable housing for low- and moderate-income individuals, as shared living situations are generally well below the prevailing market rental rates. Also, shared housing programs can improve the existing housing stock in another way. Frequently, the elderly homesharer's home is in need of repair that is not affordable on a fixed income. Income gained from the rental of a room, however, can be applied to upgrading the condition of the house. For these reasons, redevelopment agencies view the funding of shared housing programs as helping to meet their mandated goals.

A final comment on funding relates to the private sector. Several shared housing programs in California have supplemented their public monies with substantial private sector support. In many areas of the state, community foundations have funded programs in either initial or ongoing phases. Several foundations have as their area of interest both senior citizen and housing programs, making senior shared housing programs an ideal recipient of their funds. It has also been possible to work cooperatively and creatively with the business community to obtain needed funding. One example related to a project developed with a local Board of Realtors. The realtors designated the shared housing program as the recipient of their annual philanthropic efforts and, in the process, received significant publicity for their members. Local, private foundations were also found to be a potential source of funding when selected carefully and approached with a thoughtful and well-articulated proposal.

ROLE OF STATE GOVERNMENT

The California Department of Housing and Community Development has served as a major funding source for shared housing programs in the state. The Senior Citizens Shared Housing Program was established under the auspices of this department in 1981. This occurred in response to the need for affordable housing being faced by California's senior (age 65 and over) population. The implementing legislation was sponsored by State Senator Henry J. Mello, who continued to play a significant role in the ongoing development of the policy. The responsibilities of the SCSHP were to determine funding allocations, monitor the selected shared housing projects, and provide technical assistance to old and

new projects statewide. The SCSHP was initially conceived as a two-year demonstration program with a $50,000 appropriation. These funds were used for
three pilot projects operated by nonprofit organizations with the program goal
to assist 500 seniors each year. In 1983 legislation was passed to place the
SCSHP in permanent status. An additional $300,000 was appropriated and was
allocated for grant awards to seven local government and nonprofit organizations.
The policy allowed programs to match seniors with other seniors or with younger
adults and established a goal of 3,000 individuals (age 65 and over) to be assisted
over a two-year period.

In 1984 the state legislature appropriated a third round of funding in the amount
of $500,000. The bill allowed new organizations to apply for grant funds without
needing to raise a local cash "match." This legislation also permitted the Department of HCD to provide funding for a qualified shared housing program to
deliver technical assistance to less experienced programs throughout the state.
It further specified that a working relationship be established with the State
Department of Aging for the purpose of administering the program. As a result,
in April 1985 grants to provide more substantial and reliable financial support
were made to 15 nonprofit organizations and public agencies to deliver shared
housing services. In the following year, one shared housing program was selected
for a special grant to provide technical assistance to agencies interested in developing shared housing programs and to other less-experienced shared housing
providers needing formative information and guidance. Subsequent legislation
during the next two years made available funds for the continuation of such
programs through a competitive proposal process. Funding for these programs
was shifted to the Housing Trust Fund. Under this fund, monies were allocated
for housing programs to serve lower-income and very low income households
as determined by HUD guidelines.

Selecting programs to receive funding was less complicated in the beginning
years because there were very few in operation. The evaluation process became
more complex, however, with the advent of greater interest in shared housing
and the proliferation of programs. Because of the need for more specific and
discriminating assessment guidelines, the following criteria were established by
which proposals were evaluated on a point-score basis:

1. "An analysis of the methods used to implement the program." The following program
   components were evaluated: outreach to participants, information and referral, counseling, placements, and follow-up. Agencies had to demonstrate an understanding of
   the mechanics and a sensitivity to the issues involved in a shared housing program to
   score well.

2. "Proportion of senior citizens (age 65 and over) matched." Since the majority of the
   programs within the state had an intergenerational focus, rather than being exclusively
   for the use of seniors, only those programs that had a 50% or greater client base of
   senior citizens placed in shared housing situations were considered for funding.

3. "The extent to which housing costs were reduced." Information in this category was based on the previous year's statistics for each program submitting a proposal. Programs given preference were those that were able to demonstrate that housing costs (based on preshare and postshare information) were reduced due to the shared experience. The state legislature found that many elderly renters paid excessive amounts of their income for housing. More than 65% of all elderly renter households paid in excess of 25% of their income for housing and more than one-quarter paid in excess of 50%. Programs documenting that housing costs were reduced through sharing were evaluated favorably.

4. "The extent to which the applicant was able to provide matching funds." Those programs that were able to show support for their programs from other funding sources were in a more competitive situation. By leveraging state with local funds, the state was able to receive greater program value per state dollar expended.

5. "The applicant's capacity to operate the program." This was measured by examining the history of the organization, experience serving seniors, involvement with shared housing, prior administration or government grants, and expertise of staff.

6. "The cost-effectiveness of the program." The cost to the state of placing a senior in a shared living arrangement was derived by determining the ratio of SCSHP grant dollars to seniors matched. To receive the maximum point-score, an agency had to match one senior for each $125 of SCSHP grant funds requested. If an agency placed a large percentage (at least 50%) of frail elders, a higher amount ($156) of grant funds per senior "matched" was allowed for the same maximum point-score.

The California Department of Aging (CDA) also has a serious concern for the housing situation of the elderly in the state and for how housing programs and resources can enhance the development of long-term-care service delivery systems at the local level. The CDA has taken the initiative to compile and update listings of shared housing programs throughout the state. Although the ultimate responsibility for allocation of state monies for shared housing lies with the Department of Housing and Community Development, the Department of Aging has an important collaborative role to play. The CDA cooperates with the HCD in reviewing and commenting on the Request for Proposal (RFP) process including the evaluation instrument, the ranking of the applications for funding, and the conduct of site visits to monitor the grantees during the contract year. This cooperation between state agencies has resulted in efficient management of state shared housing monies.

TECHNICAL ASSISTANCE

While conducting monitoring visits to the shared housing programs funded under the SCSHP, state HCD staff determined that it would be useful to have one qualified program take a leadership role in providing information and technical assistance to beginning as well as veteran programs. As a result, SCSHP funds were awarded to the Human Investment Project (HIP) in San Mateo to serve in this capacity on a statewide basis. Following up on a questionnaire sent in the fall of 1986 to shared housing programs throughout the state, the HIP staff focused their technical assistance in two areas: the first established seminars to be held in strategic locations around the state dealing with common shared housing program problems, for example, funding, marketing, and dealing with difficult clients; the second area of assistance was the production of a "how-to" manual that was to be a compilation of materials and experience developed by shared housing programs statewide. This manual, "Homesharing: Successful Strategies," was distributed to all 51 programs and was made available to other agencies on request.

During a second year of the technical assistance contract with HIP, a set of video training tapes was produced for distribution, and the first statewide conference on shared housing was convened. Topics covered on the training tapes included interviewing the "problem" client and using mediation as an effective tool in "problem" matches. The state conference is discussed in more detail below.

NETWORKING INITIATIVES

In reviewing the written evaluations of the Technical Assistance Seminars held in 1986–87, it was clear that the various shared housing programs felt a professional need to meet together with others in the field to discuss common problems and creative solutions. In fact, informal networking meetings were already being held in various parts of the state to address the critical problems and issues. One such group, the Bay Area Shared Housing Coalition in the San Francisco area, was organized in 1983 and had been meeting twice each year. A similar group in the San Diego area had been meeting quarterly for several years.

The most ambitious network, in terms of frequency of meetings, was convened by staff from the Area Agency on Aging in Orange County in the greater Los Angeles area. Fifteen programs were scattered throughout Orange County, which contained a population of 2 million residents. These 15 programs held monthly meetings, and their objectives were to orchestrate joint promotional efforts, receive training as a group, and even share clients. They also instituted a progressive group "mixer" where clients met informally with each other. This type of activity allowed clients to meet many prospective housemates at one time instead of going through the more typical referral process with a housing counselor. The progressive "mixer" departed from the usual format in that meetings occurred at all 15 program sites at different times of the day. Through careful scheduling, a client could meet many people living in different cities during one day.

Perhaps the most important networking effort for homesharing in California was the first statewide conference held at Asilomar in April 1988. This conference was sponsored jointly by the State Department of Housing and Community Development and the Human Investment Project. Twenty-eight shared housing programs were represented by staff personnel and board members. State Senator

Henry J. Mello, considered to be the motivating force behind the shared housing legislation in California, was the keynote speaker. Some of the significant topics addressed at this conference included an overview of shared housing on the national level, changes in the Housing Authority's Section 8 Certificate program, use of CDBG and Redevelopment funds, perspectives on the problem client, automation for small and midsized agencies, and creative publicity efforts. The two-day event concluded with a group consensus to establish a statewide association that would meet on an annual basis. The rationale for this initiative, as outlined by participants, was to establish greater credibility for the concept of shared housing, greater political strength, a more positive image through increased visibility, and a resource for the sharing of information through a centralized network and clearinghouse.

It is clear that there is a significant amount of professional activity taking place in California in the shared housing field not only in relation to the provision of services but also in respect to the enhancement of skills and knowledge of agency staff and to the development of stronger organizational linkages.

PROGRAM SURVEY

To expand the understanding of shared housing gained from the broader state perspective, a study was conducted to elicit responses from the perspective of individual matching programs. The purpose was to obtain descriptive data and viewpoints from the operational level that would further identify and clarify trends, issues, and concerns as well as specific practices that have proven effective in delivering shared housing services. This research was thought to be needed in a field that was still in a developmental phase and in which operational and accountability practices were still, for the most part, idiosyncratic. By 1989 two national surveys had been undertaken, (see, for example, Chapter 3 in this volume) as well as several case studies (Pritchard, 1983; Chapter 10 in this volume), but research had not kept pace with practice developments in respect to this rapidly evolving housing concept. The aim in this survey, therefore, was to describe the service delivery activity and also attempt to capture the vitality and uniqueness of the efforts being carried out over a broad regional area.

Methodology

A research strategy was designed to collect descriptive data from shared housing projects throughout California. Because of the changing nature of these projects, the intent was to focus on critical aspects of operational functioning through selected quantitative data and also through more qualitative information that could clarify the issues and concerns more comprehensively. To accomplish this goal efficiently, a survey instrument was developed to record the perceptions of shared housing project directors. Considering the absence of standardized reports and uniform data categories in this field, this research approach was thought to have the possibility of yielding pragmatic and thoughtful information about shared housing operations.

The sample population was obtained from the California Department of Aging's *Listing of Senior Citizen Shared Housing Projects* (1986). All known shared housing programs in California were included in this inventory. Data were collected over a two-year period (1986–88) to take advantage of an updated "listing" and include all agencies with substantial programs that had survived the initial challenges of funding and staffing deficiencies. Ultimately, all 51 shared housing programs contained in the state listing for 1986 were included in the sample population.

The survey instrument consisted of 20 questions. Sixteen questions required specific answers, and three were open ended and asked for individual comments and perspectives. The last question requested demographic information about the project. The survey technique was to ask project directors to respond to the questions based on their understanding and experience with shared housing. Some questions were factual and entailed information readily available, and other questions asked respondents for their perceptions of the most salient characteristics of a particular phenomenon or the frequency of occurrence. This instrument was initially field tested and revised by submitting it to three homesharing programs for an assessment of its clarity, relevance, significance, and limitations.

Thirty-seven of 51 programs (73%) returned completed questionnaires. The answers were quantified where possible and content analysis used for more detailed responses. When responses were quantified, the percentages obtained relate either to the number of programs in the sample (N = 37), or when several specific answers were requested for one question, the total number of answers submitted for that question was used to determine the percentage.

Findings

A fundamental concern of homesharing programs has been to recruit sufficient numbers of applicants. One of the most critical questions, and one that requires further study, is how to sensitize and interest the older population in homesharing as a viable housing option. Project directors were asked to list what they perceived as the three most effective recruitment methods. The methods identified were advertising in various media (television, radio, newspapers); disseminating agency flyers, newsletters, or bulletins; and making presentations to groups and organizations in the community. It was thought that these methods were more effective than most other techniques including "mixers," that is opportunities for potential homesharers to meet in a neutral group setting. Two other means of recruitment not requiring specific agency efforts, agency referral and word of mouth, were also considered useful but of lesser importance in identifying new homesharing candidates.

Related to the basic effort to recruit applicants was the further need to recruit sufficient numbers of both homeseekers and homeproviders. More directors (20, 54%) reported substantially fewer numbers of homeseekers than homeproviders. Thirteen (35%) respondents reported fewer homeproviders. Others did not report a significant difference. The situation of homeseekers is complex and varies not only related to individual personality factors but also according to local market conditions for affordable housing. Homeseekers are frequently under pressure to make a housing adjustment very quickly and become easily discouraged if not matched immediately. Other elderly homeseekers do not choose shared housing as an option for a variety of personal reasons. Although some of the reasons were reported—desire for privacy, distrust of others, and inflexibility—a greater understanding of this phenomenon is needed.

In looking at the motivation of older persons to choose homesharing as a housing alternative, program directors were asked to identify the major reasons for participation or nonparticipation. For homeproviders, the need for additional income (32%) was mentioned most frequently, followed by the desire for companionship (30%) and the need for services in the home (22%). Concern for security (13%) was a lesser motivating factor. Homeseekers were seen as having similar motives. They were strongly motivated by financial concerns (45%), followed by the need for companionship (26%) and, to a lesser degree, security (9%). Homeseekers were perceived as potential service providers in relation to participation in shared housing, rather than as needing services.

Why don't more older persons view shared housing as a viable option? Program directors reported that from their perspective the primary reason was the desire for independent living and the need for privacy (46%). Another important reason was the concern for security, which involved a basic distrust of strangers (21%). Third, they reported the problem of individuals with inflexible personality characteristics who avoid living in interdependent relationships (17%).

A major task of the shared housing staff is to evaluate new applicants effectively in order to identify individuals with inappropriate mental or social characteristics. Lacking a really effective screening instrument, fact gathering and interviewing techniques were normally employed. Asking for personal references adds another screening dimension to this imperfect process. More than two-thirds of the programs (25, 68%) have opted to use this screening device. Of this group, 19 required references from both homeseekers and homeproviders whereas 6 required references only from homeseekers.

Another technique to help create the basis for a successful match is to facilitate a meeting between the prospective sharers at which expectations are discussed specifically and systematically. This is accomplished by having the prospective sharers participate in negotiating a formal agreement before finalizing the match. An agreement stipulates the financial considerations, household responsibilities, privileges, boundaries, and services to be provided. By engaging in these negotiations, potential concerns and issues can be addressed before becoming points of conflict. Despite the apparent value of having formal agreements between the participants, only 7 programs (19%) required this procedure as part of the matching process. Although 30 programs (81%) did not have this requirement, 16 (43%) of them did strongly suggest to their match participants that they develop an agreement informally. Thus this practice, although encouraged extensively, has not become a standard procedure in most programs.

Once a match has been initiated, another important method used by the agency to maintain the continuing viability of the arrangement is to schedule follow-up contacts to monitor the situation and deal with issues of conflict and stress. Twenty-eight (76%) directors reported that their programs employed this tactic, and 20 (54%) made their follow-up contacts during the first month. However, 22 (59%) of these agencies made their follow-up contacts by telephone rather than face-to-face interviews.

Despite agency efforts to arrange the most compatible match and to plan for potential difficulties, a large percentage of dissolutions were perceived as occurring during the first three months. Directors reported three major reasons for dissolutions. The most frequent reason cited was incompatibility (31%). The next most frequent cause of dissolutions was related to a variety of planned and unplanned housing adjustments that can simply be labeled "change of circumstances" (24%), for example, relatives deciding they wanted the sharer to live with them or the individual accumulating enough money to rent his or her own apartment. Health-related problems of various kinds (21%), such as illness, institutionalization, or death, constituted the third most important cause of dissolutions. Another important contributing factor was the expectations that the sharers had agreed to initially but were not actually fulfilled once the match had begun (11%).

Arranging viable matches is a fundamental goal of shared housing matching programs. Respondents, however, identified a number of obstacles that interfered with their being able to match clients effectively. The first type of difficulty was seen as client deficiencies (34%): insufficient funds, high expectations, and personality issues. A second important barrier related to deficiencies in the program itself (26%): insufficient funding, space, and staffing. Third, and related to these concerns, was also the need to improve the effectiveness of staff through learning more effective methods, skills, and techniques (11%). A fourth problem identified was an insufficient number of applicants (10%), which affected the ability to perform the most appropriate matching. Finally, it was noted that it was not financially possible to initiate enough publicity to attract sufficient numbers of clients to the programs (6%).

Directors were asked two questions about the kinds of clients their programs were prepared to serve: "Were there many applicants interested specifically in temporary shared housing (up to three months)?" "Did they arrange intergenerational matches?" Thirteen directors (35%) thought that up to 10% of their applicants were more interested in temporary matches, and another seven respondents (19%) thought that their programs were asked to provide temporary placements for between 11% and 20% of their clients. Another major potential source of clients was the population of younger adults. Intergenerational matches were arranged by all but two of the projects in the sample population.

To understand more about the operational practices of the shared housing programs, directors were asked about several key areas: service fees, use of computers, funding, and legal concerns. Only two agencies (5%) requested small registration fees if the clients could afford them. Many of the agencies, however, would accept donations. Most directors thought that requesting fees would be an inhibiting factor to participation by low-income clients.

In respect to computers, 13 agencies (35%) had incorporated computers into their shared housing program's operations. Of the 13, 9 (24%) reported that they were using the computers to enter and maintain client demographic information. Eleven (30%) used the computers for general administrative tasks. None of the respondents indicated that he or she had a computer program that could match homeproviders and homeseekers successfully. Several projects, however, have found the computer very effective in identifying individuals with compatible characteristics, for example, neighborhood, smoker or nonsmoker, needing and willing to provide services. Using the homeprovider's key compatibility characteristics, the computer can generate a list of homeseekers with corresponding characteristics. This reduced list can then be analyzed more efficiently to develop an effective match.

Directors were also asked whether their funding for the shared housing program was adequate to achieve their goals. Three programs (8%) reported that they received no funding for shared housing. These programs operated entirely through the use of volunteers. Nine programs (24%) reported that their funding was sufficient to meet their stated goals. However, 25 directors (68%) indicated that their current level of funding was insufficient to carry out their program mandates. For those 25 programs, the areas most affected by inadequate funding were staffing and the ability to generate publicity and other community educational initiatives. With more funding, respondents said they would hire additional staff, increase their publicity and scope of services, and, where not currently available, obtain a computer for more efficient operations. Most funding (80%) for these programs was obtained from public sources with Community Development Block Grant and Older American Act monies being the most prevalent and with some state and local government general-purpose funds being allocated specifically for shared housing. Private sources contributed 20% of the funding support, most of this coming from fund raisers, United Way, and private foundations.

The final area pertained to whether the agency had experience or had concerns related to legal problems. Shared housing projects were perceived by some respondents as very vulnerable to lawsuits stemming from matches that became exploitive or emotionally disturbing. Another legal concern was the inhibiting effect of zoning laws in some areas. It was also reported that one public agency that wanted to initiate a shared housing program in an urban community was unable to do so because the city attorney refused to approve it.

Three open-ended questions were designed to provide the opportunity for the directors to elaborate on their operational practices. They were specifically asked to discuss any unique or innovative aspects of their programs, areas needing research, and other significant issues or problems they wanted to address. The basic need to attract sufficient numbers of applicants provoked many creative techniques. Three noteworthy ones included using want-ad-type formats, distributing housing information booklets, and developing a systematic marketing plan. Another approach was to expand the scope of services to encompass additional vulnerable populations, such as the physically disabled, AIDS patients, and younger clients. Several directors thought that their use of computers was breaking new ground in shared housing. Using volunteers exclusively to operate the project was considered unique by one director. Another agency made a comprehensive psychosocial assessment of each client to understand problems and needs so that housing counseling could be focused most effectively.

Respondents identified many areas needing further research and understanding. The challenge of making the most successful match possible was a major concern. More effective assessment tools are needed to evaluate and match homeproviders and homeseekers. More information is also needed to identify the specific variables or determinants of successful matches. For planning and accountability purposes, it was also important to develop a standard definition of "successful" matches or to develop another way to describe matches that appeared to have positive outcomes. Respondents were also concerned about improving financial accountability, that is, the costs to develop a match and cost-effectiveness.

According to the respondents, more research is also needed to understand the motives of older persons in regard to homesharing with attention directed to different socioeconomic groups. Is homesharing really an option of last resort for seniors? Are there incentives that might play a critical role? Generally, how is it possible to sensitize the senior population to the benefits of homesharing and to stimulate their interest in this housing alternative? Are there ways to educate or motivate seniors to consider shared housing more seriously?

Other topics identified for further study included the questions of liability and zoning laws. Many projects were concerned about the possibility of lawsuits. More information was needed on the legal status of the agency as a broker and facilitator. Similarly, zoning policy precluded shared housing in some areas. More information was needed to understand the complexities of this legal phenomenon. Finally, research was needed to study the experience of homesharing with special populations, for example, the homeless, AIDS patients, the disabled, and single parents on public assistance. Matching single parents and their children was mentioned as an especially important area to understand more fully.

The third area of inquiry asked respondents to identify issues and problems they perceived as most significant from their perspectives. Their comments primarily focused on areas seen as critical to effective shared housing service delivery. Obtaining adequate funding was a major concern and one that absorbed significant amounts of staff time. Directors believed that shared housing required greater funding attention and resources. Additional funding, if it were available, would not only be used to augment and refine existing services but, in some cases, to develop group homes for greater diversity in trying to meet the need for affordable housing. A more immediate concern was to hire and pay the staff adequately. Respondents also wanted to be able to increase the size of the staff to be more responsive to all clients. This would entail being able to interview potential sharers, facilitate matches, and conduct follow-up contacts in a more substantive manner. These basic matching functions, publicity, and outreach efforts, as well as the details of accountability, required more trained staff to increase the level and scope of services.

Directors were also concerned about the obstacles that prevented their agencies from achieving the goal of providing an affordable housing option to the elderly population. One obstacle was inherent in the present older cohort's reluctance to engage in homesharing. Homeproviders were often ambivalent about having a stranger in their homes, and homeseekers wanted to live where they could have their personal items and furnishings with them. In some cases the home-providers' homes were not suitable because of physical deficiencies. Also, there appeared to be fewer homesharing opportunities for younger persons, men, single parents with children, and minorities. Further complicating the problem, some funding sources would not fund matches that included younger adults or would not count younger adults in terms of accountability goals.

The need for in-home services was increasing as a motivating factor for homeproviders to engage in homesharing. This population, however, often desired substantial services but in return offered inadequate compensation. To complicate this problem further, not enough homeseekers were interested in providing in-home services in exchange for some combination of room, board, and a salary. In fact, project directors were concerned that in many cases there were not sufficient homeseekers in their applicant pool, that they were usually outnumbered by homeproviders.

Finally, respondents were concerned about a basic lack of public education for the elderly about shared housing as well as comprehensive information generally about housing choices in a community.

Discussion

What do the data and the perceptions of shared housing directors tell us about the status of shared housing throughout a large region? First, it appears that the spurt in growth of shared housing projects during the early 1980s has leveled off in California. Fifty programs were identified in the 1984 California "listing." Several of these programs were discontinued and several others added, bringing the updated total in 1986 to 51. The heaviest concentration of shared housing projects was located in large urban areas.

Although the need for affordable housing for the elderly continued to increase, shared housing projects that relied primarily on outside funding for their survival and viability struggled to maintain adequate support. This housing resource has attracted the attention of local and state funding agencies but only to a limited extent. Very few programs were funded substantially enough to provide adequate staffing and to publicize the concept broadly and effectively.

Despite these funding difficulties and several other problems and issues that are reviewed in this chapter, shared housing as an affordable housing option for older persons is thriving throughout the region of California. As noted earlier, organization, networking, and expertise were developing rapidly and were contributing significantly to raising the level of effectiveness throughout the state. Professional interaction at regional and area meetings and conferences demonstrated the experience, interest, and enthusiasm of shared housing personnel. Several established projects prepared operational manuals that describe the matching process and address the administrative and accountability dimensions of running a successful shared housing program.

One seemingly intractable problem was evident throughout the findings. Despite a serious need for low-income housing, seniors, generally, were not motivated to select shared housing as an economical solution. It appeared that there was an unwillingness to live with nonkinship individuals and forego one's privacy even though it caused severe financial difficulties. There is some evidence, however, that shared housing has had more success in certain geographical areas. Low apartment vacancy rates, large numbers of low-income seniors, long waiting lists for Section 8 rent subsidies, and the absence of other housing alternatives create a situation in which shared housing offers the only affordable option. In this case the desperate need for housing provoked by market conditions frequently overcomes other ambivalent concerns.

In contrast, some communities have the opposite circumstances operating— low rents and high vacancy factors—but shared housing programs have other problems to confront. In these situations in which the pool of homeseekers is smaller, individuals considering shared housing have frequently been clients with emotional problems, current or former substance abusers, ex-offenders, or those with a combination of adverse social and personal characteristics. Considering a match of one of these "problem" clients with a frail elderly homeowner often involves a complex set of concerns, and when this population of clients comprises a substantial number of the applicant pool, the program is faced with serious challenges. Other than requirements of funding sources, there are few guidelines for dealing with problem clients. In California, programs receiving SCSHP contracts "may not discriminate on the basis of physical or emotional disability." This policy delegates to the individual program the responsibility for determining how to absorb and how best to serve this population. With limited funding, many shared housing programs do not have the expertise or sufficient time to deal with the variety of special needs presented by "problem" clients. One of the sensitive issues that arises is how to handle the question of disclosure of the problem factors between the prospective homeseeker and the homeprovider. This is a challenging area and one that should attract research attention because it is becoming more critical due to a larger population of problem applicants that includes an increasing number of homeless clients.

A critical problem in the long-term care system relates to the demand for in-home services at affordable costs. The shortage of such services in many locations has motivated homeowners to turn to shared housing for a solution to their dilemma. Frail elderly homeproviders above the poverty level and not eligible for government-funded in-home supportive services frequently need personal or chore services. A limited number of homeseekers are able and willing to provide this service for appropriate compensation. When a suitable service agreement between a homeseeker and homeprovider is arranged, the character of the match is different in that it implies a different set of expectations in addition to the usual ones (Jaffe, 1989). This could trigger the need for more monitoring and involvement on the part of the shared housing program (Jaffe and Howe, in press). It also underlines the need for shared housing programs to be part of the service delivery system and to collaborate with other agencies involved in long-term care.

The question of what circumstances constitute a "successful" match has been approached from different perspectives. Directors indicated through their responses and comments that a match that meets the needs of the participants, regardless of length, is successful. Funding sources and monitors concerned with accountability may quarrel with that interpretation, believing that the investment in creating a match should produce long-term benefits to the matched individuals. The research findings, however, reveal the basic transitional nature of shared housing matches. Individual circumstances affected by health, family, financial, and personal issues are continually changing and often result in dissolutions after a relatively brief period. There seems to be a need for these temporary solutions whether they were planned or unplanned. Other matches may have a much longer life. More understanding of early dissolutions is needed to determine whether screening techniques need improvement, whether intervention would have helped, or whether this phenomenon is inevitable but, nevertheless, serves an important purpose.

A related issue that emerged from the survey concerned the question of follow-up services. Shared housing programs focus their resources and efforts on identifying, screening and matching applicants. Many programs are also concerned about follow-up to insure that the match gets off to a good start and to prevent early dissolutions. Counseling and monitoring efforts perform an important role in fostering longer-term matches. According to the survey, the majority of these follow-up contacts were made by telephone. Whether this type of contact is as effective as a face-to-face contact needs to be studied. Unfortunately, funding and staff deficiencies mitigate against these added, labor-intensive services even though they might swing the balance between potentially successful or abortive matches. This type of service could provide an excellent opportunity to use well-trained volunteers.

The California experience also underlines the need for the development of some greater conceptual understanding of the nature of shared housing. Shared housing has grown beyond the basic matching programs to encompass group homes and apartment complexes designed for sharing. In addition, there are many naturally occurring homesharing arrangements that evolve without formal matching processes (Schreter and Turner, 1986). The potential and actual populations that may use shared housing extend beyond the elderly to younger adults as well as special populations including single parents with children, the homeless, the disabled, the terminally ill, AIDS/ARC, and various ethnic groups. Thus the shared housing model in California is expanding both in terms of the kind of housing arrangements involved and the population characteristics.

Finally, one basic area for further refinement relates to the need for consensus building on the appropriateness of important concepts and models in shared housing. Although many of the methods and policies are becoming more consistent, there is a great deal of diversity in areas such as goal definition, funding criteria, evaluation techniques, and descriptive language. Service delivery, communication, and accountability can be enhanced as the most effective and efficient procedures are identified and disseminated. One example would be the possibilities inherent in computer technology and how to adapt it more effectively to the tasks of shared housing. Research has an important role to play in analyzing and reporting on the activities and developments in this field.

SUMMARY

Shared housing as a distinct area of professional interest in the housing field should continue to expand in California and in other geographical areas. Some regions have already developed extensive networks, such as the mid-America region, New Jersey, and Minnesota. Technical information and successful experiences are disseminated throughout these networks at conferences and training sessions and through newsletters and research reports. Increased leadership from significant national agencies, such as the Administration on Aging and the National Shared Housing Resource Center, could also produce significant improvements in the organization and delivery of shared housing services. Expansion, however, will be most affected by either a worsening in marketing conditions for low-income housing or a breakthrough in how to attract seniors to the possibilities of homesharing.

A key theme that has emerged from the California survey is that there are obstacles to the stability and growth of the shared housing enterprise. On the demand side, one must ask: what methods can be used to enhance the acceptability of shared housing as a housing alternative for the elderly? On the supply side, the key question is: how can funding sources, public and private, be sensitized to consider shared housing more seriously as a means to increase affordable housing resources by using existing housing stock? It seems apparent from this analysis that relatively small amounts of funding can have substantial impact when directed to local shared housing programs.

The basic need for appropriate, affordable housing to contribute to the quality of life of the elderly is a vital concern and has broad implications. Shared housing has an important role to perform in providing an economical and potentially enriching housing alternative. The challenge to the practitioners, researchers, and other professionals involved in this field is to close the knowledge and practice gaps and to provide the most effective and efficient services possible. More creative and substantial strategies are needed, however, to reach and present the elderly population with the potential advantages of homesharing so that this resource can be considered realistically as a possible housing option.

REFERENCES

California Department of Aging. *Listing of Senior Citizen Shared Housing Projects in California*, June 1986.

Jaffe, D. J. *Caring Strangers: The Sociology of Intergenerational Homesharing*, Greenwich, Conn.: JAI Press, 1989.

Jaffe, D. J., and Howe, E\ "Case Management for Homesharing." *Journal of Gerontological Social Work*, in press.

Pritchard, D. C. "The Art of Matchmaking: A Case Study in Shared Housing." *The Gerontologist* 23 (1983):174–79.

Schreter, C., and Turner, Lloyd. "Sharing and Subdividing Private Market Housing." *The Gerontologist* 26 (1986):181–86.

6

Michigan Match: A Homeshare Experience

Melanie A. Hwalek and
Elizabeth A. Longley

This chapter provides a description and comparative analysis of seven state-supported homeshare programs in Michigan. It describes the different ways the programs operated and compares their designs and outcomes. The seven programs all received some funding through the passage of state legislation. Some of the programs were initiated because of this legislation. Others had been operational before receiving state support.

MICHIGAN SHARED HOUSING LEGISLATION

In 1983 the Southeast Michigan Council of Governments (SEMCOG) established a Shared Housing Task Force to research the possibility of implementing shared housing throughout Southeast Michigan. With a grant from the Hudson-Webber foundation and their own dollars research began. Using expertise from shared housing experts throughout the nation and local service agencies, the SEMCOG formed Homeshare in October of 1984. With limited funds from the State of Michigan's Office of Services to the Aging (OSA) and their own funds, five agencies committed to the program for two years.

At the same time Representative Ray Murphy, who sat on the original task force, introduced legislation mandating the OSA to examine the feasibility of establishing a state-supported shared housing program. Under this act, P.A. 357 (1984), model shared housing projects were to be developed, and the OSA was to report to the legislature on the progress of the demonstration projects, the market for shared housing among Michigan's elderly, and the impediments faced in the development of the program. P.A. 357 defined the following components as necessary parts of the shared housing programs funded by the legislature: (1) An older person must be involved in the match, (2) the seeker(s) and provider(s)

will share the expenses of maintaining the housing, and (3) the rights and responsibilities of the older persons sharing housing shall be delineated in the form
of a shared housing agreement.

The act gave the OSA responsibility for designating shared housing demonstration sites and monitoring the activities of those sites. P.A. 357 also mandated
that the demonstration projects be evaluated to determine the benefits and possible
impediments to the programs. The OSA was also mandated to evaluate the
original demonstration sites. Much of the data reported in this chapter is based
on that evaluation and relates to the original demonstration period of November
1985 to January 1987.

Original funding of $200,000 for the demonstration period was provided by
the Michigan State Housing Development Authority (MSHDA). The MSHDA
also provided continuation funds for 1987 (February 1 through September 30,
1987) in the amount of $110,000. Funding for 1988 (October 1987 through
September 1988) was a $200,000 joint effort between the OSA and MSHDA.
Funding for the shared housing projects has been included in 1989 in the amount
of $164,400.

Michigan is one of the few states that has been actively involved in the funding
and coordination of shared housing. Since 1985, the OSA's role has evolved
with the overall success of the programs from that of funding agent to active
involvement in securing funds at state and local levels for the continuation of
the projects, establishing performance standards for agencies involved with
shared housing, and facilitating networking between individual agencies. Due
to a reduction of funding in 1989, however, the OSA's administration will be
that of a pass-through funding agent.

DESCRIPTION OF THE STATE-SUPPORTED PROGRAMS

Shared housing demonstration grants were awarded to the following com-
munity agencies in November, 1985: the SEMCOG in Detroit, Detroit Senior
Citizens Department, Tri-County Office on Aging (TCOA) in Lansing, and Upper
Peninsula Commission for Area Progress (UPCAP).

Through the agencies, seven programs actually received funding. The SEM-
COG grant provided support for five programs in southeastern Michigan in
addition to supporting the coordination of homeshare programs in the area. In
this section, we describe the administrative structures of each of the seven
programs.

Senior Citizens Department of the City of Detroit

The Detroit Senior Citizens Department had a homeshare program from November 1985 until September 1987. The program served the Detroit area and
the eastern part of Wayne County. The original grant to the Detroit Senior

Citizens Department served the following cities in southeastern Michigan: Detroit, Highland Park, Hamtramck, Harper Woods, Grosse Pointe, Grosse Pointe Shores, Grosse Pointe Park, Grosse Pointe Woods, and Grosse Pointe Farms.

Detroit is the largest city in Michigan and has a large proportion of low-income and minority elderly. Highland Park and Hamtramck are smaller cities whose boundaries are completely within the boundaries of Detroit. Both of these towns have large proportions of poor and minority elderly. Harper Woods is a small city just north of Detroit. Its elderly population can be described as primarily white and middle class. The "Grosse Pointes" are located just east of Detroit. The population of elderly in these small towns are predominantly upper middle and upper class.

The project office was located within the Senior Citizens Department in downtown Detroit. The homeshare staff consisted of a full-time project coordinator, two part-time homeshare counselors, and one full-time secretary. According to the project coordinator and the director of the department, the small staff was not sufficient to handle the entire service area.

The grant from the OSA to this project totaled $40,875. Only the project coordinator and secretary were paid through this grant. The two homeshare counselors were supported by funds from the Detroit Area Agency on Aging through the federal Older Workers Program (Title V). Fiscal and other administrative assistance was provided to the project as an in-kind contribution of the Senior Citizens Department of Detroit.

In addition to having shared housing, the Senior Citizens Department of Detroit operates other housing-assistance programs and a general information and referral service for seniors. These services were part of the regular activities of the Senior Citizens Department and were not supported by the homeshare grant. Homeshare applicants who needed these programs, however, could easily be referred. Alternatively, seniors calling about other types of housing assistance could also be referred to homeshare.

The decision to try to match a particular seeker and provider was made by a joint decision of the counselors and the shared housing coordinator. Common preferences, needs, and requests of the two parties were among the considerations of the staff when matching seekers and providers. If the two individuals were interested in learning more about each other, an introductory meeting was held. Usually, the homeshare counselor was present at this meeting, at which a general impression was obtained about the two applicants and about the likelihood that a match would be successful. If the two applicants were interested in trying to live together, a trial match period was set. After a successful trial period, the lease agreement was developed, under the direction of the homeshare counselor.

In addition to making matches, this project published a monthly newsletter called *Home Sharing Detroit*, which was distributed to local senior citizens.

Between November 1985 and January 31, 1986, 73 seekers and 234 providers applied to this homeshare program. A total of 13 matches were made, and 7 were recorded to be still in existence. Of the seekers, 63% were female, and 85% of the providers were female. Seekers' annual incomes ranged from $600 to $14,000.

Due to budget problems the department opted not to continue this program in 1988. The Office of Services to the Aging, through the Area Agency on Aging in Detroit, contracted with a new agency in March 1988. This agency, the Walter P. Reuther Centers, is a multi–Senior Service agency with the same service area as Detroit's Senior Citizen Department. Since this agency has been coordinating this project for a short time, it is difficult to report on similarities and differences in the procedures.

Oakland Livingston Human Service Agency—Oakland County

One of the shared housing projects administered by the Oakland Livingston Human Service Agency (OLHSA) serves Oakland County in Southeastern Michigan. The county houses the city of Pontiac, as well as many smaller townships representing high-, medium-, and lower-income groups. The northern part of Oakland County is largely rural. The 1980 census estimates that there are 89,793 people of age 65 and over in the county, 11,471 of whom are both 75 or older and living alone.

This homeshare project operates as a consortium of the following four agencies: Community Services of Oakland, Farmington Hills Senior Adult Program, Waterford Senior Citizen Center, and the OLHSA. The goal of the consortium is to promote the shared housing program in all of Oakland County.

The main headquarters of this homeshare project is at the main office of the OLHSA in Pontiac. At the OLHSA office, there are two part-time homeshare counselors and one supervisor who spends 40% of her time on shared housing. In addition, one volunteer and one student provide a few hours of service on a weekly basis.

The OLHSA received a total of $10,517 from the OSA, through the grant given to the SEMCOG. Almost one-half of these funds were distributed to the other consortium agencies, according to the number of matches that were made. Much of the staff time on this project is contributed by the OLSHA or the other agencies in the consortium. In addition, office space, support staff time, supplies, and so on are contributed to the project by the OLHSA.

In addition to the shared housing project, the OLHSA operates a wide range of services for senior citizens as well as other populations that are not paid through the OSA/SEMCOG grant. Included among services offered to seniors are outreach, chore services, energy assistance, weatherization, senior discount program, congregate meals, health screening, educational programs, counseling, and information and referral.

Applications and matchmaking are done by each agency in the consortium. Matches are made by the individual projects, and unmatched applicants are discussed at periodic consortium meetings with the goal of making additional matches. Between November 1985 and January 31, 1987, a total of 76 seekers and 99 providers applied to the project through the consortium agencies. As of January 31, 1987, 22 matches had been made through this program, and 13 were still ongoing. Of the seekers, 64% of the applicants were female; 72% of the provider applicants were female. Applicants' annual income ranged from zero to $90,000.

Oakland Livingston Human Service Agency—Livingston County

The Livingston County project is the second homeshare program administered by the OLHSA. It operates as an independent site serving Livingston County, just west of Oakland County. Almost all of Livingston County is rural. The 1980 census estimated 7,042 people of age 65 and over to be living in the county, and 756 were at least 75 years of age and living alone.

The project received $4,207 through the SEMCOG to operate the program. This grant amount is only enough to support one staff person who spends one-half of her time on project-related activities. The single staff member acts as both administrator and homeshare counselor and represents this site at the SEMCOG-coordinated meetings.

As a field office of the OLHSA in Livingston County, this agency offers most of the services for the elderly that are offered by the main agency office. As with the other OLHSA office, none of the other services provided by the agency are paid through the OSA grant.

Seekers and providers are selected as a potential match by the one staff person. Very little collaboration with other staff is available at this site, although the OLHSA-Oakland office provides advice and support whenever possible.

Between November 1985 and January 31, 1987, this homeshare project had 55 applications from seekers and 50 from providers. It made a total of five matches during this time, and one is still together. It is probable that the small size of the grant and consequent limitations on staff size have contributed to the relatively few matches made by this project. Of the seeker applicants in Livingston County, 66% were female; 76% of the provider applicants were female. Annual incomes of the applicants ranged from zero to $72,996.

The Information Center (TIC)

The homeshare project administered by TIC operates from two offices. It serves all communities in southern and western Wayne County. The headquarters for this homeshare project is located at the main TIC office in Wyandotte. The project staff consists of a part-time homeshare counselor and one part-time volunteer counselor. In addition, three regular agency staff members contribute part of their working hours to the project. TIC received $10,368 from the OSA through the SEMCOG grant. This supports the salary of the paid, part-time homeshare counselor. About 42% of project costs are paid through the general funds of TIC. These additional funds do not include in-kind contributions such as contributed time of the regular staff and supplies.

In addition to the shared housing project, TIC provides general information and referral services and operates housing assistance and care management programs for seniors. None of these additional services is supported by the OSA grant. Matching particular seekers and providers is done through informal sharing of information among the project staff. Once a potential match is located, the staff make calls to the two applicants. If both are interested, their telephone numbers are exchanged. The applicants are encouraged to talk with each other over the telephone and to call TIC after their telephone conversation. If the telephone conversation is positive, the two applicants are encouraged to arrange a meeting, preferably in a neutral location. If the meeting is positive, the seeker is encouraged to visit the provider's home. Thus several meetings between the seeker and provider are recommended before the match is made. Also, a trial match period is suggested. Although the staff make themselves available to be present during the meetings, this is not a requirement. Once the match is made, the TIC staff assist with the housing lease and make periodic follow-up telephone calls to assist with problems that may have arisen.

Between November 1985 and January 31, 1987, this homeshare project had 104 applications from seekers and 111 from providers. It made a total of 18 matches, and 11 are still together. Of the seeker applicants, 74% were female; 82% of the provider applicants were female. The annual incomes of applicants ranged from zero to $26,000.

The Housing Bureau for Seniors

The Housing Bureau for Seniors homeshare program serves the elderly residing in Washtenaw County, west of Wayne County. Washtenaw County houses the city of Ann Arbor, but the remainder of the county is mostly rural. According to the 1980 census, there were 16,853 people of age 65 and over in this county, 2,134 of whom were 75 or older and living alone.

This project is administered by the executive director and one part-time homeshare administrator. There are six senior citizen volunteers who act as the homeshare counselors. They are involved in interviewing and screening applicants, making introductions, and counseling applicants in the matching process and after the match is made.

This program was operational before the OSA grant was awarded, when the agency received $4,958 through the SEMCOG grant. Additional costs of office space and supplies are paid by the Housing Bureau. The Housing Bureau also provides information on the location and availability of subsidized senior citizen housing in the county in addition to the homeshare program. These information services are not supported by the grant from the OSA.

The decision to try to match seekers with providers is made at group meetings of the homeshare counselors and administrators held three times a month. During these meetings, names of new applicants are added to a bulletin board of unmatched seekers and providers for possible matching. In this way, information on applicants screened by different counselors can be shared on a regular basis, since the volunteer counselors spend only one-half of a day each week at the program.

Between November 1985 and January 31, 1987, there were 72 seekers and 50 providers who applied to this project. A total of 19 matches were made during this period, and 14 matches are still in existence. Of the seeker applicants, 73% were female, and 77% of the provider applicants were female. There was not enough data from this project to provide information about the annual income of applicants.

Tri-County Office on Aging

The Shared Housing for the Elderly project of the Tri-County Aging Consortium (TCOA) serves Ingham, Eaton, and Clinton counties, south of the center of the state. Ingham County houses the state capitol of Lansing. The remaining parts of Ingham County and Clinton and Eaton counties are primarily rural. The 1980 census estimated that 31,754 people of age 65 or older lived within these three counties. Approximately 4,550 of these seniors were at least 75 years of age and living alone.

The TCOA project staff consists of one full-time project coordinator and a part-time secretary. For a few months, a part-time peer-volunteer counselor assisted the project by counseling matched participants. A part-time student intern also assisted with some project activities. The TCOA received a total of $38,825 from the OSA. In addition, the agency contributed staff time, travel costs, supplies, office space, telephones, and equipment.

Unlike the SEMCOG-coordinated projects, this shared housing project did not begin until it received the OSA grant in January 1986. The TCOA, however, was aware of the need for shared housing in the area because of the many calls from seniors requesting this type of living arrangement.

Because of its close proximity to Michigan State University and Lansing Community College, one major focus of this project was to locate students as possible homeseekers. With students as seekers, it would be expected that a large number of matches would dissolve at the end of the school year. Reports from the project staff, however, indicated that some older students maintained long-term residence in shared housing arrangements.

In addition to having this homeshare project, the Tri-County Consortium on Aging oversees subcontractors who provide a variety of services to the elderly (not paid by the homeshare grant). These services include information and referral, day care, legal services, employment, volunteer, transportation, homemaker, home health, and special services for Spanish-speaking and Native American seniors. The agency itself provides planning, needs assessments, information and referral, coordination, and advocacy on behalf of senior citizens in the service area. It also operates a nutrition program, including home-delivered meals, a Job Training Partnership Act (JTPA) employment program for low-income seniors, a care management program for high-risk frail elderly, respite care, a shelter advisor, and tax assistance.

Matching is done primarily by the homeshare administrator/counselor. Each qualified applicant is charted on a spreadsheet, which is reviewed whenever a new name is added. The preferences of the applicants are the major criteria used to match a seeker and provider, although the intuition of the project administrator/counselor also enters into the matching decision. The project is unique in its use of the Statewide Tenants Records Bureau to conduct credit checks and personal reference checks on seeker applicants.

Overall, seekers have been more difficult to locate than providers, and providers living far from Lansing were encouraged to place their own ads in local newspapers to find seekers. The TCOA staff assisted providers in the follow-up of these ads. Almost 300 initial inquiries challenged the limited staff in processing applications. Budget constraints limited the project's use of the agency computer. The project made 18 matches from the 49 seeker applicants and 67 provider applicants that entered the program between November 1985 through January 31, 1987. Of these matches, 12 are ongoing.

Upper Peninsula Area Agency on Aging

The Upper Peninsula Area Agency on Aging shared housing project serves Delta, Iron, and Marquette counties in the central part of Michigan's Upper Peninsula. The Area Agency on Aging, which administers the project, serves all 15 counties in the Upper Peninsula. According to the 1980 census, the 3 counties that the project covered had 14,460 people of at least 65 years of age. About 1,950 of these seniors were 75 or older and living alone.

The shared housing project is implemented by one full-time staff member who serves as both administrator and homeshare counselor. The OSA provided $35,450 to this project. Additional volunteer efforts were contributed to the project particularly in assisting with moves when matches were made.

The homeshare counselor consulted with the SEMCOG-coordinated projects at the beginning of program development. Forms developed by the SEMCOG were used with modifications tailored to apply to the needs of this program. As with the TCOA project, the proximity of this site to Northern Michigan University and Bay de Noc Community College resulted in placing some emphasis on locating students as possible seekers.

In addition to having shared housing, the UPCAP also provides a variety of services to seniors through 91 sites throughout the service area. Services provided by the UPCAP that were not supported by the shared housing grant include homebound meals, congregate meals, respite care, care management, a summer program for low-income seniors (SELLS), an older worker program, other housing assistance, escort, transportation, homemaker aides, and shelter advisors.

Prospective matches are made by the project coordinator. Once identified, the seeker and provider decide whether they would like to meet each other. When two interested parties are located, the coordinator is responsible for arranging an introductory meeting. Often, this includes transporting the seeker or provider, or both, to a common location. The decision to try shared housing is made by the seeker and provider. When it is made, the coordinator assists in the arrangement of the housing lease and sometimes assists in the moving process. Because of the rural nature of this service area, screening a prospective applicant can take an entire day.

Because of the additional need of providers identified during the screening and application process, the project coordinator also provided information and referral to other services in addition to homeshare. Calls received from counties outside of the targeted areas were served to the extent possible, given the limitations of staff size and funding. Between November 1985 and January 31, 1987, the program received 45 applications from seekers and 65 from providers. It made 10 matches, of which 6 are still in existence.

COMMON ELEMENTS AMONG THE SEVEN PROGRAMS

There are many common elements among the seven programs that make for successful programs. They include the fact that all are part of an information and referral agency, exist within an agency that has a close tie to the aging network (three contracts are actually with Area Agencies on Aging), and have large service populations that provide extensive pools of seekers and providers. Perhaps one of the most significant elements is that shared housing is only one program of many for these agencies. Should funding shortages occur, the program will not necessarily be eliminated.

Although each of the seven programs have unique characteristics and procedures, they all operate according to a counseling model, whereby counseling services are provided in addition to matching seekers and providers. For the most part all seven projects follow the same basic steps in implementing their homeshare projects. These steps are inquiry to the project by a client; intake or preapplication, which screens the seriousness of the applicant; interview and application, at which time detailed information is received from the applicant; and screening, which includes reference checks and, at some sites, medical checks. After all preliminary information is received and reviewed by staff, in some cases introductions are made by staff; in others, referrals and names are given to clients. After the provider and seeker meet and decide to participate in homeshare, most agencies help coordinate a homeshare agreement.

After the lease agreement is signed, the matching process ends. Most of the homeshare counselors, however, follow up on the matches, either formally or informally. As problems arise, the counselor provides support and assistance.

If the match is discontinued, the applicants are able to return to the pool if they are interested in trying the matching process again.

Throughout the homeshare process, the staff often counsel applicants. The staff believe that counseling is a necessary part of this program. The most frequently given reason for providing counseling as part of the homesharing process is that callers must understand what homesharing is about. Callers sometimes think that sharing a home means getting a live-in housekeeper. Others think it is simply renting a room.

Through counseling, other needs of the applicants can be identified and the counselor can refer the person to other needed services. When the homeshare counselor is present at the initial meeting of the seeker and provider, counseling helps some applicants decide on a housemate. It also helps some to adjust to their new living arrangements. In some cases, the homeshare counselor may become a "family" therapist, assisting the homesharers through difficulties in learning to live together.

Although each program is required to have proper liability coverage, these agencies have found that through an extensive application-screening process, the careful selection of matches, follow-up, and counseling, any legal burdens that might exist in this type of program, have been eased.

ISSUES IN THE DEVELOPMENT OF HOMESHARE PROGRAMS

Funding

There are many similarities among the seven programs funded through the original homeshare legislation. Unfortunately, underfunding was a major similarity. Because of the lack of sufficient funding, the projects were forced to be creative in their financing and programming. Using volunteers and student interns was one common method for increasing the program staff. But although volunteers and students can contribute excellent skills and motivation to project activities, they are usually available for limited amounts or lengths of time. If the program expands without additional funding, more volunteers and student interns would be needed. More volunteers place additional work loads on the paid staff in screening potential volunteers, in training, and in coordinating the matching process.

Other avenues of creative financing must be considered for programs such as these, which were originally supported through state funding. In these programs, legislative funding was reduced each subsequent year of programming. Because of competing needs among social programs, it cannot be expected that a state legislature would provide all necessary support for a public homeshare program, even though such a program can be cost-effective compared with the alternative of building senior housing. One of the demonstration projects used federal Title V Older Workers funding to support the salaries of senior citizen counselors.

Other additional funding could be obtained from local governments and private foundations. Local funding has been obtained in Michigan by some agencies with commitments from communities and counties for appropriation of general monies, federal block grant funding, and state small cities block grants.

A method of additional funding not likely to be successful is a sliding fee for homeshare services. Many of the seniors in the programs were living near or below the poverty level and could not afford to pay for homeshare services. Making the program a private enterprise is also likely to fail, because of the counseling model adapted by the projects. When one is working with seniors, it is important that the level of trust be established with the program staff. In these projects, the staff completed extensive screening and reference checks on potential seekers. Furthermore, in many instances, the staff were involved with the move itself, and some even provided a type of "family therapy" when problems arose between seekers and providers after the match was made. These are time-consuming and costly services not likely to be affordable within a private fee-for-service program.

Staffing

Related to the underfunding of the programs is the consequent small staff involved in the projects. In four sites, the budgets were less than $15,000 and were not large enough to support even one full-time staff member. The other three sites received funding between $35,450 and $40,875. These amounts could support, at most, one full-time coordinator and part-time clerical assistance.

A small staff offers the advantage of easier matching because one or two people meet all of the applicants. With only one or two counselors, information about applicants can be easily shared. This is important because often psychological characteristics are more important than life-style preferences in predicting a successful match. With a single counselor screening all applicants, the potential interpersonal "chemistry" between a seeker and provider can be efficiently assessed.

Similarly, matchmaking becomes difficult when programs have a large staff. The staff must come together as a group and must describe the applicants they screened. Information sharing is limited to basic information such as whether an applicant smokes or has pets. More psychological characteristics important to matching are represented by the relevant staff's interpretation of the applicant's characteristics.

With limited staff, however, the potential impact of the program cannot be adequately estimated. A limited staff results in limitations in the outreach needed to locate potential seekers or providers. With only one paid staff person, some of the projects were limited in the number of potential providers that could be screened, especially in rural areas where a visit to a provider's home could take an entire day. Speed of screening is important because seekers are often in immediate need of housing and cannot afford to wait a few months before being matched. If screening takes too long, the seeker may have already found alternative housing and can no longer be located for participation in homeshare.

The limitations of a small staff had an important negative impact on those demonstration projects that were capitalizing on students in need of housing. Because of the limitations in the number of providers who could be screened, often students had already located housing by the time a potential provider was found. With a more adequate staff, a system could be established whereby a number of providers could be prescreened during the summer months and a number of students could be invited to meet the providers when they returned from summer vacations.

Location of Program within a Multiservice Organization

All of the demonstration projects provided services in addition to homeshare. Most of the projects were housed within a multiservice agency that offered a wide array of services for seniors. The staff of multiservice organizations were often skilled at assessing the needs of the frail elderly and could help the applicants gain access to other services offered by the agency. Such multiservice agency involvement is critical to the counseling model of homeshare, since frail elderly who are likely to be potential providers often have multiple needs that cannot be met solely by the seeker. The location of the projects within multiservice organizations also resulted in the unexpected impact of providing applicants with information and referral to other services besides homeshare.

Involvement of Sites within the "Aging Network"

All of the projects were involved in the "aging network" in Michigan and knew where to locate services needed by applicants. Because of their involvement with other services to the aged in Michigan, the staff from other parts of their agencies or from related agencies were easily informed about homeshare and were able to refer some of their clients into the program.

Extent of Staff Involvement with Seekers and Providers

All of the seven programs provided the same set of services: intake, initial interview, screening, matching, follow-up, and counseling. They differed, however, in the emphasis they placed on these program components. Some programs would actually transport seekers to providers' homes, but others would not. Some programs would be involved in the initial meeting and would provide follow-up family-type counseling, whereas others believed they should have limited involvement with the interpersonal dynamics between seekers and providers.

It is not important for all programs to have similar staff involvement because each project has its own agency philosophy. It is important, however, that the applicants have a clear understanding of the program's philosophy concerning the staff's involvement in the matching process. Applicants should know the extent to which they can turn to homeshare staff for assistance.

Interactions among Different Programs

The five programs within Southeast Michigan were coordinated by the SEMCOG into a network of homeshare agencies. This coordination was useful for sharing information about successes and for group problem solving. The network of agencies provided input into the development of forms, brochures, and training manuals. The five agencies involved in the network believed that the network meetings were very helpful in enhancing the development of the program.

There were two projects geographically isolated from the others. These projects had the benefit of using network-produced materials but could not share in joint problem solving. This isolation was somewhat alleviated by the OSA staff coordination and site visits and a training session held in February 1988 that opened up the lines of communication with all of the agencies.

Differences in Service Area

The seven projects were varied in the types of areas they served. The types of service areas impacted on the types of problems encountered by the programs. The Detroit project, for example, served a large metropolitan area. Problems encountered by this project included high rates of fear of crime from seekers among potential providers, transportation issues for seekers, and transient seekers, to name a few. Problems encountered by rural projects included the distances the staff had to travel to providers' homes. Furthermore, distances between seekers and providers in rural areas made initial meetings difficult.

Because of the differences in problems related to the type of service areas, projects must have the ability to adapt their program design to meet the special needs of their populations. The homeshare program must have an understanding of the unique needs of their populations and be able to accommodate these needs. The Tri-county program, for example, decided to help providers in remote areas place advertisements in their local newspapers to locate seekers living close to them. The homeshare staff would provide a sample ad that potential providers could adapt for their own use. In this way, potential providers could get assistance from the program staff without the staff having to travel long distances to visit the homes.

CHARACTERISTICS OF SUCCESSFUL SYSTEMS

Because of their successful implementation, it was important to determine factors that made these projects successful. This information was obtained by personal interviews with most of the project staff, both paid and volunteer (Hwalek, 1987).

The most frequently cited factor in the success of the programs was the quality of the project staff and volunteers. Dedication, hard work, belief in the program, flexibility in light of limited resources, cooperation, and aggressive pursuit of program goals were used to describe characteristics of the staff involved in the program. Two respondents said that the program was successful because the applicants believed the staff were truly interested in their needs. Excellent agency directors and the networking approach of the SEMCOG were also mentioned as reasons that the programs were successful.

Overwhelming public interest and the need for housing were also frequently cited reasons for the success of these programs. One respondent thought that the fact that shared housing was on the senior platform in Michigan enhanced the success of these efforts. Another respondent concluded that now the staff have at least an alternative to mention to callers who are in desperate need of housing in the midst of the severe shortage of subsidized housing in Michigan.

Programmatic factors were also cited as reasons for the success of these projects. They included good planning, good marketing techniques, going out to the homes of potential providers, having regular meetings, success in obtaining additional funding, having a volunteer on the staff who is in a match, the comprehensive assessment process, and the connection with the tenants' bureau to assist with screening.

Finally, some characteristics of applicants were cited as reasons for success. They included loneliness of seniors, seniors whose families live far away, and the ability to place people who had no homes.

FUTURE OF SHARED HOUSING IN MICHIGAN

Since the inception of the program, shared housing in Michigan has been extremely successful. Because of the success of the original demonstration projects, other agencies throughout the state have, with foundation funding and their own resources, implemented shared housing programs. The Office of Services to the Aging will continue to administer limited funding to the original demonstration agencies. Administration funds at the OSA have been depleted, however, and, therefore, technical assistance, coordination, and training will no longer be available. Despite these cuts in resources, it appears that there is significant interest and enthusiasm among the shared housing agencies and that shared housing is here to stay in Michigan.

REFERENCES

Hwalek, M. *Final Report on the Evaluation of Four Shared Housing Demonstration Projects for the Michigan Office of Services to the Aging.* Detroit: SPEC Associates, 1987.

7

Ontario's Homesharing Program

David H. Spence

Homesharing is defined in this chapter as the matching of two or more unrelated individuals into a private, family home or apartment, based on a set of common preferences and needs. To facilitate this matching process, the Ontario Ministry of Housing has established a number of municipal homesharing agencies. Although these agencies maintain a thorough listing of persons seeking and providing accommodations, their services go far beyond those of a typical housing registry. Through intensive counseling and interviewing, agencies are able to link together compatible persons to share accommodations. Follow-up assistance and mediation are also integral to the housing approach. Should it be determined that an individual is not suited to homesharing, he or she will be referred to more appropriate housing and social services in the community.

The Ministry of Housing first developed an interest in the concept of homesharing in 1985, with the sponsorship of 3 matchup agencies on a pilot basis. There are now a total of 15 such agencies operating across the province. This chapter examines the historical development of the ministry's program, assesses the nature of the communities involved in program delivery, profiles the organizational structure and performance of agencies funded under the program, and briefly discusses the key indicators of a successful match. In addition, the implications for homesharing operations, aging policy, and the knowledge base for gerontology are presented. Although there are a number of shared group residences or cooperative households now operating in Ontario, under different funding mechanisms, the focus of discussion in this chapter is limited to the matchup model of homesharing.

HISTORICAL OVERVIEW

Rationale for Ministry's Involvement

Owing to an increasingly low rental housing vacancy rate, the high cost of new rental construction, and a severe shortage of available land, coupled with an increase in the number of households, an urgent need has developed for governments to consider other less conventional solutions to stimulate the supply of affordable rental accommodations. Homesharing represents one approach that can help to address a small part of the housing problem. Specifically, the concept appealed to the Ontario Ministry of Housing for a number of reasons.

First, it offers the potential to intensify and make better use of the existing housing stock. It has been estimated that about 852,760 of the total 2,970,000 residential dwellings in the province of Ontario were underused in 1981 (Statistics Canada, 1987).[1] Many of these dwellings would lend themselves to at least one form of residential intensification, such as homesharing, the creation of a second self-contained unit, or the establishment of a rooming or boarding house.

Second, homesharing is a financially attractive option to both prospective homesharing clients and funding agencies. Additional units of affordable rental housing can be created at virtually no cost to the homeprovider and at moderate cost to the government. For funding agencies, the concept does not involve large capital outlays. The operational costs are relatively low, and if it is determined after a period of time that demand for sharing cannot sustain the program, funding may be gradually phased out.

Third, the concept is relatively simple to operationalize. The administrative service infrastructure required to operate a homesharing program is generally in place at the municipal and community agency levels. Within certain constraints, the concept can be easily adapted to address the specific conditions and needs of a given locality.

Fourth, the option provides an additional housing choice for seniors who want to retain their independence and remain in their own home or community. Through additional companionship and assistance with household chores, the quality of life for older adults can be improved and possibly extended. Faced with a rapidly aging population throughout Canada, and North America for that matter, many governments are exploring innovative options that may help to avoid premature institutionalization and lower public health care and housing costs.

Establishment of the Pilot Projects

Before the ministry's involvement, homesharing was not a totally new concept to Ontario. The first homesharing service in Canada began in the Niagara region of Ontario in 1980 and was followed by another service in 1983, which was located in metropolitan Toronto.[2] Funding for these agencies, however, was somewhat limited and piecemeal. Both agencies had a very specific focus on seniors, with one performing peer matches in rental apartments only.

There was a definite need for the concept to be introduced and tested in other parts of the province, under different delivery models and to other client groups. Because of this, funding was approved to develop three projects in two munic- ipalities: metropolitan Toronto and the region of Ottawa–Carleton.

PARAMETERS OF THE MINISTRY'S PROGRAM

When the first three pilot agencies were established, program funding was shared equally by the participating local or regional municipalities and the Min- istry of Housing. Approximately $15,000 was provided by both government sponsors, resulting in a minimum total operating budget of $30,000 for each of the three projects.

As the pilot projects developed, it became evident that additional financial support would be required to operate homesharing services more efficiently. At the same time, interest was expressed in establishing homesharing services by a number of other municipalities, in addition to the initial three pilot locations. As a result, the ministry's funding structure has been revised and enhanced twice, since 1985, to accommodate this growing demand.

In late 1986 the first provincial government homesharing program was offi- cially announced. Through this arrangement, $20,000 was provided to partici- pating municipalities per year for two years to cover 50% of program costs.

Under the current program guidelines, established in October 1987, munici- palities may now receive a total of $40,000 per year for three years to cover up to 75% of the total operating expenses of the homesharing service. It is expected that the municipality and other local sponsors contribute the remaining 25% of the annual operating costs.

Since the beginning of the pilots, the provincial grants have been supplied to municipal corporations, who may in turn operate the service directly or select another community-based agency to administer the service on their behalf. Mu- nicipalities have been selected as the appropriate delivery agent of homesharing programs for a number of reasons. They represent a stable, constant entity, with established and formal linkages with other local, regional, and provincial housing and social services. Municipalities are aware of and understand the range of housing problems facing their community. They are closest to, and most familiar with, the broad range of client groups and the specific needs of each.

The grant, supplied to the municipal matchup agencies, may be used to cover any legitimate program development and operating expense. Eligible costs in- clude staffing, general administrative expenses, promotional activities, and com- puter hardware rental or acquisition.

At present, program funding is renewable on a yearly basis, for a maximum of three years. In 1989, about one year before the end of the three-year term, ministry funding will be reviewed and evaluated with consideration being given to possibly extending program assistance for an additional period.

The number of grants available to municipalities has also increased since the inception of the initial demonstration projects. Although there are 15 programs now underway, it is anticipated that a minimum of 22 homesharing agencies will be operational by April 1989.

To be eligible for funding under the ministry's homesharing program, interested municipalities are requested to submit a proposal to the ministry for review and approval. The proposal should indicate the municipality's willingness to contribute funding toward the homesharing service and outline the way in which the service is to be integrated with regional, community, and neighborhood housing and social services.

Once approved for funding, staff are hired and a local advisory committee is established. The purpose of the advisory committee is to provide advice on agency policies and procedures and to oversee the operation and management of the service. The committee typically consists of representatives from the municipal council and staff and local housing, health, and social service networks. Through the advisory committee the needs of the specific client groups are identified and considered when setting the directions of the program.

The ministry program guidelines allow for some flexibility in the local administration of the service in terms of the eligibility criteria and procedures employed. To insure that there is some consistency in the operation of homesharing services across the province, however, agencies are required to follow relatively standardized interview procedures and quarterly reporting requirements.

COMMUNITY CONTEXT

Matchup programs are now underway in the cities of East York, Etobicoke, Scarborough, Toronto, York (all within metropolitan Toronto), London, North Bay, Peterborough, and Sault Ste. Marie and the regional municipalities of metropolitan Toronto, Niagara, Ottawa-Carleton, Sudbury, Waterloo, and York. (See Figure 7.1.)

These agencies are reasonably well distributed across the province. Three of the 15 services are situated in northern Ontario, whereas most of the remaining programs are located along the more heavily populated southern corridor. In particular, 6 of the 15 services are functioning within metropolitan Toronto, an area with a total population of about 2,155,000 people (Ontario Ministry of Municipal Affairs, 1988b).

The population of municipalities operating homesharing services across the province ranges from 51,000 persons in North Bay to 606,000 people in Toronto (Ontario Ministry of Municipal Affairs 1988b).[3] In terms of population base, the agencies fall within three general categories: five agencies are situated in municipalities with populations between 50,000 and 150,000 people, six agencies operate in communities between 250,000 and 400,000 persons, and four home-

Figure 7.1
Homesharing Agencies in Ontario

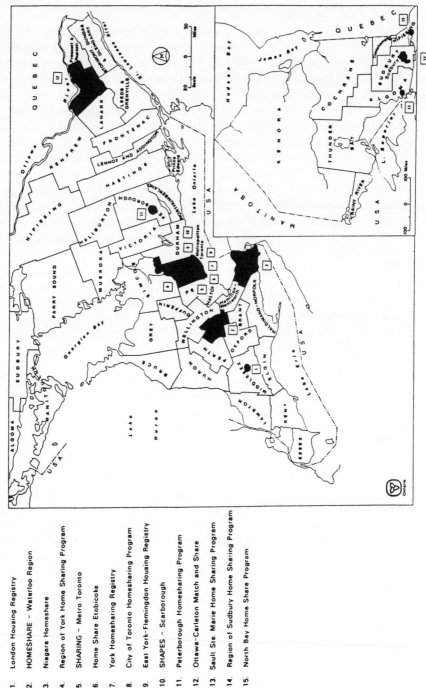

1. London Housing Registry
2. HOMESHARE – Waterloo Region
3. Niagara Homeshare
4. Region of York Home Sharing Program
5. SHARING – Metro Toronto
6. Home Share Etobicoke
7. York Homesharing Registry
8. City of Toronto Homesharing Program
9. East York–Flemingdon Housing Registry
10. SHAPES – Scarborough
11. Peterborough Homesharing Program
12. Ottawa–Carleton Match and Share
13. Sault Ste. Marie Home Sharing Program
14. Region of Sudbury Home Sharing Program
15. North Bay Home Share Program

sharing programs have more than 450,000 persons within their catchment or service area.

Six of the 15 programs are offered to a larger geographical area through a regional municipality. This approach may also prove to maximize the number of prospective clients and consequently result in more matches being arranged. Careful assessment of the need for regional delivery or expansion is advisable, however. It may demand greater costs in terms of staff travel time or in establishing site offices when necessary. Also, many prospective clients may be unwilling to relocate to another community within the larger region or district.

Based on the ministry's experience to date, it is considered that, whether homesharing services are offered on a regional or citywide basis, a minimum urban population is required to sustain the activities of the central or primary office. Specifically, it is suggested that agencies stationed in communities of more than 50,000 persons are more likely to succeed. Agencies functioning in areas with populations much smaller than 50,000, particularly if the target group is limited to seniors, may find it difficult to build and maintain the sizeable client pool necessary to make successful matches.

Typically, those homesharing services that are offered to a larger regional area have been concerned more with housing seniors than other segments of the population. Six of the seven programs that primarily serve older adults are sponsored by regional municipalities, whereas all eight of the services assisting a more general clientele are sponsored by the local or city tier of government.

This may be attributed to the fact that regional governments are cognizant of the higher proportions of elderly persons in many rural areas (Hodge, 1987). Often seniors in these rural communities are exposed to a limited number of housing alternatives and social services (Ontario Ministry of Municipal Affairs 1988c). Homesharing is one means of improving the choice of accommodations and increasing the level of informal service(s) available to them.

The population demographics and consequent housing needs of cities, however, are somewhat different from those in rural areas. Generally, the pressures placed on the rental housing stock in urban centers are much greater, as reflected in the relatively low vacancy rates and high rental costs. Homesharing agencies in cities, such as metropolitan Toronto and London, tend to concentrate more on crisis housing situations (Corke, 1987). Many homeseekers are on lower incomes and require some form of income assistance. These homesharing clients usually span the entire population spectrum from older couples and "empty nesters" to students, singles, single parents, the disabled, the working poor, welfare recipients, and the homeless. Although homesharing in Ontario was never originally designed to provide a solution for crisis situations, in the absence of feasible alternatives, it often fills a service gap in urban settings (Metropolitan Toronto, 1987). People that may have not previously considered homesharing as an option may be forced to rethink their housing choices.

Another factor that has contributed to the development of homesharing services in certain parts of Ontario is the presence of strong political will and commitment.

In several cases, local mayors and councilors have been instrumental in creating municipal support initially and maintaining a high degree of visibility for the service on an ongoing basis.

ORGANIZATIONAL STRUCTURE OF HOMESHARING AGENCIES

Funding Sources and Staffing

As discussed, the core source of agency funding stems from the ministry's homesharing program. This three-year core funding adds an element of financial security and stability for homesharing agencies. As a result, most agencies are able to concentrate on the business at hand, rather than constantly attempting to secure ongoing funding from various agencies on an ad hoc basis.

Unfortunately, a lack of consistent funding appears to have been the key obstacle that thwarted the adequate growth and development of many home-sharing agencies in other parts of Canada and in the United States (Milone, 1987; Shared Housing Resource Center, 1988).

In addition to the required municipal contribution, other sources of revenue for Ontario's homesharing agencies include other provincial government bodies such as the Ministry of Community and Social Services; previously, the federal government through its New Horizons Program designed to help seniors serve seniors and through its Immigrant Settlement Program; the United Way; charitable community services and clubs; local seniors organizations; educational and religious institutions; and foundations. Unlike many programs in the United States, very few of Ontario's agencies receive donations from private companies. With the exception of one agency, which charges a nominal fee, the homesharing services are provided to clients free of charge. The current fiscal operating budgets for Ontario's homesharing agencies range from a high of $108,900 to a low of $40,000. The median annual budget is $53,300.

In terms of staff, two agencies have the equivalent of two and one-half paid staff, whereas five programs have two staff persons, and the remaining eight programs have one and one-half full-time positions. Most of the programs make use of community volunteers, and several have also hired summer students to assist them in the preparation of specific projects, such as the development of a marketing plan or a community needs assessment.

Municipal Sponsorship and Delivery

Eleven of the 15 municipalities have vested in the responsibility for the development of the homesharing service with their community and social services departments. In the 4 cases, the municipal housing or planning departments assume this role. Generally, although not without exception, the social service departments participate in the development of homesharing agencies for seniors.

As the elderly persons use disproportionately more health and social services than the population as a whole (Ontario Ministry of Municipal Affairs, 1988c), municipal social service departments are justifiably interested in evaluating the impacts of the less costly, informal types of support and assistance often provided through a sharing arrangement. The housing and planning departments, on the other hand, are usually more concerned with the efficient management of the housing stock, land, and infrastructure for the broader population.

Clearly, there is an argument for homesharing to be viewed from either a housing or social policy perspective (Kardish, 1987; Morrow, 1987). I believe that the greatest potential for agency success and longevity lies in securing support from both perspectives.

In several cases in which the Ministry of Housing has cofunded the operation of a service with a municipality, the regional office of the Ontario Ministry of Community and Social Services has also contributed funds. This has had the effect of strengthening and solidifying the operating budget. Also, there is greater assurance that both housing and social policy objectives will be attained.

The agency selected to operate the service varies significantly. Five home-sharing programs are administered directly to the public by the participating municipality through the social service, planning, or housing offices. Munici-palities cofunding the other 10 programs have hired community-based agencies to operate the service on their behalf. These agencies consist of four community information centers, two social planning/development councils, a family coun-seling center, a local office of the Victorian Order of Nurses, a church, and one group that has been incorporated specifically to deliver a homesharing service.

No particular delivery agency has been found to be more effective than the others. Any local government or nonprofit agency that has expressed the interest and commitment and has in the past exhibited a sufficient degree of stability and performance in delivering other services may be selected to assume the home-sharing responsibilities. Those homesharing agencies, however, that are part of a large multiservice organization may, from the outset, be more able to refer their clients readily to other related housing and nonhousing services. Finding stable, affordable housing is often a necessary precursor to solving many other related problems. Providing similar services on site (e.g., employment, family counseling, legal assistance, education, and training) could substantially reduce the bureaucratic and administrative confusion that many homesharing clients often endure.

AGENCY OPERATIONS AND PROCEDURES

Description of Services Provided

A survey of the ministry-sponsored agencies, undertaken in July of 1988 (Ontario Ministry of Housing, 1988c), identified the specific type and extent of services administered by each of Ontario's homesharing programs. This section merely highlights the survey findings.

The survey indicated that all programs offer counseling and referral services to clients as a standard procedure. The type of referrals made, however, is dependent on the client focus and orientation of the operating agency. Points of referral ranged from other homesharing agencies and housing registries to legal clinics, educational institutions, family counseling centers, income maintenance programs, youth services, seniors centers, rent-review offices, assisted housing, day care, unemployment, and alcohol and sexual-abuse clinics.

In addition, all agencies visit the homes of providers, follow up the matches once arranged, and mediate problems, if they arise. With one exception, homesharing agencies recommend the use of agreements between homeseekers and homeproviders and provide assistance in drafting such contracts, if required. Also, trial periods between prospective sharing partners are encouraged by almost every agency.

Most services suggest that homeseekers and homeproviders initiate a preliminary meeting between themselves, and a few agencies facilitate introductions between clients with the homesharing staff present. Less frequently offered services include requiring medical references from doctors and police checks on prior convictions.

In addition to matching individuals together in shared living arrangements, 9 of the 15 homesharing services now operating also refer clients to private self-contained accommodations such as an accessory, self-contained apartment in a single family home or an apartment in a low-rise building. This "placement" function represents a logical extension of services for some agencies, especially when an accessory apartment arrangement, for instance, may involve some degree of "sharing" through an exchange of services. Although originally this additional service was more prevalent with programs catering to a broad population group, there has been a gradual shift by seniors' agencies toward offering placements as well. Placements, however, are encouraged on a much less frequent basis than homesharing. The main objective of the ministry's program has been, and will continue to be, matching individuals into shared accommodations.

Client Focus

Under the homesharing program, municipalities are permitted to identify the specific client group(s) that will be served within their communities. Agencies need not confine their services to seniors but should be particularly sensitive to the needs of older adults.

Seven of the 15 services currently operating place a primary emphasis on seniors. Four of the 7 agencies require that at least one person in the match be 55 years of age or over. Another of these 7 services has a dual focus on both seniors and single parents. The remaining 8 agencies cater to a more general client group consisting of seniors, singles, single parents, students, and newcomers to Canada.

In three instances, agencies have shifted away from concentrating on seniors to serving a more general population group. Particularly in the smaller communities, there has been a need to broaden the client focus to increase the size of the client pool and consequently the potential number of matches made and to provide a greater range of choice in homesharing partners for seniors registered with the programs. The Peterborough Homesharing Program, for example, arranged only three matches in its first 14 months of operation. As a result of broadening the target population combined with associated promotional activities, the agency substantially increased its client pool and made 22 additional matches within the next nine months of operation. This improved performance was achieved without substantially sacrificing the original seniors' trust of the program. Although the focus has shifted toward the general population, 13 of the 22 matches still involved persons over the age of 55.

Although the types of services of all programs are similar, those that serve mainly seniors tend to provide a more intensive and supportive form of assistance. Consequently, greater time and attention are required by the homesharing staff for each client.

Agencies and advisory committees should carefully weigh the trade-offs involved in offering a specific versus a more general client orientation. This is important because, unfortunately, the more qualitative aspects of homesharing services, such as counseling and referral, are often ignored by funding agencies. Regardless of the definite benefits of the many other services provided to homesharing clients, the political decision to continue funding the local program usually boils down to the number of matches being made.

Marketing and Promotion

Homesharing agencies use a wide variety of methods to recruit their clients. Based on the most recent quarterly reports prepared for the Ministry of Housing in June 1988, the most frequent source of program awareness for prospective homeproviders and homeseekers was through human interest stories and classified ads in newspapers and referrals from family, friends, and former clients. Brochures and flyers and radio and television spots are also popular means by which agencies create public awareness of the programs. Many other clients are referred to the homesharing agencies by other housing services, community shelters, health care and educational facilities, and social service and welfare offices.

Most agencies are becoming more professional and experienced in terms of their promotional and recruiting skills. A sophisticated method of referral is now developing between homesharing programs, particularly those located in the metropolitan Toronto area. Other more innovative methods such as social gatherings for groups of prospective homesharers, transit ads in subways and buses, and promotional videos are being tried, with a reasonable degree of success.

PROFILE OF AGENCY PERFORMANCE

This section presents a descriptive profile of the homesharing services and their achievements. Statistics offered are derived from the quarterly reports of June 30, 1988, as prepared by the homesharing agencies for the Ontario Ministry of Housing. Thirteen of the present 15 agencies were in operation at that time.

Length of Agency Operation

The average length of operation as of June 1988 for the 13 agencies was 1.6 years. Although the 3 original pilot agencies had been operating for about 3.0 years, 4 others had been functioning between 1.5 to 2.0 years, 3 between 1.0 to 1.5 years, and 3 for less than 6 months.

Referrals

During the quarterly operating period of April–June 1988, 2,273 referrals were made by 13 homesharing agencies: 1,797 to other housing-related agencies and 476 to nonhousing related services. The nature of these referrals has been extremely diverse.

Matches and Placements Made

In total, 1,207 cumulative matches and placements had been made by the 13 agencies. Of them, 744 were matches involving approximately 1,900 persons. Two hundred and eighteen, or about 29% of these matches, are still ongoing.

An average of 36.4 matches had been made per year by each agency; however, the median number of matches was only 16.0. One agency located in Scarborough has been outperforming all others with 204.0 matches annually. This is primarily due to the large population served and geographic area covered. Although this agency's client focus is relatively broad, two groups are commonly targeted: students and newcomers to Canada. Both groups have immediate housing needs and perhaps require less initial housing counseling and support than the elderly clientele served by many other agencies.

Although those agencies serving a larger population usually achieve a higher number of matches per year, this rule of thumb does not always hold true. Two agencies in smaller-sized communities of 50,000 to 60,000 persons, for example, have been considerably more successful in making matches than several located in medium-sized urban centers with populations exceeding 300,000 people. In these instances, the smaller municipalities have a broader target population with less restrictive eligibility, whereas the programs in larger communities cater primarily to seniors.

To date, 463.0 placements have been made by nine homesharing agencies for an average number of 25.0 placements per year. The majority of these placements have been made by one agency located in London, Ontario. Most programs do not regularly place persons into private accommodations, as is reflected by the low median number of 6.0 placements per year for the nine agencies.

Profile of Matches

With reference to those homeproviders matched that quarter, 62.6% were singles, 17.9% were single parents, and 19.5% involved two parents or a couple. In terms of homeseekers, 91.5% were singles, 5.9% single parents, and 2.6% were two parents or a couple.

Of the total number of homeproviders matched, 49.6% were seniors. Only 16.9% of the homeseekers were seniors, which is lower than the percentage of provincial population made up by the 55 and over age category.

Forty-eight or 42.9% of 112 matches arranged that quarter were intergenerational, consisting of a person over 55 years of age sharing accommodations with a younger individual. Also, 18 or 16.1% of the 112 matches involved some form of service exchange between the homeseeker and homeprovider for a reduction in rent.

It is interesting that the program coordinators considered that at least 15 matches, or 13.4% of the total matches made during the quarter, enabled the elderly provider to remain in the community for a longer time and thereby avoid premature institutionalization. Also, 11.6% of the matches made it possible for homeseekers to move from subsidized accommodations: 1 from a public or assisted rental housing unit and 12 from temporary shelters. These numbers indicate the dramatic potential that homesharing can have in terms of lessening the financial pressures placed on governments in providing shelters and care for seniors and lower income adults and youth.

Duration of Matches

Of the ongoing matches, 38.5% have lasted under 3 months, 23.4% between 3 and 6 months, 23.4% between 6 and 12 months, and 14.7% beyond 1 year. It should be mentioned that the duration of ongoing matches has increased significantly during October 1987 to June 1988, when 47.8% of the ongoing matches fell within the first 3 months. This indicates that as the programs generally mature, so should the length of ongoing matches. Nevertheless, it is believed that this trend may soon reach a plateau or optimum duration.

The terminated matches have been shorter: 53.8% have lasted under 3 months, 25.1% between 3 and 6 months, and 16.3% between 6 and 12 months. Only 4.8% of the terminated matches lasted longer than 1 year. Again, however, this represents a substantial increase in the length of matches since the end of September 1987, when 61.8% of all terminated matches lasted less than 3 months.

Reasons for Homesharing

Most homesharing providers that were matched chose to share accommodations for financial reasons: 47.2%. Other reasons included life-style or companionship, 25.3%; stability and security, 14.1%; assistance required, 9.9%; integration or language and improved quality of shelter, 0.7% each; and "other" reasons, 2.1% of the total reasons stated.

Similarly, 42.9% of the matched homeseekers selected homesharing for financial reasons. Life-style or companionship, stability and security, improved quality of shelter, integration or language, and assistance required followed at 18.8%, 13.1%, 8.9%, 7.9%, and 4.2% respectively. "Other" reasons were 4.2% of the total responses. Generally, life-style or companionship and stability and security are more important reasons for sharing among the senior home-providers and homeseekers.

Although incompatibility ranks highest as the reason for termination of matches, 31.75%, the incidence of incompatibility has decreased significantly from 41.0% since the end of September 1987. Other reasons for matches ending are change in seeker status, provider moving as planned, and quality of accommodations at 31.75%, 11.0%, 9.5%, and 2.5% respectively. In this instance, "other" reasons were 13.5% of the total number of reasons for terminating matches. It should be reinforced that in many cases the termination of a match is often beneficial, resulting in a positive change of events for at least one of the parties, such as a new job or improved quality of accommodations (Ontario Ministry of Housing, 1987; Metropolitan Toronto, 1987).

Profile of Registered Accommodations

The homesharing services have had a substantial impact on intensifying the existing housing stock. During the April–June 1988 quarter of program operation, 46.2% of the homesharing cases and 66.7% of the accessory apartment cases involved accommodations that were provided on the market for the first time.

In addition, the accommodations offered through the ministry's homesharing program have been very affordable, relative to other forms of housing. The average rent for shared accommodations in metropolitan Toronto as of June 1988 was $320 per month, including utilities. In other areas of the province, outside of metropolitan Toronto, the homesharing rent was $235 per month. Accessory apartments or placements, advertised through the programs, were offered at $575 and $350 per month for metropolitan Toronto and other areas of Ontario, respectively. In contrast, the average rent for a vacant one bedroom apartment in the metropolitan Toronto area in October 1987 was $850 per month (Canada Mortgage and Housing Corporation, 1987:6).

COMPONENTS OF A SUCCESSFUL MATCH

In January 1988, as part of the background research for the preparation of a ministry procedures manual for provincial agencies (Ontario Ministry of Housing, 1988a), homesharing coordinators were interviewed on a number of pertinent topics. One such topic involved the identification of objective and subjective factors that contributed to the making of a "successful match."

The objective factors were simply based on those individual preferences that compatible homeproviders and homeseekers found to be the most important considerations in the matching process and brought to the attention of agency coordinators. They included good housekeeping standards, age, gender, cultural background, pets versus no pets, location of accommodations, accessibility to transportation, smoking versus nonsmoking, employed versus unemployed, furnished versus unfurnished accommodations, and the potential for service exchange or provision.

Beyond these objective criteria, coordinators offered their additional subjective impressions of the key factors that lead to a successful match. These factors included compatible personalities, flexibility in negotiating day-to-day aspects of shared living, honesty and respect, ability to communicate problems openly, similar life-styles, each party's expectations met, length of match agreed upon beforehand, balance struck between privacy and companionship, and adherence to household rules negotiated between sharing partners.

Although all of the above variables represent very important or key matching criteria, the success of the match often depends on the personality of the coordinator. Her or his degree of perceptiveness and understanding in identifying the specific needs of the clients and insuring that those needs are properly met is the crux of arranging a compatible match. Through adequate counseling and advice, homesharing partners are better able to develop mutual and realistic expectations of homesharing at the outset of the process and thereby avert much of the potential for conflict in the later stages.

IMPLICATIONS

Implications for Homesharing Operations

Based on the information presented in this chapter and on the ministry's experience to date, a number of important implications for homesharing operations may be discussed. During the development of these services a definite need has emerged for insuring that adequate ongoing funding is available to homesharing programs. If an agency is to function effectively, it is suggested that a minimum of one full-time staff member be hired, regardless of the size of the local community in which the service is located. Without this degree of commitment, it is extremely difficult to insure that counseling, referral, and promotional activities are afforded adequate attention.

Sufficient resources should also be directed to the creation of promotional strategies and activities. Carefully designed and targeted advertising materials are essential in developing and maintaining heightened community awareness. To assist the agencies in their outreach efforts, the ministry has prepared a pamphlet, pamphlet stand, and poster concerning homesharing. Also, a newspaper advertising campaign and a video are in production.

Another factor that has contributed to the orderly development of homesharing agencies in Ontario is the central delivery of the services. Through the ministry's program support initiatives, such as the standardized interview and quarterly statistical report forms, a computer program for matching clients and generating statistics, and an operational procedures manual, it has been possible for agencies to converse in a common language using agreed-upon definitions, terms, and procedures. In addition, the similar approach employed by homesharing agencies in Ontario will aid in the comparative analysis and evaluation of programs in the future.

It is also imperative that local and regional politicians be well informed of the issues associated with the homesharing service. Involving politicians in the ongoing management of the service, through their active participation on the advisory committee, has proven invaluable in attaining the local profile necessary.

In Ontario, at present, there is no agency that is the equivalent of the National Shared Housing Resource Center in Philadelphia. Under consideration, however, is the development of a Provincial Association of Homesharing Coordinators. This would provide a mechanism for coordinators to exchange their views and assume a greater degree of control over their own activities and directions. Working in cooperation with the ministry, the association would be responsible for the development of a quarterly newsletter and the sponsorship of an annual conference on homesharing. It is considered that strengthened linkages between agencies and agency participation in the policy decision-making process are vital to the continued growth and development of homesharing agencies across the province.

Implications for Aging Policy

By no means is homesharing a panacea for solving our housing problems, but it does serve as a viable, satisfactory approach for a significant number of individuals. The concept must be viewed in its proper context: as one small part of a comprehensive housing strategy designed to assist both elderly persons and other groups of the population (Spence, 1987; Kardish, 1987).

In terms of aging policy, homesharing must be seen as one of many housing options on a continuum of care between independence and dependence (Corke, 1987). Along with other innovative alternatives, such as "granny flats" or "garden suites," accessory apartments, cooperative households, and sheltered and congregate housing, homesharing provides an additional choice for individuals who are able to retain their independence, yet require some degree of social or financial support.

Several homesharing programs in Ontario, geared toward seniors, are formally integrating their operations with other existing social service networks. Niagara and Sudbury regions, for instance, are delivering their respective homesharing services out of a single, centrally located municipal office in conjunction with their home support and satellite home programs. These improved service linkages will undoubtedly help to streamline the delivery of the matching and referral process and facilitate public access to the program.

It is also imperative that agencies considering the financial sponsorship of homesharing services come to grips with the fact that substantial lead time is required before a service is operating at a peak level of performance. Based on the ministry's involvement, at least one full year is needed to develop procedures, properly market the program, and build a substantial client pool. Once local demand has been proven and a decision made to proceed, commitment should be given to the provision of stable funding for two years to allow agencies a legitimate opportunity to test the feasibility of the option.

Implications for Future Research

There are several areas in which further research may help us to gain additional knowledge about and insight into the concept of homesharing and in turn provide the information necessary to make well-informed policy decisions. One of the most important issues that needs to be addressed more fully, at least from a funding viewpoint, is the cost-effectiveness of matchup services for seniors, as well as others. Certainly, governments cannot be criticized for being concerned with the financial implications of homesharing. In the past, however, many evaluations have consisted of simply dividing the total operating budget by the number of matches made to arrive at an arbitrary decision on the future of a program.

The impact that homesharing has on reducing the public cost of, and need for, other community services must also be more thoroughly considered. Specifically, what effect does homesharing have on keeping people out of costly institutions, subsidized housing, and temporary shelters? In addition, what real impact do informal support services, provided through sharing, have on decreasing the need for other formal, public services. Only recently has data of this type been collected in any systematic fashion. Longitudinal studies are also required to assess the financial impacts over a longer duration.

Research also needs to go further in terms of examining the qualitative aspects of homesharing. In particular, greater attention should be devoted to determining the level of client satisfaction in homesharing arrangements, relative to other forms of accommodations. The potential impact the concept may have on improving the quality of life, and possibly the length of life for individuals involved, has also been largely overlooked to date.

Several other items should also be evaluated and monitored over the longer term. Among other things, they include the potential benefits for older adults of broadening the focus of a program from seniors to the general population; the impact that additional interviewing, screening, and counseling may have on match quality and duration; and the most effective means of reaching homesharing clients, particularly seniors, to relate the advantages of the homesharing concept.

NOTES

1. In this context, an *underused dwelling* may be defined as a unit that contains at least four rooms more than the number of occupants residing in the unit. A five-room dwelling with one occupant, for example, would be categorized as underused. A "room" does not count bathrooms, hallways, or vestibules.

2. Both these agencies are now funded under the ministry's home sharing program. In addition to the 15 services operating in Ontario, there are approximately 6 other homesharing agencies currently underway in other provinces in Canada.

3. Although one homesharing agency offers a service to the entire metropolitan Toronto region, it is limited to matching seniors into peer or intergenerational situations. This restriction has the effect of reducing substantially the number of individuals that may be potentially assisted below the number that may be reached through Toronto's more generally targeted program.

REFERENCES

Canada Mortgage and Housing Corporation. *Rental Market Survey: Toronto Census Metropolitan Area*. Toronto, Ontario, October 1987.

Corke, Sue. "The Ontario Experience with Home Sharing and Group Living Arrangements." In *Home Sharing and Group Living Arrangements for the Elderly: Summary Notes on Workshop Presentations Held at the Fifteenth Annual Scientific and Educational Meeting of the Canadian Association on Gerontology*. Toronto: Ontario Ministry of Housing, 1987.

Hodge, Gerald, with Collins, John B. *The Elderly in Canada's Small Towns: Recent Trends and Their Implications*. Occasional Paper No. 43. Vancouver: University of British Columbia, 1987.

Kardish, David. "Municipal Planning Perspectives." In *Home Sharing and Group Living Arrangements for the Elderly: Summary Notes on Workshop Presentations Held at the Fifteenth Annual Scientific and Educational Meeting of the Canadian Association on Gerontology*. Toronto: Ontario Ministry of Housing, 1987.

Metropolitan Toronto. *Assessment of the Neighbourhood Housing Assistance (Homesharing) Projects in Metropolitan Toronto*. Toronto: Metropolitan Community Services Department, November 1987.

Milone, Donna. "An Overview of Home Sharing and Group Living Arrangements in the United States." In *Home Sharing and Group Living Arrangements for the Elderly: Summary Notes on Workshop Presentations Held at the Fifteenth Annual Scientific and Educational Meeting of the Canadian Association on Gerontology*. Toronto: Ontario Ministry of Housing, 1987.

Morrow, Lynn. "Municipal Social Policy Perspectives." In *Home Sharing and Group Living Arrangements for the Elderly: Summary Notes on Workshop Presentations Held at the Fifteenth Annual Scientific and Educational Meeting of the Canadian Association on Gerontology.* Toronto: Ontario Ministry of Housing, 1987.

Ontario Ministry of Housing. *Home Sharing and Group Living Arrangements for the Elderly: Summary Notes on Workshop Presentations Held at the Fifteenth Annual Scientific and Educational Meeting of the Canadian Association on Gerontology.* Toronto: Ontario Ministry of Housing, 1987.

————. *Manual of Operations and Procedures for Ontario's Home Sharing Agencies.* Toronto, 1988a.

————. *Ontario Home Sharing Agencies: Survey of Services Offered.* Toronto, 1988b.

————. *Survey of Program Activities of Home Sharing Services in Ontario.* Toronto, 1988c.

Ontario Ministry of Municipal Affairs. *Health and Social Services for Retirement Communities: Draft Report.* Toronto, 1988a.

————. *Municipal Directory, 1988.* Toronto: Queen's Printer for Ontario, 1988b.

————. *Rural Service Centres: Draft Final Report.* Toronto, 1988c.

Shared Housing Resource Center. *Survey of Shared Housing Programs in the United States: A Summary of Findings.* Philadelphia, 1988.

Spence, David. "Community Need and Demand for Home Sharing Services." In *Home Sharing and Group Living Arrangements for the Elderly: Summary Notes on Workshop Presentations Held at the Fifteenth Annual Scientific and Educational Meeting of the Canadian Association on Gerontology.* Toronto: Ontario Ministry of Housing, 1987.

Statistics Canada. *1981 Census of Canada.* Cited by Ontario Ministry of Housing, *Report of the Ontario Task Force on Roomers, Boarders and Lodgers.* Toronto: Queen's Printer for Ontario, 1987.

Part III
CASE STUDIES

8

Homesharing for Homecare

Elizabeth Howe and Dale J. Jaffe

Other chapters in this book have indicated that older people use homesharing to meet a variety of needs. The pressure of inadequate financial resources may encourage someone to rent out a room, or the need for help with daily activities such as shopping or housework may suggest the usefulness of having someone else living in the house. As a result, during the past 10 years or so, formal homesharing programs have emerged in communities all over the country to help older people find others with whom to share housing.

As Barbara Robins and Elizabeth Howe suggest in Chapter 3, in some communities it is primarily financial pressures that make people consider sharing. High rents may make renters look for less expensive options than apartments. High home values and high property taxes may make older homeowners look for additional sources of income. As a result, programs in such communities define their missions as primarily meeting housing needs. On the other hand, in other communities housing costs may not be an issue, but among the frail elderly and their children, need for services at home makes them consider sharing. In these places, programs are likely to evolve with a service orientation. Many programs see some of both kinds of demand (see Jaffe and Howe, 1988).

In this chapter we want to focus on the second reason for homesharing—as a means of providing inexpensive home care. This can be explored on two distinct levels. The first is concerned with programs. What leads some homesharing programs to become predominantly service programs? How do service programs work, and what are the social benefits they provide? The second level is concerned with individuals. Who gets involved in service matches and why? What are the advantages and limitations to individuals of homesharing as a way of providing such services?

To address these questions, we consider the homesharing program in Madison, Wisconsin, as a case study. An in-depth exploration of the nature of this program and its matches can help to provide an understanding of the nature and dynamics of both service programs and matches. This in-depth picture can then be compared with what we know more generally about homesharing.

Madison's homeshare program is particularly appropriate for this purpose because in a national study of 38 homesharing programs, it was found to have one of the largest proportions of matches in which services were exchanged for room and board—96%, compared with an average of 40% for all programs (Howe, 1985; Jaffe and Howe, 1988).[1] Madison's program can be most easily compared with 7 other programs that had very high numbers of such service matches (over 70%) but in 9 other programs, between 48% and 68% of the matches involved service exchanges as well. Even programs that were primarily concerned with meeting purely housing needs often had a smattering of such arrangements.

In homesharing programs in general three types of matches emerge. *Independent matches*, as their name suggests, involve two independent people who come together as the homeprovider and the roomer. *Transitional matches* bring together an older person who has some need for help with activities of daily living with a live-in who provides assistance in exchange for room and board. Finally, in *dependent matches* the homeseeker provides a great deal of care to a very impaired older person, usually in exchange for room, board, and a small salary.

As with many other service-oriented homesharing programs, Madison arranges both types of service matches—transitional and dependent. In 1983, 83% of matches were of the former type, and 14% of the latter type. In other service-oriented programs, the proportion of dependent matches ranged from none to about a quarter, and in one case, even up to 40% of all matches.

Madison's program is not typical of all homesharing programs, but it does seem to be fairly characteristic of service and mixed programs. In terms of the homesharers themselves, homeproviders are mostly women. Like other service-oriented and some mixed programs, it makes almost entirely intergenerational matches. Students, in the case of Madison and several other communities, and somewhat older unemployed single people are the pool from which homeseekers are often drawn, although we will see some differences on this score later. Still, as will be suggested later in the chapter, there are many other similarities nationally among both programs and matches.

We begin by looking at the level of the program and its operations. After briefly looking at its background, we explore why demand for Madison's program primarily comes from frail elders and consider who applies, who gets matched, and how. Then we shift to an examination of individual service matches to see how they work and attempt to identify the benefits and the limitations of homesharing as a way of meeting needs for home care. Overall, this case study suggests that homesharing can be an effective and flexible way to meet the service needs of some frail elderly. The greater those needs are, however, the less likely it is that homesharing can be the only answer. Moreover, evaluations of the cost-effectiveness of homesharing may be somewhat different between participants and societal policy-makers.

DATA AND METHODOLOGY

The sources of information for this exploration of service homesharing are eclectic, and the methods of analysis used here are largely qualitative. The data on Madison's homeshare program come from a variety of sources. To understand the nature of applicants and the process of matchmaking, data were collected in part from case files. This provided information on 276 applicants to the program between August 1, 1982, and July 31, 1983, as well as on all matches as of May 1983. In addition, staff were interviewed about the process of making matches.

Information on the matches themselves was collected through in-depth, open-ended, but structured interviews in the summer of 1983 with 19 homesharers and 16 live-ins, covering 34 past and current matches in all. Of them, 29 are the basis of this analysis.[2] To complement these interviews with the participants, we also conducted interviews with other people who provided support to the residents. They included seven children, one grandchild, four friends, one legal guardian, and one social worker. These interviews were done in the summer and fall of 1983. In many cases these people played central roles in supporting the homesharers and were very much a part of the "matches."

All interviews were tape-recorded and then transcribed. Quantitative tabulations of factual data such as the length of matches could then be made. Using a systematic set of topics as a framework, qualitative notes were also made on each interview, allowing for comparison across individuals or matches.

Comparisons between Madison's program and other homesharing programs are based on the results of a 1984 survey of a random sample of 38 matchup programs drawn from the National Shared Housing Resource Center's *National Directory of Shared Housing Programs for Older People* (1983). The survey was intended to explore the administration of these programs and consisted of a telephone interview with the director of each. Thus it can be used for comparisons of programs but not for comparison of the nature of individual matches. Information on matches in other programs is largely gleaned from more in-depth case studies of particular programs, several of which are represented in this volume.

MADISON'S HOMESHARE PROGRAM: BACKGROUND

Madison is a city of 170,616 (1980) population. It is the seat of a large university with an enrollment of 43,075 students in 1983, as well as a number of smaller colleges and technical schools. It is also the home of the state government of Wisconsin. In the past it has also had sizeable blue-collar industries

such as meat processing and machine tools, although in recent years these industries have been in decline. It is a pleasant, generally middle-class, low-density
community. Among people over age 65, median income in 1980 was approximately $6,400 per year for the standard metropolitan statistical area (SMSA),
about 125% of the state's median income for the same age group. The 1981
annual housing survey estimated that 64% of households whose heads were over
age 65 owned their own homes. The nature of the rental housing market, especially for students, varies a good deal from year to year, but such housing
can be scarce and expensive.

The homesharing program is sponsored by Independent Living, a voluntary
agency providing a range of services to the elderly. In 1983 the homeshare
program had a paid staff of two and one volunteer. It was initially funded through
the Community Employment and Training Act (CETA) and the local United
Way, but by 1983 it had secured a three-year grant from the Gulf + Western
Foundation. In all these respects it was fairly typical of other service and mixed
programs, 44% of which were sponsored by agencies serving the elderly, with
generally small staffs and a variety of rather uncertain sources of funds.

As a component of an agency serving the elderly, the homeshare program's
original goal was to make homesharing arrangements for the elderly. Its goals
have always been service oriented, concerned, for example, with providing
inexpensive in-home care and preventing premature institutionalization. The
staff, however, quickly learned that there were few elderly homeseekers and
many older homeproviders. If the latter were to be matched, the program had
to recruit younger people as live-ins.

In 1983 the program made 43 matches. This is at the high end of the range
for service-oriented programs (mean, 26 matches per year) and close to the
average of 45 per year for mixed programs.[3] When the size of the population
of the community is controlled for, there is tremendous variability in matches/
population—from 1,399 to 37,533—but Madison, at 3,968, is in the midrange.
It is difficult to get accurate data on length of matches, but a rough estimate
suggests that the average match length in service and mixed programs may be
about eight months; so Madison, at seven months, is not particularly unusual.

Thus as service-oriented programs go, Madison's Project Homeshare is probably not very unusual. Nevertheless, service-oriented programs in general are
somewhat out of the ordinary, making up only about one-fifth of all homesharing
programs. Using Madison as our prototype, let us look at why such a program
develops and how it works.

THE DEMAND FOR SERVICE-ORIENTED HOMESHARING

One central fact about the demand for homesharing in general is that in the
United States today, sharing living quarters with people other than family members is an unusual living arrangement. As a rule, the elderly are as reluctant to
consider it as any other population group. At present, only 2.5% of people over

age 55 share living quarters with nonrelatives (Schreter and Turner, 1986:182). Generally, they seem to share only when severely pushed by income or health needs or by loneliness (Howe, 1985).

This reluctance to share means that homesharing programs tend to be small. Moreover, as Robins and Howe argue in Chapter 3, their staffs must be aware of and responsive to the forces in particular communities that make people consider shared housing.

Since homesharing is an unusual living arrangement, what makes people in Madison consider it, and why do they primarily want service matches? Home-providers and homeseekers are distinct groups with different reasons for sharing. It is the homeprovider applicants who are overwhelmingly older people—average age 79—looking for help with activities of daily living. This group is really seen as Independent Living's primary clientele, and it is they who define the program as service oriented. Homeseekers, on the other hand, are virtually all young—average age 27—and are looking primarily for inexpensive housing.

A variety of factors channel to the agency the potential homeproviders who primarily need help with services. To reach them, Independent Living has actively promoted the program through general advertising, media coverage, and presentations to a wide range of churches, social service agencies, and other organizations serving the elderly. The net is cast wide but still draws in primarily frail elders. Fully 46% are referred by social service agencies. They are mostly people who live independently until an illness brings them into the formal service system, and it becomes evident that they cannot continue to manage alone. The 31% who are referred by family are often in the same situation, since children are often either reluctant to, or unsuccessful in, urging assistance on their parents until they are in considerable need. Indeed, even after they have applied to the program, elders are often so reluctant to share that 24% of those people who were not matched never even completed the application process. Many of these people were referred by children but, when brought to the time of decision, decided that they just did not want to share after all.

This pattern of delay and frailty is probably reinforced by the perception of Independent Living in the community. Independent older people who wish to increase their incomes by renting rooms to students can do so through the university housing office; whereas Independent Living may be primarily viewed as an agency providing services to the elderly. Indeed, some of the applicants who "referred themselves" heard about the program because they were using other services from the agency.

Several results follow from this recruitment pattern. One is that some applicants are too frail to be served adequately by homesharing. Only 15% of homeshare's elderly applicants were judged to need little assistance; more than half needed a great deal because of chronic illness or extreme frailty. Of older people who were not matched, 20% were too frail, and 6% actually died before a match could be made. Of those people who did end up in matches, 92% said they had applied because they needed help with services.

But elderly potential homeproviders are obviously only half of the homesharing picture and cannot be helped if there are no helpers. Homeseekers, by contrast, come for completely different reasons. The primary draw is their need for inexpensive housing. In Madison two groups are looking for inexpensive housing and are willing to share: students and other young people who are unemployed or working at low wages. Independent Living recruits actively at all local colleges, and 42% of applicants heard about the program through a college source.

Nevertheless, inexpensive housing was not the only reason they chose to share with an older person rather than with contemporaries, and without some additional reason beyond financial need, they may have been unlikely to consider a service match because of the extra work involved. Among homeseekers who actually were matched, 18% said in addition that they wanted to help someone, and 29% thought the experience would be useful to their career training. Students come from fields such as medicine, nursing, and social work. Several had an ideological commitment to helping the elderly remain independent; nine were actually working in nursing homes or hospitals during the time they were live-ins.

HOW ARE MATCHES MADE?

In 1983 Project Homeshare had 119 applicants as homeproviders and 157 as homeseekers. These figures are fairly close to the 145 and 148 averages for all service-oriented programs. It is the job of the program to "match" one with the other. Ultimately, in Madison 32% found someone to share with, considerably higher than the average of 17% for all service programs. Two aspects of this process are particularly critical for understanding the capacity of the agency to make service matches and the nature of those matches.

One critical variable is that the agency uses a "counseling" model for structuring the matching process, and this probably increases the likelihood that frail elders will find a live-in. The counseling model involves a considerable expenditure of time and energy on making each match. After applicants fill out initial application forms, the staff visits the home of a potential homeprovider and checks references of homeseekers. Then they consider which applicants might be suited to each other, usually suggesting several options to the homeprovider who is viewed as the primary client. Often the staff meet with potential partners at this stage, and if a match looks likely they help the sharers work out a contract specifying what contribution each person will make to the match. Once the match is established, the agency follows up once a month for several months and then at about three-month intervals to see if there are any problems that need attention. Altogether, it may take as many as 130 telephone calls and office visits, 30 home visits, and 30 consultations with professionals from other agencies to make a dozen matches.

Not all programs use such a complex matching process (Jaffe and Howe, 1988). Programs that primarily help independent elders to find "roomers" who provide no services, generally do not use such an elaborate process. But if frail older people are to be matched, it is probably necessary to take the time to work with both partners. Indeed, five of the seven other service-oriented programs have procedures as elaborate as Madison's. The central reason is that both sides are potentially vulnerable in the exchange. The older person must be protected against possible exploitation or inadequate services. The live-in should not be faced with the care of a resident whose full needs have not been made clear. So the agency must work with the live-in, the homeprovider, the children, and referring professionals to define needs and to work out a contract specifying the exchange of room and board for specific services. Then they must follow up to see that the arrangement is actually working. In a program like Madison's such a process probably emerges naturally as a result of the needs of frail clients, and once established, its ability to make matches for at least some such clients contributes to maintaining the steady flow of referrals from other agencies serving the frail elderly.

Despite the use of a process that makes it possible to work out matches involving fairly elaborate exchanges, it is still difficult to find live-ins for frail elders. This is the second critical variable that determines not only the number of service matches set up but also their duration.

Homeseekers are not generally expected to be full-time caregivers, and the more time and work that is involved, the harder it is to find anyone willing to enter the role. Thus it is not surprising that 65% of the older applicants who were not matched with a live-in needed a great deal of assistance, compared with only 36% of those who did end up in a match.

The trade-off, in Madison at least, is that homeseekers are willing to provide services but only if the commitment is for a limited period—usually nine months or a year at the most. Many are in a period of transition in their lives—from their parents' home, in school, in their first job, or during an engagement before marriage. Although they are in a new environment, they may find it useful to live with an older person, providing services in exchange for room and board. But at the end of the set time, they generally expect to make the transition to "ordinary" independent living arrangements.

Within these constraints, a counseling approach to matchmaking can result in service matches, sometimes even for very frail homeproviders. Nevertheless, homesharing is significantly limited in how well it can meet major service needs at least through barter exchanges. Not only in Madison but in a dozen other cities as well, programs have found that if they wish to encourage this kind of assistance, the homeprovider must pay the homeseeker a salary in addition to providing room and board. Consider the programs described in this volume. Jon Pynoos and Arlyne June found that in San Jose 17% of the matches involve payment of some salary (see Chapter 10). In Madison, the stipends in total care matches averaged $140 per month in addition to room and board, for an imputed income of about $4,300 per year. Alfred Fengler and Nicholas Danigelis show that in Burlington, Vermont, the homesharing agency has institutionalized what they call "personal care" matches in which live-ins are paid on the average of $700 per month and basically become full-time caregivers (see Chapter 9).

WHAT HAPPENS IN SERVICE MATCHES?

Once the match has been set up, the focus must shift from the program to the individuals in the match, since the homeprovider and homeseeker are more or less on their own to work out a relationship. What kind of relationship develops in service matches depends largely on the health and needs of the homeprovider. Curiously, contrary to what one might expect from the discussion of match-making, matches in which the resident needs less help often prove to be more problematic than those in which the resident needs a great deal of help.

In Madison, when the older person was only somewhat impaired, resident and live-in traded services such as shopping, preparing meals, vacuuming, and laundry for room and board. Instrumentally, many of these transitional matches worked, but emotionally, it was often difficult to work out a relationship that satisfied both people. The enforced closeness of living together and of providing the required services made a purely formal, "businesslike" relationship inappropriate. Friendships and familial relationships were the other possible relationship categories familiar to sharers, but the built-in dependence and contact often precluded the gradual development of voluntary and equal friendships, whereas too little common history often made "family" an unrealistic model.

Since both people in the match needed the benefits it could provide, more than one-half of both live-ins and residents in these transitional matches worked at adapting to the other person's tastes and habits. Yet hopes and expectations on both sides were hard to meet. At a practical level, one-third of these home-providers thought the live-in did not live up to the terms of the contract. Often they were anxious to avoid confronting the other person and simply let the problem fester until the match was irretrievably broken, although in these cases intervention by the agency could sometimes have dealt effectively with the problem. More difficult was the problem of the second third who wanted more companionship than the live-in was willing to provide. In many of these cases the residents chose homesharing in part because they wanted companionship, but often they were not willing to be explicit about it during the matching process. Once in the match, they exerted indirect pressure on the live-in to spend time with them, often making the live-in feel guilty or angry.

On their side, live-ins, in the process of transition to greater adult independence, generally worried about being too much restricted by their responsibilities to the resident. Sometimes conflict also arose from their resistance to being mothered by their homeproviders.

Some of these problems were enough to bring a match to an end prematurely, and this happened in 43% of the cases. Many, however, were more in the nature of irritants. Each person needed the practical assistance they got from the match, so that 57% stuck with it. Despite the fact that only 14% of the relationships in these matches were close and comfortable, several lasted between one and two years, and the rest came to natural endings in shorter periods. Even so, only one-quarter of all transitional matches were characterized by their members as unqualified successes, and the rest were divided equally between outright failures and qualified successes.

In these transitional matches the homeproviders, while in need of some assistance, were still basically independent. Indeed, it was the combination of independence and dependence that made these matches so troublesome. It is difficult to create an instant comfortable relationship between two people who are brought together by need but who also continue to assert their independence from each other.

On the other hand, in matches in which the homeprovider was much more impaired and dependent, a different dynamic developed that bound the live-in more closely to the resident in a "dependent" match. These residents had severe health problems—Alzheimer's disease, stroke, multiple disabilities, or extreme frailty—and needed a lot of assistance. Although it was difficult to find live-ins for such clients, they did make up 28% of Independent Living's matches, and by and large the matches worked out surprisingly well.

In these matches the resident's greater need for care was dealt with in two ways. In four matches in which the resident had involved children and adequate financial resources, the live-in became one member of a support system that included professional nursing care during the day, with the live-in responsible primarily for help at night. The children, who sometimes lived out of town, played an active role in arranging for care and in monitoring the arrangements. The cost of such an arrangement is substantial. The nursing care alone would cost between $14,000 and $18,000 per year, and a stipend for the live-in might cost an additional $1,700 (1983).

In these matches the live-in's relationship with the resident's children was a central element. Although there sometimes were tensions and disagreements, generally a businesslike trust developed between them. With the residents themselves, the relationships were warm but somewhat distant, a compound of friendship and professional caregiving.

In four other matches in which money and active children were lacking, the dependent match relationships were different. These homeseekers were usually the key persons caring for the homeproviders. There were no nurses or children. The live-in managed the household, shopped, cooked, did errands, sometimes provided personal care, and gave warmth and companionship. In some instances they were even cast in the role of making fateful decisions about nursing-home placement for their homeprovider.

The relationships that developed were extraordinary. These live-ins were unusually dedicated people. Ordinary friendship with its norms of equity was really precluded because of the heavy dependence of the resident. In some instances the resident's mental impairment meant that they could not even recognize the live-in. Live-ins did not take refuge in professional distance, however, but were engaged and caring, stating that the relationships were equitable in terms of love if not in terms of work.

Although these live-ins shouldered a greater burden of work and responsibility, their situation gave them greater freedom than other live-ins had. The balance of power in the relationship lay with them rather than with the homesharer or his or her children, and they were not so much subject to the irritant of making an ordinary relationship work. In fact, it was this very freedom and the knowledge of the power they held that bound them morally to continue the relationship until the resident died or could no longer live independently. None of these matches was characterized as a failure by the people in them, and 57% were classified as unqualified successes. Live-ins who said their matches were "qualified" successes referred less to their relationship with the homeprovider than to their feeling that they had not been prepared for how dependent the resident would actually be.

MATCHES: HOW TYPICAL IS MADISON?

Matches in Madison's project homeshare seem to be a great deal like those in other homesharing programs that make service matches. There are some differences. Madison's matching process may be somewhat more effective in terms of total matches, although comparison with San Jose and Milwaukee indicates that Madison was not serving a more frail group of older people. The primary difference in Madison was that live-ins were younger than those in other programs. In Chapter 13, Dale Jaffe and Christopher Wellin's study of Milwaukee's program found, for example, that the age range of homeseekers was much wider, and they were more likely to be marginally employed people or recent immigrants than students. Pynoos and June (Chapter 10) found that homeseekers in San Jose were much more likely to be elderly themselves, with 62% over the age of 60; similarly, in San Diego, according to Pritchard (1988), 50% of the live-ins were over age 55. It would certainly not be surprising if older live-ins responded differently to the homesharing situation.

Overall, however, comparison with studies that have looked at the nature of homesharing matches suggest considerable similarity in the way service matches work. Jaffe and Wellin, in their analysis of Milwaukee's service-oriented program in Chapter 13, found that sharers in 45% of the matches struggled with problems of unmet expectations or incompatibility. Unmet expectations in relation to concrete services accounted for some of these problems, although in general, the more in need of services the homeprovider was and the more elaborate the terms of the exchange, the less problematic the matches seemed to be. Substantial need for services to maintain independence seems to be associated with more realism about what a match can provide. On the other hand, the unmet desire for more companionship was a much greater cause of friction; 75% of live-ins in problematic matches felt pressed to spend more time with their residents.

Fengler and Danigelis found that in Burlington, in more independent matches common expectations were a key to success, and implicit demands for companionship were a source of conflicts just as life-style differences between older and younger partners were (see Chapter 9). In a somewhat similar vein, Pritchard (1988) found that, in San Diego, 6% of the matches actually ended because of unmet expectations, and 27% more did so because of incompatibility.

Together, these studies produce a picture of service-oriented homesharing that is similar to that found in Madison. This can give us greater confidence in our evaluation of the advantages and limitations of homesharing as a way of meeting the home-care needs of the elderly.

ADVANTAGES AND LIMITATIONS OF SERVICE MATCHES

Both the advantages and the limitations of homesharing for the individuals involved should be fairly evident by now. Madison's homesharers identified the advantages clearly themselves. They are largely practical. The largest number of residents identified the practical assistance provided and the greater security of having someone else in the house. Since 58% had been told by doctors or hospital personnel that they could not continue to live alone, this instrumental orientation is hardly surprising. Live-ins, for their part, stressed the benefits of inexpensive housing and the useful experience.

These advantages represent concrete monetary benefits to both participants. We estimated (Howe, Robins, and Jaffe, 1984) that in 1983 in transitional matches a live-in who did outdoor chores, cleaned, cooked, and helped with medications represented a saving of about $4,600 per year to the homeprovider over the cost of hiring help. In dependent matches the savings from having a live-in who was the sole provider of care could run as much as $56,000 per year, even deducting the $140 per month that Madison's live-ins were paid on the average. Such an amount is probably only a "paper" savings, however, since one of the main reasons that live-ins became sole providers was that their residents could not afford other help. If the live-in was only one of several helpers, one of whom was a nurse's aide, the cost savings would be much less. On the part of the live-in, the room and board was estimated to represent a savings of about $2,600 per year; in dependent matches the stipend, though minimal, would be about $1,700.

But not all of the benefits of homesharing are monetary. One of the advantages is the greater flexibility of services provided by a live-in over those provided by formal services. A home-chore person may do housework and maybe even shopping but probably would not shovel snow. If a resident needs help with medication late at night, this assistance may be difficult to arrange without someone living in the house. Services may also be better. Thus a person in the house may be more reassuring for security than a Lifeline beeper or a burglar alarm.

Although the advantages may be self-evident, the strongly instrumental cast of the evaluations may be somewhat less expected. There is a natural tendency among the staff of homesharing programs to think of matches as successful if they grow into friendships or familylike relationships. This is certainly a desirable outcome, and a significant minority of homesharers hope for such results themselves, but it is important to recognize that service matches can be instrumentally successful even if they do not become close or even altogether comfortable relationships. Certainly, the members of many of Madison's matches seem to be making this point, and the more problematic nature of Milwaukee's matches in which companionship was a major expectation would support it as well.

The limitations of homesharing seem to be equally self-evident. Living alone is one aspect of an older person's independence. Sharing, especially in exchange for services, is not usually considered to be a ''normal'' or valued living arrangement but is, instead, an admission of increasing dependence and loss of autonomy. Thus it is hardly surprising that older people often come to consider homesharing only after they have become so frail that it is difficult to find someone to help them. Nevertheless, at that point it may be considered a better alternative than living with children, moving to a retirement home, or especially entering a nursing home, an alternative most elderly dread.

Sharing a home to arrange for concrete services seems to be more workable than sharing to gain a companion. The process of working out an explicit contract is much better suited to arranging the housework than it is for a set amount of ''togetherness.'' It may seem obvious that friendships must develop and grow naturally and cannot be created on order, but clearly this is exactly what some homesharers hope for. This is not an absolute limit. Friendships do develop in homesharing matches, but this is probably more an unintentional side benefit than a deliberate result.

Because of the difficulty of arranging service matches, programs must also accept the fact that homeseekers are often in a transitional phase of their lives, which makes homesharing attractive only for a limited period. Thus in Madison it is normal for matches to last on the average seven months, and this does not seem to be atypical of other programs as well.

Clearly, the limited term of matches does make homesharing a somewhat cumbersome way of providing home care for frail elders. Homeproviders in transitional matches usually have chronic disabilities but could continue to live in their own homes for a considerable period of years with some assistance. If they choose to meet their needs by sharing, they must be willing to accept the constant change and uncertainty of having a new live-in every year or so. In Madison 44% of all homeproviders in 1983 had had two or sometimes even three matches. Here again, a practical assessment of necessity is at work, but not every older person has the psychic energy to adapt to a new live-in every nine months.

Overall, from the standpoint of individuals actually willing to get involved in service matches, the disadvantages of sharing seem to be outweighed by the advantages for 62%. But on the whole, homesharing does a better job of meeting practical service needs than needs for emotional support or companionship. In addition, older people who do it must have a fair amount of flexibility and determination to make it work.

ADVANTAGES AND LIMITATIONS OF PROGRAMS

For a program, the advantages of arranging service matches are also fairly obvious. The major return is that the program helps, if only in a small-scale way, to provide home services that help the frail elderly to live independently in their own homes.

As we have already seen, in Madison's program about 60% of the home-providers came into the program from nursing homes or on doctors' orders. All of the residents in dependent matches would have been in nursing homes had they not had elaborate care arrangements at home, in which live-ins played either a central or a helpful role. Several such matches did end with institutionalization. Residents in transitional matches were probably not generally at risk of nursing-home care, although without some kind of home care, some of them might reluctantly have considered it. They clearly needed home care, however, and most had only limited resources to pay for it, so a barter arrangement was particularly attractive to them.

Besides securing the tangible and practical help provided by homesharing, the program staff may also have the satisfaction of making matches that develop into friendships or quasi-familial relationships. Although we have shown that this is not always a realistic expectation for the people in the matches, it is easy to see how the agency staff would see this as one of the rewards of matchmaking. To be able to argue to oneself that a homesharing relationship has transcended the boundaries of the purely instrumental increases the psychic rewards of the work. Since many people who work for such programs work for small salaries or as volunteers, these psychic rewards are important for maintaining commitment to the organization.

The hope that matches would be long lasting and close may also be, in part, a response to the limitations of homesharing. Making service matches is a difficult, intensive, time-consuming business. Because people are reluctant to share housing, programs are generally small; it takes on the average about 10 hours of staff time to make one service match. Because of all of these factors, it may be difficult to justify homesharing programs to funding sources as cost-effective. Again, to be able to argue to funding sources that long-lasting relationships do occur is to add an additional, important element to the "benefit" side of the cost/benefit tally sheet.

Moreover, any program that sees people looking for service matches must recognize that simply in terms of numbers of people helped and the ease of finding helpers, the less the burden on the homeseeker, the easier it is to make a match. It is difficult to find live-ins to be the primary caregivers for very frail older people. Even Madison had only 4 matches of this type out of 29 total matches, 24 of which were service matches of some kind. The burden is simply too great, and it is not realistic to expect that many homeseekers can be recruited with the dedication of the ones interviewed for this study. Fairly independent older people who need only limited, practical assistance are the best prospects, but frail elders can also be served if the live-in is one member of a team providing "total care." If live-ins are to be primary caregivers in dependent matches, salaries in addition to room and board are probably essential.

Programs that have many applicants needing services do seem to have more difficulty finding live-ins and making matches and are somewhat smaller (average of 26 matches) than housing-oriented programs (average of 43 matches). Service programs that make multiple matches for "regular" clients may find that they expend disproportionate resources on a small clientele. Most programs are always under pressure to expand their constituency. But as long as "demand" in the community is for service-oriented rather than housing-oriented homesharing, programs have little choice about where their expansion can occur.

Service-oriented programs can take some actions to adapt effectively to an environment in which most demand comes from older people needing services. They can try to encourage an understanding of both the suitable uses and the limitations of homesharing among both funding and referral sources. They can also do the same for elderly applicants and their children. Indeed, this is something that is done naturally if the matching process is organized according to the counseling model, in which desires and expectations on both sides are clarified and formalized in a contract. The program can also help to support the matches by following up on them and helping to deal with conflicts before matches reach a stage where they break down.

If a program wants to try to make dependent matches, it should encourage the payment of adequate salaries to attract live-ins. In addition, in this kind of match more support for the live-in may be useful. It could take the form of case management to help arrange for additional services such as adult day care or meals on wheels. Or it could involve training or counseling to help the live-ins deal with their homesharers or their children.

Programs can take systematic steps to increase applicants, especially homeseekers, as well as the proportion of applicants who get matched. Nevertheless, it is probably nearly inevitable that programs making service matches must accept both the reluctance of older people to share, unless pushed, and the difficulty of finding help if they are frail. For programs that have both housing and service demand, this may not pose a significant problem, but for those that make only service matches, this may result in small programs and a constant need to sell homesharing to both funders and clients.

SOCIAL BENEFITS OF HOMESHARING

From the point of view of older people willing to consider homesharing, it can be a workable, flexible, inexpensive, and sometimes pleasurable way to meet home-care needs. Certainly, from their point of view a homesharing program could easily be considered cost-effective.

But participants are not the only evaluators of homesharing. In most cases the homesharers themselves do not pay the cost of the program, so programs must depend on public and voluntary funding sources to survive. These programs are not elaborate or costly by the standard of many social programs. Indeed, their small, personalized, and informal nature is one of their advantages from the client's perspective. Nevertheless, since the financial benefits primarily accrue to the homesharers themselves, it is legitimate to ask whether there are additional public benefits incurred that justify public and voluntary funding of these programs.

Although staffs are concerned about helping all elderly who could benefit from homesharing, broader societal policy-makers may be more concerned with saving public money. Tax money is used both for nursing-home care for elderly who qualify for Medicaid and for traditional home-care services for less frail elders who may be at risk of entering nursing homes.

The homesharing clients most likely to be in nursing homes would be those in dependent matches. Service-oriented programs have, on the average, four such clients, but if Madison is any indication, only about half of them might qualify for Medicaid assistance. Nursing-home care might in 1983 have cost about $98,000 per year, or $196,000 for two people. Thus even if dependent matches are the hardest to make and the least common, only a few can potentially result in considerable savings of public funds.

It is more difficult to estimate likely public expenditures on home-care services since they vary a great deal in comprehensiveness and eligibility standards. In 1983 Wisconsin's Community Options Program (COP), which used Medicaid waivers to prevent inappropriate institutionalization of the elderly, allowed an expenditure of as much as $8,400 per person per year for home care. If an average service-oriented homesharing program had 18 transitional matches, and if we assume that one-quarter of them would have been eligible for a program such as COP, the cost could have been as high as $37,800 per year.

By comparison, what is the cost of homesharing? We did not collect information on this in the survey, but figures exist for a few programs. Taking the average cost per match for Madison and the Twin Cities (Robinson, Martin, and Shafto, 1983), the cost of the average service program of 26 matches would be about $30,000 per year. Just the staff cost for making and maintaining a match, assuming it lasted for a year, would be about $190.[4]

Thus potentially, a homesharing program costing $30,000 per year, only a quarter of whose recipients might qualify for some kind of public aid, might still save as much as $233,800 in public costs for social services and nursing-home care, for a social benefit of $203,800. But decisions to fund programs are not necessarily made by making calculations of this kind, and a policy-maker might wonder about the high opportunity cost of funding a home-care program whose demand is uncertain and must be stimulated. In an ideal world, some form of congregate care might well be more appropriate for frail elders at the "dependent" end of the spectrum (Howe, 1985). On the other hand, congregate care is not very common and, as a more institutional alternative, is expensive. Homesharing is not only becoming more common, but the cost is small. Moreover, there is an argument to be made for encouraging diversity in the options that older people have for meeting their need for assistance with activities of daily life. Given the substantial need for home care for the elderly in many communities, this exercise in weighing costs and benefits does suggest that homesharing can be a cost-effective way, not only for sharers but for society as well, to serve the older people willing to try it.

NOTES

The research on which most of this chapter is based was done as a program evaluation supported by Independent Living of Madison, Wisconsin (Howe, Robins, and Jaffe, 1984). We would like to thank our colleagues Jane Osterman, who collected some of the data, and Barbara Robins, who was involved in the conceptualization of the evaluation and the design, administration, and analysis of the survey of other homesharing programs that grew out of it.

1. In the in-depth study of matches discussed later in the chapter, only 83% of the matches were service matches. This is largely the result of the sample of homesharers interviewed. The nature of this sample is discussed in the section on methodology.

2. The total number of matches used here was 29 for two reasons. Some of the live-ins and residents were involved in more than one match. For 12 matches both parties were interviewed. In 15 cases only the homeprovider could be interviewed because the match was over and the live-in had moved away. In another 7 cases the resident could not be interviewed because of senility or other health problems, and only the live-in was interviewed. Thus throughout the interviews 34 matches were discussed. Of them, 5 of the matches could not be used because not enough information on them was available. In some cases they had simply not been discussed in enough detail. In a few cases, such as an interview with a homeprovider with Alzheimer's disease, the results of the interview were too difficult to interpret.

We should also make clear that the number of matches used here differs slightly from that used in some other reports of our research. This chapter, which reports on 29 matches, is based on the evaluation of Independent Living's homeshare program (Howe, Robins, and Jaffe, 1984; also reported in Howe, 1985). That analysis did not use the face-to-face interviews done by Dale Jaffe. In his report of his own findings (1989), however, he used 30 matches, and of the total of 34 matches identified, the matches included and excluded were slightly different from what was used in the program evaluation. Finally, for the analysis of the national survey of homesharing programs by Barbara Robins and Elizabeth Howe (see Chapter 3; Howe, 1985; Jaffe and Howe, 1988), the total number of matches in the Madison program during the year May 1982 to May 1983 was used.

This also happens to have been 29 matches, but they were not exactly the same matches as those identified and discussed in Jaffe's interviews. His study covered 85% of all of the matches in existence in May 1983, and any given interview might cover a present match as well as one or several past ones. These variations account for the difference in the proportions of the three types of matches reported in footnote 1.

3. This figure of 45 matches per year is typical of most "mixed" programs. There is one very large program that makes about 450 matches per year, however. When it is included, the mean for all mixed programs increases to 90 per year.

4. This assumes it takes 10 staff hours to make a service match and maybe 5 more to monitor it during the year. It also assumes a staff salary of $25,000.

REFERENCES

Howe, Elizabeth. "Homesharing for the Elderly." *Journal of Planning Education and Research* 4 (1985):185–94.

Howe, Elizabeth; Robins, Barbara; and Jaffe, Dale. *Evaluation of Independent Living's Homeshare Program*. Madison: Independent Living, 1984.

Jaffe, Dale. *Caring Strangers: The Sociology of Intergenerational Homesharing*. Greenwich, Conn.: JAI Press, 1989.

Jaffe, Dale, and Howe, Elizabeth. "Agency-Assisted Shared Housing: The Nature of Programs and Matches." *The Gerontologist* 28 (1988):318–24.

National Shared Housing Resource Center. *National Directory of Shared Housing Programs for Older People*. Philadelphia, 1983.

Pritchard, David. Personal Communication, 1988.

Robinson, Timothy; Martin, Richard; and Shafto, Michael. *Share-A-Home: Final Report*. Minneapolis: The McKnight Foundation, 1983.

Schreter, Carol, and Turner, Lloyd. "Sharing and Subdividing Private Market Housing." *The Gerontologist* 26 (1986):181–86.

9

Homesharing Service through Social Exchange: The Case of Project HOME

Nicholas L. Danigelis and Alfred P. Fengler

Project HOME is a Chittenden County, Vermont, homesharing service that attempts to match elders and frail individuals who want to remain at home with a homeseeker who may pay or barter for lodging or who may be paid to perform caregiving services for the homeowner.[1] Beginning services in the spring of 1982, Project HOME has grown from a small program almost totally run by volunteers with no budget to a major community service organization with three and one-half paid staff members, anywhere between four and six volunteer staff members, and a budget of more than $70,000. Even now, as an established service organization complete with advisory board and as a recipient of United Way funds, Project HOME remains a curious hybrid: It operates within bureaucratic limitations of budgeting, procedures for operation, and some division of labor, while it continues to depend on a dedicated core of volunteers for its key service-delivery functions.

The increase in the number of clients served parallels the dramatic increase in the organization's size. In its first year of operation 85 people applied to Project HOME, which was able to make only 4 matches. By the fifth year of operation there was a threefold increase in applicants to 251 and almost a twentyfold increase in matches to 75 for the year. In addition, there are currently more than 500 counseling inquiries a year that involve requests for information about homesharing or related service requests, suggesting that Project HOME has become an important clearinghouse for information pertaining, but not limited, to elders' (and others') living situations. Thus the Project HOME staff provide information and referral for other more appropriate agencies or services.

A major reason for the success of the program was the early acknowledgment by all persons associated with Project HOME of the guiding principle of social exchange. The idea of reciprocating goods and services not only was essential to the origins of the program but also remains essential to the philosophy of the current staff associated with Project HOME. The following analysis shows how Project HOME evolved on the basis of social exchange within the organization and between the organization and the researchers evaluating it. First, it is necessary to describe the key actors, events, and processes in the program.

THE ORIGIN AND HISTORY OF PROJECT HOME

Origins: Serving Two Groups of Elders

The idea for Project HOME was developed in 1981 by members of the county Retired Senior Volunteer Program who saw dual needs that a single homesharing service could meet. One problem was the serious housing shortage in the county's major city. According to the Retired Senior Volunteer Program (RSVP) director at the time, residents were encountering only a 1% housing vacancy rate. The second need, not critical given the numbers of projects in which RSVP volunteers were involved but critical with respect to the direction the program would take in its development, reflected the mission of the RSVP to provide meaningful activities for its volunteers. Thus the original idea behind Project HOME was to service two groups of people: elderly in need of shared housing and older RSVP volunteers who would help to match these elders with each other and thus experience a meaningful volunteer role. To provide administrative continuity, a part-time RSVP staff person was temporarily assigned to this project to get it off the ground.

Shortly after the RSVP decided to begin Project HOME, in the fall of 1981, the RSVP director contacted the researchers, one of whom she knew in a professional capacity, and asked if they would help construct a homesharing application form in exchange for use of the information on the forms in research endeavors relating to homesharing. They agreed and, during the early winter of 1982, after consulting with the RSVP director and the RSVP staff person assigned to coordinate Project HOME, developed a draft application form and shared it with the director and her coordinator. Once copies of a final draft were ready, the researchers held a training session for the RSVP volunteers who would be using the application form to interview prospective homesharers. Around April 1, 1982, Project HOME, through word of mouth and public service announcements, began to accept applications from elders desiring to share housing.

The First Year: Learning How to Match Clients

For a few brief months Project HOME resembled a cottage industry in that it functioned as a part of the whole RSVP program, using a staff member from the RSVP part time, depending on RSVP volunteers, and operating out of RSVP office space. Not surprisingly, like many cottage industries Project HOME required much more attention than the early staffing resources could accommodate.

The director of the RSVP, in fact, decided that to develop a matching instrument; to train the volunteers to interview potential applicants; to recruit, advertise, and arrange the actual match, there needed to be a single individual to coordinate the activities. Thus in October 1982, about six months after the program had begun accepting applicants, the RSVP hired a part-time staff person with help from an $8,000 community service grant from IBM. The funding provided for this part-time director to work some 20 to 30 hours a week for one year.

The new HOME director was employed through the RSVP and was thus responsible to the RSVP director. At the same time the HOME director was, in theory, separated from the daily operation of the RSVP and unlikely to be compromised by the daily distractions of the larger organization. In practice, the HOME director's desk was in the same office as RSVP personnel and next door to the RSVP director's office. Since volunteers were involved in HOME as interviewers, the goals of the RSVP and HOME were compatible, and the needs of two groups, homeowners and volunteers, were being served through the same project.

A key problem facing the new director was that no matches had been made at the time she was hired. A great deal of the problem lay in the tremendous imbalance in the pool of applicants: 23 of the first 29 applicants to the program were homeproviders, there were hardly any elderly applicants willing to move, and the few there were could not be matched. For the university researchers, nevertheless, there was enough preliminary indication that the study of Project HOME and its service mission was important enough and could be based on a sufficiently strong data base for an application to an outside agency to fund an evaluation of the program. Thus in the fall of 1982 they applied to the Andrus Foundation for financial support to evaluate Project HOME.

During this first year of its existence, more than a dozen RSVP volunteers worked for Project HOME, interviewing applicants. By the end of the first year, some 83 applications had been received, but only four matches were made. Nevertheless, Project HOME had begun and was making itself known in the community among service providers and clients alike.

The Second Year: New Directions

The first part-time director of Project HOME served for only half of the one-year grant awarded by IBM, leaving the program near the end of Project HOME's first year for personal reasons. In general, the first year of Project HOME was a difficult period for the program, because it was trying to sell the concept of homesharing to elders in the area at the same time it had little experience in matching applicants with one another and had not developed a systematic matching procedure.

At the beginning of the second year, a new part-time director was hired, and for several weeks both the old and new directors worked together. The new director had experiences and interests directly relevant to homesharing: She had worked with older people as a chaplain and had training as a journalist. Her grandmother and mother's various experiences in a variety of living conditions helped spark her interest in living environments for older people. At the time she became director, she was also homesharing herself. Finally, the job required her to do things she liked and thought she was good at such as interviewing, serving people, and being responsible for program development.

Also during the spring of 1983, the university researchers were informed that funding from the Andrus Foundation was forthcoming. As a result, they initiated a roundtable discussion in which the old and new HOME directors, the director of the RSVP, and the original RSVP coordinator for Project HOME discussed the progress and direction of Project HOME.

Three important things happened during this critical second year: an expansion of the target population, a complete overhauling and expansion of the application form, and an expanded role for the director.

First, from the beginning, the new director believed that although Project HOME was a service for the benefit of elders, the program could not continue to depend only on elder homesharer clients; the very low numbers of matches attested to the fact that getting older people to leave their own homes was terribly difficult, if not impossible. As a result, she opened up applications to well and disabled nonelders who were in need of shared housing and who would be willing to share with elders.

Second, after service in the field for nearly one year, the original application form had showed itself to be inadequate for purposes of matching applicants, especially the new, younger group, and for evaluating the program's efforts to match individuals. Together, the new director and the university researchers developed a much more comprehensive application instrument comprised of a separate application form and interview schedule for homeproviders and a separate form and schedule for homeseekers.

Finally, because the IBM grant was scheduled to run out during the middle of the program's second year, the RSVP and HOME directors discussed options for uncovering new sources of funding. Since the RSVP director believed that HOME needed to support itself in this respect, she maintained that the HOME director needed to take the initiative and proceed to make grant applications when appropriate, with the understanding that the RSVP would help in any way it could.

Despite having no experience in grant writing, the HOME director set to her task, and within only a few months of the lapse of the IBM grant, Project HOME received support from the state of Vermont's Independence Fund to continue Project HOME. Between the time the IBM grant lapsed and the Independence Fund grant started, the RSVP provided monetary support to carry HOME's administrative costs, and afterwards, the RSVP made up the difference between the Independence Fund grant and what HOME needed to operate.

While all of these important changes were occurring during the second year, the number of volunteers fluctuated somewhat, but around a half dozen were doing interviews on a regular basis and another half dozen were supplementing these more active volunteers with interviews at less frequent intervals. By the end of the second year, Project HOME had received an additional 86 applications and had made 18 more matches. Among the matches, 3 involved clients who had already homeshared through Project HOME earlier.

The Third Year: Declaring Independence

The third year was characterized by a tremendous growth in the number of Project HOME clients in the wake of continuing financial pressures. In response to these stimuli, there evolved a restructuring of roles within HOME's small staff and, finally, independence of the program from the RSVP.

During the third year, as the director and her volunteers stepped up advertising and successes with clients became known, the program received a large influx of applicants. At the same time, the problem of money continued to be an ongoing concern, especially during the summer of 1985 as the one-year Independence Fund grant was nearing an end. Simultaneously, therefore, the HOME director was being asked to spend more time serving more and more clients while spending more time writing grant applications to insure that the program continued. The dilemma was solved by the HOME director spending more time on grant proposal writing and a small core of experienced, capable volunteers taking greater responsibilities in matching applicants with one another.

At the same time that funding was getting to be an issue, the RSVP director was becoming increasingly concerned that Project HOME was outgrowing the RSVP's original expectations, because HOME volunteers were providing direct service—which, in her words, "is not the purpose of RSVP." Thus during this very busy third year, both financial and organizational strains were coming to the forefront in the minds of both the Project HOME and RSVP directors.

After a series of discussions concerning the alternatives, the two directors agreed that Project HOME should become an independent program that, while continuing to cooperate with RSVP, would nevertheless be a separate entity. In the meantime, the HOME director would continue to seek funding to pay for (basically) her salary.[2]

By the end of the third year, the number of Project HOME volunteers had been reduced to no more than a half dozen or so, but what was lost in number was made up for in quality of work. As the HOME director spent more time on grant writing and related administrative matters, the volunteers, in large part on their own initiative and with the blessing of the director, became involved in matching and following up matched clients as well as taking phone inquiries from and interviewing prospective clients and developing advertising strategies.

During the third year, Project HOME received new funding from the Vermont Independence Fund, and before the year was over, had become a separate entity from the RSVP. Also, 162 new applications were taken, and 43 new matches were made; 17 of the matches involved previously matched clients.

The Fourth Year: Discovering Client Needs

The fourth year was characterized by the program's formal recognition of an expansion of its mission and concomitant peaking of the number of its applicants, while the newly independent organization continued to struggle for financial support.

Regarding clients, Project HOME had, from the beginning, been attracting frail elders whose homesharing needs extended well beyond having a lodger either exchanging chorelike services or paying for a space in which to live. These elderly homeowners needed personal care requiring either previous experience (e.g., through nursing) or a willingness to commit much time and patience to caring for another individual.

In either case, the frail elder was not going to get such help from the traditional seeker who preferred paying or doing minimal work or both in exchange for a place to stay. The only solution was for the homeowner to *pay* someone to provide the necessary personal care. Fortunately, enough frail elders were able to provide a stipend in addition to living space for their caregiving homeseekers, and many younger and middle-aged seekers were found who were willing to provide caregiving services in exchange for a stipend and a place to live. In fact, during the fourth year, the number of personal-care companion applicants exceeded the number of traditional homesharing applicants.

Money, a concern from almost the beginning of the program, became especially acute after Project HOME became independent from the RSVP. Yet with funding from the Vermont Independence Fund being renewed and other, smaller sources, like the city, being successfully tapped, Project HOME continued to scrape by with enough support to pay the director and provide administrative support.

Still, because the Independence Fund was intended to provide seed money for *new* programs and Project HOME was rapidly becoming "old," the director and her staff believed that a relatively permanent source of funding was needed if the program was going to be able to focus its energies on service provision rather than dissipate them in efforts to keep itself financially solvent. Despite the day-to-day work of the core volunteers described in the previous section, the director could ill afford to become a full-time grant writer because the program had become strongly identified with her name and because she had so much knowledge about all of the homesharing applicants that it was becoming increasingly difficult to share with her volunteer staff.

Thus it was a serious setback when Project HOME's first application to the United Way was turned down during this fourth year of operation. Compounding the uncertain financial future of the program was the decision by the director to resign from her position to attend Divinity School. Although her decision to leave was firm, she kept her departure date open in hopes that the organization could get on firm footing financially before she left.

With all of the uncertainty stemming from financial concerns and the forthcoming departure of the director, Project HOME continued to maintain a high profile in the community and expand the kinds of clientele it was willing to serve. With a core staff of the director and between four and six volunteers, Project HOME processed 285 applications and made 87 matches, more than half of which (46) involved previously matched clients.

The Fifth Year: Becoming a Flexible Bureaucracy

Attacking the problem of uncertain financing in the face of ever-expanding service requests from the community and service provision for clients, the director, her volunteer staff, and the manager of the housing unit in which Project HOME was still housed decided to formalize the structure of the program by creating an advisory board of interested community members who could provide a variety of resources for the organization that it was having difficulty providing for itself.

One resource was the existence of the board itself, which would encourage outside funding agencies to view Project HOME as an established organization that was somewhat accountable to a group other than itself or its clients.

A second advantage came from the people who made up the board and the kind of specific help they were envisioned as providing. The director and her staff carefully chose board members who would provide a variety of services that it was becoming increasingly hard for Project HOME to do for itself. Thus the board charter specified four committees: Planning and Evaluation, Volunteer Development, Public Relations, and Fund Raising. The university researchers were asked to serve on the board and cochair the Planning and Evaluation Committee; two HOME volunteers were asked to serve on the board and on the Volunteer Development Committee; others were asked to serve on the board because of their expertise in public relations or fund raising and were assigned to the appropriate committees.

Two major events after the creation of the advisory board occurred during this critical fifth year. First, during the spring and early summer of the fifth year, the director and board solicited applications and interviewed candidates for the position of new director. The current director, with an advisory board and funding in place, finally had announced her intention to leave by the end of the summer to attend Divinity School. During the interviewing process, the board decided that the new director needed to have a serious commitment to service for elders and others needing homesharers but that also she or he needed to be able to run Project HOME efficiently and *manage* it. The time for large-scale entrepreneurial growth had passed, and Project HOME needed to protect what it had achieved.

After some deliberation, the board chose a woman with a background in legal-aid work who was interested in pursuing an advanced degree in public administration (she is currently enrolled as a part-time student in a local university's Masters in Public Administration program while she continues to serve as Project HOME director). In the words of one board member, the board had been looking for and, in fact, hired a "caring manager." The old entrepreneurial director and the new managerial director overlapped a month to facilitate the changing of the guard. By the end of August the old director had left, and Project HOME symbolically had entered a new era.

The second major event occurred in the fall of the fifth year when Project HOME's application to United Way was accepted and the program became a United Way agency. Project HOME continues to receive much of its financial support from United Way. During the fifth year of the program, Project HOME continued to run on volunteer power. A core of no more than five or six volunteers, along with the director, performed the usual clerical duties but also did intake interviews, discussed with coworkers and the director who to match with whom, and followed up on clients; two volunteers served on the advisory board. Some 251 clients applied to Project HOME during its fifth year, and 75 matches were made—of which more than half (45) involved previously matched clients.

Postscript

The board in its first two years has been involved in drafting a mission statement and in implementing a new small fee for service that will now be charged to all applicants and an additional fee to those who have been matched; both fees are waived in the event a client cannot afford to pay. This points to the increased concern for revenue sources as the budget continues to increase very rapidly. Much time of the advisory board is given over to the search for new ways to raise money.

Another important change has been the addition of a new full-time paid staff person to coordinate services and provide clerical support for the director and her volunteer staff. A final major change has been the expansion of Project HOME's office space: In an ironic twist, Project HOME has moved into the more spacious offices vacated by the Retired Services Volunteer Program, which moved to a new location.

A KEY TO HOMESHARING SERVICE: SOCIAL EXCHANGE

We now explore the actual interactions involved in Project HOME service delivery and evaluation by focusing on the idea of social exchange or bartering. Although barter is central to the homesharing contract between clients who desire to homeshare with one another and to the relations between the organization and its clients, we have found exchange to play a significant role also within the organization's staff and between the organization and the university researchers who have been evaluating it for more than five years.

The Origins of Social Exchange in Project HOME

Before we consider the variety of social exchange relationships fostered by Project HOME, it is important to understand that all of them evolve from (1) the reasons for the program's inception, (2) the structure of the program in its first four years, and (3) the personality of the second director whose tenure spanned the second through fourth years of the program.

Project Goals. As described in the section on the program's history, Project HOME was started to serve *two* groups of elders: those outside the organization in need of homesharing arrangements and RSVP volunteers within the organization who would benefit from meaningful service-delivery roles like interviewing. In addition, the researchers were brought in to produce an interview schedule to screen clients and to train the volunteers to administer it in exchange for complete access to interview data and all organization files.

Before even starting, therefore, Project HOME had already established exchange as the operating currency: Elderly homeowners would provide a place to live in exchange for the companionship, and perhaps some rent, that the homeseeker would give. Volunteers would give their time and knowledge regarding other elders' needs in exchange for the psychic reward of doing meaningful service for other elders. The university researchers would donate time and expertise regarding development and administering interview schedules in exchange for the information from those schedules.

Project Structure. The very loose organizational structure in Project HOME promoted great flexibility in the program's approach to service delivery on behalf of homesharing clients in two ways: First, the director received very minimal instructions from the parent RSVP organization during the time Project HOME was part of the RSVP. Thus although the RSVP coordinator provided the HOME director a continuous supply of interviewers and was sensitive to the type of creative counseling skills needed to work for HOME, and although the staff of the larger organization provided support and encouragement during the weekly RSVP staff meetings that the HOME director attended, the second HOME director often felt alone in her position, especially after the applicant pool started to swell.

On the one hand, she highly valued the responsibility, freedom, and creativity the program demanded; on the other hand, there were attendant disadvantages of being solely in charge. As she related: The freedom to ''implement procedures as I feel necessary'' had to be balanced off by almost sole responsibility for its functioning. ''I was on the creative edge by myself with other people cheering me on but not really leading me or providing me with different components I needed for my own growth.'' She emphasized this by pointing out that fund raising was interfering with what she believed to be her primary role: direct service. Once Project HOME was on its own, the HOME director was both nominally and substantively in charge.

Flexibility of structure was important in a second way, because with minimal direction from the RSVP the director was implicitly encouraged to turn to her volunteer staff and to the university researchers for suggestions, for reactions to her initiatives, or, in her words, for "brainstorming."

Director's Personality. It is in this second instance of flexibility that the director's personality becomes important: Her sense of mission on behalf of homesharing applicants took precedence over the other considerations, so the discussions that took place between the director and the interviewers and between the director and the researchers were substantive and not mere formalities. As we shall see below, a great many examples of social exchange within the organization stem from the director's efforts to seek out ideas from her staff and from the researchers.

Soon after the second director arrived at the beginning of the program's second year, it became apparent to the researchers that she was willing to experiment in an effort to improve the program's service delivery. To understand how her willingness to experiment became translated into productive action, it is important to mention salient characteristics of her personality. The most relevant were her commitment to service for elders and others in need, her entrepreneurial orientation, and her willingness to compromise and learn from others.

Her background as a chaplain and her later decision to enter Divinity School correctly suggest a strongly religious orientation in the director's personal makeup. Her religiosity, however, manifested itself in nondenominational terms. Thus Project HOME for the director was a program with a "mission" (her word) to serve elders, disabled, and others who had serious housing needs. As a result, it was natural for the director to open up the client pool to nonelders shortly after she became director. Her basic commitment to service precluded her putting arbitrary limits on the recipients of that service, so a variety of clients were taken on as potential homesharers; for those who were inappropriately looking for homeseekers (e.g., frail elders with no resources and serious physical or mental disabilities, renters wanting to use the program as an apartment-finding service), she expanded Project HOME's service to include referrals to other local agencies.[3]

Not surprisingly, the director of Project HOME was also an entrepreneur. Students of social organization draw distinctions between entrepreneurial and managerial styles of organizational leadership. The former is based on the assumptions that significant changes are needed or desirable in the organization; an entrepreneurial leader will innovate to get them accomplished. The latter, on the other hand, is based on the premise that leadership is required that will maintain the organization in pretty much its present form; a managerial leader will preserve what already exists.

As for her willingness to compromise, the best evidence of her flexibility in this regard comes from the fact that, although she was willing to move forward and take risks (e.g., opening the program to younger sharers, attempting to match frail elders with paid caregivers), the director also was establishing a consensus form of decision making. Initially, with the researchers and then later with the volunteers as well, the director sought input from those with whom she worked, "brainstorming" with them to generate better ways to make HOME live up to her idea of a program with a mission to serve those in need.

Social Exchange: The Currency of Project HOME

Much has been written about social exchange in the relationships between dating and marriage partners (Vander Zanden, 1984), friends (Liebow, 1967), and even large-scale organizations and societies (Blau, 1977). We suggest that the idea of exchange lies at the root of Project HOME's success in melding together various disparate groups to produce the service that allowed the program to flourish during its early years rather than die off as so many programs might have done under similar circumstances (i.e. shortage of funds).

The essential argument we propose, borrowed from George Homans (1961) and Peter Blau (1964), is that people do things with and for other people as long as something is expected in return. As a result, a *norm of reciprocity* will develop that tends to direct the interaction between the two parties and continues as long as the parties see benefits from the interaction. As we will demonstrate, the exchanges occurring in Project HOME involved the giving and getting of not only material but also emotional commodities.

In the case of Project HOME, social exchange can be seen in a variety of relationships, not the least of which are the relationships between the program staff and the program's clients and between the homesharing clients themselves who propose to live with one another. Our emphasis in the remainder of this chapter is on two major relationships: The first is between the director and her volunteer staff, and the second is between the director and the researchers.

The Program and the Volunteer Staff

The First Year. During the first year of the program, the volunteers' major program contacts were with, first, the volunteer coordinator on loan from the RSVP and, then, HOME's first director who stayed for about half a year. In each case, efforts were made by these two individuals to provide encouragement and emotional support for the volunteers, but there really was very little else that they could do. The volunteers' major source of accomplishment was going to have to be the fruits of their interviewing efforts: the matching of HOME applicants.

The roles that volunteers play in Project HOME have varied on the basis of where the leadership in the program lay. Initially, the volunteers were seen by the RSVP director not only as service *providers* but also as key *recipients* within the program. In terms of their roles as service providers, the directors of both HOME and the RSVP were satisfied with the expertise, enthusiasm, and commitment of the volunteers.

As for being service recipients themselves, while interviewing homesharing applicants, volunteers were expected to receive the benefits from having done important work for people in need. In the language of social exchange (Homans, 1961:51–82), we suggest that an important requirement for the volunteers to continue to work for Project HOME was a sense of accomplishment or reward. In this case, the reward would stem from two sources: the camaraderie involved in working with other committed volunteers *and* the reason for their volunteering at HOME—seeing their elderly clients get matched and improve their living situations.

The former benefit was clear to any observer present at the interviewer training sessions conducted for the volunteers. Although the training itself was unremarkable, the researchers noticed before and after the sessions especially that the volunteer interviewers appeared to enjoy one another's company, socializing and trading interviewer experiences. The latter source of psychic reward was not immediately evident, however. Although the interviewers were interested in the welfare of the applicants they were interviewing, there did not appear to develop among the volunteers the sense of accomplishment that originally had been anticipated by the RSVP staff and the volunteers themselves.

There are two reasons for this: First, early in its existence Project HOME was hardly matching anyone because of the restrictions placed on sharer possibilities emanating from an elders-only applicant pool. Therefore, the main cause for celebration (i.e., matching applicants) occurred only rarely. When clients were matched, the sense of excitement among all concerned—RSVP director, HOME director, volunteer interviewers, and the researchers—was very great, highlighting even more the large numbers of clients for whom matches were not forthcoming.

Closely related to the lack of matchmaking in the first year or so of the program was the problem of volunteer alienation from the whole matchmaking process. If one considers alienation as arising from a separation between oneself and the total work picture, somewhat like the way traditional assembly-line workers have participated in only one small part of the whole production process, it is easy to see that the volunteers' initial role in Project HOME's matchmaking was limited by their taking inquiries from, interviewing, and making recommendations regarding the potential suitability of the applicants with whom they personally have had contact.

More than once at interviewer training sessions during the first two years of the program the researchers were asked by volunteers, "Whatever happened to 'so and so'? I know she's not been matched, but she is a dear and really needs a sharer." Because the researchers were conducting follow-up interviews of applicants at the time, they often could supply information to the volunteers, but the whole feedback process was random. Thus initially, the volunteers, instead of feeling a sense of accomplishment from their interviewer roles, were frustrated because so few clients were being matched and because they were getting little feedback on those who were not getting matched and in whom the interviewers had developed a proprietary interest.

Evolving Volunteer Roles. When the second director began work, her decision to open up the program to nonelders had important secondary consequences for the volunteers as the number of matches began to go up quickly. On the one hand, having "their" clients find homesharing matches made the volunteers happy, because they now could see that interviewing applicants was part of a successful process in an increasing number of cases. On the other hand, the large upsurge in applicants put increasing pressure on the director to juggle in her mind a geometrically expanding number of sharer-matching possibilities. With a small homeseeker pool, as existed when applicants were limited to elders, the director was able to consider the relatively small number of possible matches and weigh them carefully without confusion.

Now, as the number of seeker clients approached the size of the homeowner pool (which itself was increasing substantially), the director was finding it increasingly difficult to focus her attention on coordinating volunteer efforts, doing intake interviews herself, deciding on which clients should be introduced to each other in the hopes of their agreeing to homeshare, and writing grant applications to keep the program solvent. One obvious solution to the director's time problems was to expand her position to full time; when the State Independence Fund money was awarded to the program, one of its provisions was for the director to be full time. Still, the director's efforts were being spread very thin.

A forte of the director was her ability to motivate the people with whom she worked. In this particular instance, it did not take much motivation by the director, because the volunteers themselves, seeing the general strains on the director's time, were eager to play a greater role in Project HOME's service delivery.

It is hard to pinpoint the exact process that led to increased volunteer participation in Project HOME, but what is clear is that by the beginning of the program's third year, the makeup of the volunteer group had altered in two important ways. First, the number of volunteers had shrunk to less than half the original dozen or so. Second, the volunteers themselves had organized the work among themselves in a basic division of labor. As the HOME director told it:

A year ago I had 12 interviewers who seldom came into the office with me. I was doing all the office type work and all decision making. Now I have only 2 to 4 volunteers out in the field doing interviews and have 4 home office volunteers who like the administrative part. . . . So all of us are becoming involved as case workers and we are becoming more like the RSVP model where I am the director and they are like coordinators.

Thus the director now had an office staff of volunteers as well as volunteers in the field.

The director's relationship with the volunteers also had changed. As the director said of the office workers: "They are much more intensely involved with the program than before. . . . They have completely reorganized the filing system and the way we do the application process." In terms of the latter, for example, the volunteers were now requesting that applications be returned to the office so that references could be checked out before anyone was sent on an interview.

Another initiative by the volunteers was the weekly staff meetings in which the director was invited to participate as a coequal. Initially, the director met only monthly with the staff, but projects were being delayed because of the time gap between meetings. According to the director, the volunteers "felt a need to get together more often. I said I would be willing to meet every week. They set the time and these meetings have been going on since March, even through vacation season."

Among other things accomplished in the weekly meeting context were decisions to eliminate introductory luncheons between potential sharers; have a recognition get-together for staff, researchers, and clients; put together fliers and a brochure on Project HOME; and do a slide presentation for a television publicity show.

The small core of volunteers had now become very close and supportive of one another. The director was no longer the central focus of support for the individual volunteers, and they were now equally likely to turn to one another for support. They were far more likely to take the initiative on assignments than was previously the case. With her own increased responsibilities, like grant-proposal writing, the director of HOME came to see herself more in a nurturing and supportive role vis-à-vis the volunteers. As we reported earlier, since Project HOME has taken on a board of advisors, volunteers also attend board meetings and participate in the board's Volunteer Development Committee.

Social Exchange and the Volunteers. Since the third year of the program's existence, therefore, the volunteer role has grown appreciably; with this growth have come important consequences for the volunteers' relationship to the program. In an ironic twist, the RSVP director's initial desire to make Project HOME a meaningful service vehicle for RSVP volunteers has reached fruition because Project HOME volunteers themselves took the initiative to *make* their work more meaningful with the full support of a director who was willing to experiment with a reorganization of staff tasks.

At the heart of this successful exchange between program and volunteers lie two important factors. First is the goal of service delivery to clients in need. Without that important objective, it is doubtful that Project HOME could have maintained the hold that it did on its volunteer staff. Second is the HOME director who was willing to use the volunteers in roles that made full use of their skills in a wide variety of roles. The result of the program's important objective and its leadership in the hands of an entrepreneurial director was tremendous growth in a program that at one time was moribund.

The Program and the Researchers

The Initial Exchanges. The researchers, like the volunteers, were operating both as service providers and recipients: The time spent in constructing and arranging for copies of the application form, training the interviewers, and acting as unpaid consultants was expected to result in access to the completed interview application forms and enough preliminary information to make a grant application for funding of a systematic evaluation of Project HOME feasible.

Early in the process, the evaluation component of HOME was accepted by the director of the RSVP in exchange for help in developing the intake form, which presumably would help the RSVP coordinator on loan to HOME "make" homesharing matches. The intake form, therefore, was to play a dual role: For the RSVP and Project HOME, it was to facilitate the decision-making process concerning which applicants get introduced to each other by giving the staff important insight into each applicant's background and interests. For the researchers, the intake form would provide important background information so that general profiles of stayers and movers could be drawn, and the particular characteristics that help a client get matched would be isolated.

When the second, longer intake form was developed by the researchers with the collaboration of the second HOME director, the exchange continued. The increased length made it possible for the researchers to process a greater amount of information measuring life satisfaction and familial and community social support. At the same time, more information was requested concerning any disabilities of the applicant. This was in response to an expressed need of the HOME director to "identify more clearly how disabled and dependent a person is."

In a very real sense, the initial exchanges between the staff connected to Project HOME and the researchers were easily expressed in an accounts receivable and accounts payable sort of way. The researchers provided expertise in questionnaire construction, typing and reproduction of the intake forms (Andrus support included clerical costs for both intake and follow-up interviews), and training of the volunteers who would be doing the intake interviews. Project HOME provided collation of the intake forms by the volunteers; volunteer interviewers; access to all client data, as long as client confidentiality was respected; and access to the volunteer staff and the director for structured and unstructured interviews as part of the program evaluation.

New Exchanges. From the outset, the researchers were studying not only the client data but also the program that was providing the service delivery. Until the second HOME director took over in the spring of 1983, the researchers' role as program evaluator was fairly clear-cut and "uncontaminated." Once the researchers began to work with the new director, however, the distinction between evaluator and program volunteer became harder to maintain. The first example of the blurring relates to the roles the researchers' research assistant came to play in her relationships with the program director and volunteer staff.[4]

The major ostensible roles of the assistant were to do the follow-up interviews with matched and unmatched clients of Project HOME and to record and transmit daily information concerning the work of the director and her staff to the investigators. As a result, in yet another example of exchange, the research assistant performed various clerical tasks for the Project HOME staff, attended their meetings, and generally provided the staff with any input she had on various clients whom she had interviewed for the researchers.

Although primarily responsible to the university researchers, the assistant therefore also was often playing a role supportive of the members of the HOME organization. The director saw the student involvement as an important component of the program, because having an undergraduate student working with senior volunteers was consistent with the intergenerational focus of the home-sharing matches that by then were being arranged.

Each of the student assistants who worked with Project HOME had been selected on the basis of not only native intelligence and curiosity but also strong interpersonal skills. It was not surprising, therefore, that each in turn was quickly welcomed by the program staff and soon accepted as yet another volunteer in the project. At the same time, each student quickly "took" to the program and its mission and, in fact, *did* become a volunteer at the same time she was working for the researchers.

One example stands out concerning the second, two-part intake form, which was detailed and long. Each time the assistant would come back from her work with the director and volunteers, she would begin to air the interviewers' complaints about the large number of questions and the problems associated with the personal nature of questions dealing with friendships of the applicant. On the one hand, it was important for the researchers to know—whether directly or indirectly—how the volunteers who were in the field felt about the intake schedule; so in this respect the researchers were glad to hear the assistant's report. On the other hand, the report often carried with it the argument by the assistant that the researchers really ought to shorten and edit the schedule; that is, the assistant was now a spokeswoman for Project HOME.

Although this conflict concerning the assistant's role did create some difficulties, overall the fact that the assistant had become involved enough with the program and thus spoke with its best interests in mind really produced more benefits of insight than problems. Indeed, regarding the example of the intake schedule above, the volunteers' (and the student's) complaint was well founded, and after a year's trial, the researchers agreed to shorten it. In fact, it was the research assistant working in conjunction with the volunteers and director who put together the working draft of the new schedule.

Thus even the problems associated with the assistant's role conflict often ultimately produced positive change for the program and for the researchers. In the case of the intake schedule change, the volunteers became happier with the shorter, less intrusive schedule, and although the researchers lost some potentially useful information through the cutting process, they retained almost all of the critical background and attitude questions and were rewarded by higher-quality intake data overall.

The second instance in which the blurring of roles occurred related to the way the researchers fed back information from preliminary data analyses to the director and her staff. In the context of describing the exchanges between herself and the researchers, the HOME director spoke of this feedback:

The researchers are open to my needs and the programs' needs. . . . The data has been valuable to me in making changes I need to make. There has been a real positive interchange. It has been a nice cooperative relationship. . . . They have provided personal support in developing the program as well as printing and staff time to getting the applications done. Information is available immediately to make alterations to serve the people.

There was an expectation, as seen in the last sentence of the previous statement, that as information was collected it would be fed back to the director for modification and improvement of the program. As this happened, the researchers were put in the role of consultants as well as evaluators. Such a process, we maintain, was a necessary part of the healthy, cooperative relationship established between service provider and researcher, but it did lessen the impartiality and nonintrusiveness of the research evaluation. Thus as the program evolved it was in a small way a result of the participation of the researchers as volunteer consultants.

A final way in which the researchers' roles became blurred stems from actual volunteer work that the researchers did for the program. Here we do not mean the initial agreement to exchange their expertise and resources for information, although such an exchange helped develop the norm of reciprocity that characterized the ongoing relationship between the researchers and the director. Rather, we refer to publicizing and promoting the program.

This occurred in three ways. First, starting in the summer of 1983, only a few months after the second director had begun working for Project HOME, the researchers began to present at professional meetings papers describing the applicants to this homesharing program, the kinds of characteristics that facilitated applicant success in finding sharers, the differences that the program made to those who homeshared, the special qualities of volunteer-based service-delivery programs, and the unique emphasis of Project HOME's contribution to the continuum of care within the home.

Although their objective was merely to present dispassionate descriptions of how Project HOME worked and whom it served, it became very clear from the first meeting that large numbers of service providers were in attendance who were seeking information on "how to do a homesharing program." As a result, in describing whom the program served and how it operated, the researchers were promulgating the program.

A second way in which they acted as volunteers occurred during the program's second year when the director decided to seek funding from the city to finance introductory luncheons for clients who were to be introduced to each other.[5] The director had found that introduction in the provider's home was very uncomfortable for both clients—the homeprovider because he or she felt as if the other person were scrutinizing and appraising the home and all of its furnishings, and the homeseeker because he or she was on the other person's "turf."

One of the researchers at the time was on an advisory council to the mayor of the city and offered to write a letter of support for the project, which he did. Whether or not the letter had any bearing on the final outcome, the important thing to note is that the researcher who wrote the letter of support believed it was not only appropriate but even important to do so. Again, research and evaluation was taking a back seat to the volunteer role, which the researchers were at times slipping into.

A related way in which both researchers acted as volunteers stems from the time Project HOME became intergenerational. In more than one of their classes, the researchers advertised the program, telling their students about the opportunities of homesharing with elders. In at least two instances, students of the researchers did apply to (and eventually find a homesharer through) Project HOME. By advertising the program, the researchers had again played the role of volunteers, rather than researchers and evaluators.

In one final way, the roles of researchers and volunteers were potentially set in opposition to one another. This occurred near the end of the second director's tenure when she was putting together the advisory board for Project HOME. Nothing seemed more natural to her (or to them) than putting the researcher volunteers on the board. So they accepted, with the understanding that their primary roles would focus on planning and evaluation. Again, during the board meetings, in committee with other board members, and on the selection committee to choose the new director, their primary role was to be a spokesperson for Project HOME. Such goals were consistent with Project HOME's goals, and in the case of the Planning and Evaluation Committee work, the researchers helped articulate the stated mission of Project HOME.

In all of the above examples of role blurring, it is easy perhaps to argue that the researchers had lost their objectivity by becoming volunteers and, as a result, failed in their efforts to be scientific evaluators of Project HOME's service delivery. Putting aside for the moment the question of whether any research can be completely *objective*, we nevertheless disagree with the idea that volunteering actually blinded them to what was happening in the program. To the contrary, we argue that the role of volunteer indeed *facilitated* evaluation of the program. First, the relationship between the researchers and the director was strengthened through their participation as volunteers. As the director relates:

I'm delighted with the relationship back and forth. I feel we are colleagues. . . . We work well together and have complementary goals and there is a lot of feedback that is valuable. . . . That friendliness and openness of wanting the program to work and evaluating it to improve it instead of calling to task and blaming things on it has been a wonderful ambience to work in. . . . Our files have been completely open to you and you have been open to us while maintaining clients' anonymity at the same time. That is the kind of relationship there ought to be.

Without this openness, the kinds of insights the director provided concerning homesharing couples, volunteer commitment, and the like would not have been forthcoming. We make this argument not so much because she would not have trusted the researchers but because there would not have been the sorts of brainstorming sessions described earlier that gave fruit to these, often spontaneously arrived at, insights. In a related way, the researchers would not have developed the sorts of insights expressed in this chapter concerning the workings of the organization without the many informal conversations they had with the director.

This open relationship between the evaluators and the evaluated was, in fact, a natural result of the desire by both groups to see the program work well. Early on, the researchers began feeding back information to the program concerning, for example, imbalances in the applicant provider-seeker ratio and the particular problems of hearing-impaired homeproviders. Such results were reported also in the paper presentations alluded to earlier, but the researchers' concern as evaluators was to provide direct feedback to the program staff so that problems in the program could be addressed. Because of the open relationship with the director, they felt no restraints in providing feedback—whether it was positive or negative; in each case, the feedback was given in hopes of strengthening the program.

A second, equally important advantage of the researchers taking on the role of volunteers was that it represented a natural extension of the idea of social exchange that permeated the program. They now were exchanging ideas concerning things such as the role of evaluation in service delivery and the imperatives facing a volunteer-based organization, so the social exchange that had begun as a fairly impartial *quid pro quo* was now unconsciously proceeding because each of the parties cared both about each other's roles and about the program. In contrast to much of what has been said in criticism of the too rational basis of social exchange theory, what was occurring in Project HOME was social exchange of a more altruistic nature. In the context of the way the program was structured, with all who were involved giving of themselves for the benefit of the clients, it would have been awkward and self-defeating were the researchers to have distanced themselves from the director and her staff.

Changing of the Guard

In an appropriate epilogue to our discussion of the social exchange relationships in Project HOME, it is interesting to note that the core volunteers (the senior volunteers who have been a mainstay of Project HOME since its inception) have remained a critical element of the program, while the peripheral volunteers (the researchers who were involved with the program in some way from its inception) have begun to disengage. As described earlier, the volunteers now have taken over the task of revising the intake schedule. After the researchers' assistant modified the early two-part form, the researchers' role in questionnaire construction steadily declined with the tacit agreement of all parties.

Similarly, as the volunteers began to take on more varied tasks in the office as well as in the field, the director began to rely on them more than on the researchers for emotional support. This is not to state that relations became strained between the researchers and the director; rather, they simply changed as the program staff became more self-sufficient in its human and material resources and as priorities of the researchers shifted to other projects. From the point of view of the program staff, the donation of needed expertise and material (training of interviewers, supplying typing and paper, and so on) were not needed any more, and the major evaluation work that could benefit the program directly had been accomplished during the first five years. From the point of view of the researchers, the most important information for the overall analysis of the program, its staff, and its clients had been gathered, and time was now needed to distance themselves from the program to do a comprehensive analysis and write-up of conclusions.

CONCLUSION

Social exchange is important not only for the clients whom homesharing programs endeavor to help but also for the service providers themselves. Taking their cue from the clients who must barter goods and services with one another if they are to effect a meaningful homesharing relationship, the director of Project HOME, her volunteer staff, and the university researchers evaluating the program have also placed a premium on the barter of goods and services.

In the process, commodities were exchanged: The volunteers gave expertise and time and received a strong feeling of service accomplishment. The researchers provided expertise, supplies, student helpers, and information in exchange for access to program files and the insights of the director. How important were these exchanges? Certainly, the bartering allowed the program to continue to serve its clients even while it was on precarious financial footing. Although Project HOME might have survived without these various exchanges, it is at least equally likely that it might not have survived. What *is* clear is that Project HOME did survive and has prospered. Other service-delivery programs, strapped for material support from traditional sources, might reflect on the lessons of Project HOME's service delivery through social exchange.

NOTES

To protect the anonymity of those interviewed for this study, names of respondents and exact dates of conversations are omitted.

1. Originally, HOME was an acronym for Housing to Match Elders.

2. The volunteers were unpaid, and space was being negotiated with the RSVP and the congregate housing corporation in whose building both organizations had offices. Application forms were provided by the university researchers, and other supplies were relatively inexpensive.

3. Consequently, Project HOME became well known among other service providers like the Visiting Nurse Association, area nursing homes, and the Area Agency on Aging.

4. In fact, the researchers employed several research assistants during the time of the Andrus grant funding. We refer to those assistants who worked with the director and volunteers as ''the assistant'' because only one served as a contact between the researchers and the program at any time.

5. The city eventually did support the lunches for a time. As noted earlier, however, the lunch plan was dropped after a while at the request of the volunteers who felt (probably correctly) that an introductory lunch at a neutral site was still stressful for the clients and was only postponing the inevitable.

REFERENCES

Blau, Peter. *Exchange and Power in Social Life*. New York: Wiley, 1964.

———. *Inequality and Heterogeneity: A Primitive Theory of Social Structure*. New York: Free Press, 1977.

Homans, George C. *Social Behavior: Its Elementary Forms*. New York: Harcourt, Brace and World, 1961.

Liebow, Elliot. *Tally's Corner: A Study of Negro Streetcorner Men*. Boston: Little, Brown, 1967.

Vander Zanden, James W. *Social Psychology*. 3d rev. ed. New York: Random House, 1984.

10

The Matchmakers of Santa Clara County

Jon Pynoos and Arlyne June

PROJECT MATCH'S COMMUNITY

Project Match operates in Santa Clara County, California, the home of the Silicon Valley. It is a land of diversity where change is the norm. It consists of sprawling suburbs, rural farms, and urban areas, centered around San Jose, the fourth largest city in California. The county covers 1,300 square miles, contains 15 cities, and has a population of 1,300,000, making it the largest in the San Francisco Bay Area. This population is aging. In 1980 the county had 141,380 persons of at least 60 years of age representing 11% of the total. The number of older residents is expected to double by the year 2000.

Santa Clara County is also an area where the supply of jobs outstrips the supply of housing, a situation that is worsening according to the Association of Bay Area Governments (ABAG), the Regional Planning Agency for the San Francisco Bay Area. Many observers believe that the very success and affluence of the Silicon Valley has resulted in a major breakdown in the affordable housing market. Costs of both purchases and rentals are high. In January 1988 the median price of a home sold in Santa Clara County was $175,500, representing a 12.5% increase in one year. According to a survey done by the U.S. League of Savings Institutions, the 1987 median sales price in the San Francisco metropolitan area was the highest in the nation. In July 1988 the local newspaper, *The San Jose Mercury News*, featured a series of articles on what was called the "housing frenzy." The articles discussed the growing phenomenon of the "supercommuters," persons who commuted more than 90 miles a day to work in order to live in housing that they could afford.

For renters, the problem was equally serious. The average monthly rental for a one-bedroom apartment was $650, and the cost of building a rental unit was

$67,500. In 1988 the rental vacancy rate had increased to 5–7% from a nationwide low of 0.5% in 1985, but there was still little available housing affordable to seniors on fixed incomes.

The statistics tell the story: (1) there are three- to five-year waits for apartments in senior housing complexes; (2) waits for Section 8 range from five to seven years, and no new applications are being accepted; (3) in San Jose alone there are 12,587 elderly households in need of housing according to the city's Housing Assistance Plan; and (4) the ABAG projects an overall need in Santa Clara County of 80,756 housing units by 1990, more than half for low- to moderate-income housing.

In response to these trends, in November 1977 the Santa Clara Council on Aging (AAA) decided to try a new approach for seniors, but something that college students had been doing for years: homesharing. The AAA called it Project Match. Although a concept inspiring much skepticism, Project Match placed 400 seniors the first year and a half of its existence. The program has since evolved and expanded in size and in new directions.

The needs that Project Match fulfills for clients and for Santa Clara County communities are best illustrated by examining the general characteristics of seniors matched during a recent period. The homeseekers are persons looking for affordable housing; some are homeless when they come to Project Match. They are invariably poor. Some are young, but most are seniors who are alone and have no place to go. They search for affordable housing in a county where it is virtually nonexistent. Most of Project Match's seekers indicate that they want to share for financial reasons. If they had to pay the average monthly market rental rate in Santa Clara County of $650, they would have no money left over to purchase other essentials such as food, clothing, and medical care.

The homeproviders, most of whom are homeowners, are persons who have housing to share. Each time that they are willing to share they create a new housing unit—a rental unit that would not be available if shared housing did not exist. Records suggest that 10% of the providers come from the 7,730 "over-housed" seniors in Santa Clara County, who often cannot afford financially and physically to stay in their homes without help.

Project Match, like other homesharing programs, fulfills a diversity of needs for clients and the communities in which it operates. To a great extent it is a response to the lack of and need for affordable housing in Santa Clara County. Even given this context of need, the program could not be successful without the development of a workable "matching" technology and the administrative machinery to accompany it.

AGENCY OPERATIONS

Project Match is a private nonprofit agency governed by a 15-person board of directors. It became incorporated as a separate entity in 1980. The Housing Match Program has three full-time and two part-time counselors. Potential clients call the agency and make an appointment for a personal interview with a housing counselor. A prescreening form is completed over the telephone. At the time of the interview, a client intake, participation agreement, and consent form are used as a basis to gather information. During the intake/screening period, clients are advised in terms of what to expect realistically from a shared housing arrangement. Counselors then search for other individuals with complementary needs and compatible preferences. There is no fee to clients, although small donations ($5 from seekers and $10 from providers) are requested.

Once the clients are interviewed and the staff are ready to propose a particular match, each client is contacted by telephone. A meeting between potential partners is arranged. After this initial meeting, Project Match contacts each client to ascertain their respective response. If a match is arranged, a match certificate is signed. Participants are assisted in setting up rules, contracts, and written agreements if they choose. Follow-up is provided after one, three, and six months from the time the arrangement is made and then every six months for two years. For matches providing live-in service arrangements, follow-up is provided every month. A significant proportion of the matches involve such arrangements.

Client records are kept on a computer. During the summer of 1988 the agency began preparations for a new computer system that would provide an improved data base and allow isolation of specific variables for client matching.

Interested homeseekers and providers hear about the program in various ways. Half of the clients are referred by a variety of community agencies, with 27% from senior centers: 10% by a shared housing program that serves only single parents and 5% from a shelter for battered women. One-fifth of the clients come through personal referrals, usually a friend of a family member who had been a client of Project Match. Of the remaining clients, 15% are referred by government agencies such as the Department of Social Services, Social Security, and the Housing Authority. Another 8% have heard about the agency through the media, mainly through public service advertisements or special interest programs on television, on radio, or in articles in newspapers and magazines.

Perhaps the single most important method of client recruitment in recent years has been the increased visibility in each community due to part-time satellite offices. The satellite offices are discussed in detail later in the chapter.

PROGRAM CHANGES

Project Match has seen many changes during its 11 years of operation. Through planning and evaluation, the board and staff became aware of additional related needs that could be met through program expansion and diversification. It was through an evolutionary process that the agency broadened its mission statement and developed a long-range strategic plan to include the potential for additional programs to meet the housing needs of seniors and also allow for policy and administrative changes in the program that could meet the changing needs of the community.

First, two new related programs were added. Both of these programs helped fulfill the agency's dual missions of creating affordable housing and preventing inappropriate institutionalization. These programs were "Home Equity Conversion," which allows senior homeowners who are "house rich and cash poor" to free up the equity in their homes to pay living expenses; and "A Group Home" in San Jose, which houses six seniors in an independent, noninstitutional setting at affordable rents. The latter was featured on ABC's "20–20" in May 1988.

In terms of the match program there have been two important revisions. First, the program began to allow intergenerational matches. Although the program had begun as a senior program, the staff became aware of a need for affordable housing among younger adults, a need that was not being met by other programs. To fill this need, the board and staff decided to allow for *intergenerational matches*, defined as matches in which only one of the housemates is a senior. Another benefit is that intergenerational matches can provide the resource pool of homeseekers for matches involving service provision.

Second, the agency opened part-time satellite offices in senior centers throughout the county. These offices have provided increased accessibility to clients who could be interviewed in their own communities, as well as increased visibility to local elected officials who were potential funding sources.

FUNDING AND EVALUATION

Project Match's original funding came from one source, the Federal Community Development Block Grant Program of the county of Santa Clara. To avoid the dangers inherent with any one source of funding, the agency subsequently developed a long-range funding plan directed toward increasing agency revenues and diversifying the funding base.

Many shared housing programs operate, as does Project Match, as nonprofit organizations. Nonprofits, by the nature of their funding, live a year-to-year existence, often dependent upon shifts in charitable contributions, governmental decisions, and various other external factors having little to do with agency performance. Nonprofits play a survival game, a game that often diverts attention and energies from agency goals.

Project Match has achieved its goal of an increased, diversified funding base. In fiscal year 1983–84 Project Match revenues totaled $94,000. In 1987–88 the agency had a budget of $280,000, of which $183,000 was allocated to the Match Program. The agency receives funds from United Way, the county of Santa Clara, the state of California, foundations, and most of the cities in the county and from private donations through fund raising. The agency constantly faces the fact that each of the 15 to 18 funding sources has many competing demands for its funds. Many of the competitors are agencies in the field of aging and housing, agencies with whom Project Match must cooperate if it is to solve the problems of its clients but with whom Project Match also must compete if it is to survive.

Thus funding is a difficult and time-consuming process, and most of all, it is unpredictable. This unpredictability is perhaps the greatest factor in making the future unstable for nonprofits providing shared housing for seniors.

Another important time-consuming process designed to insure program stability has been evaluation. Although assessment of the program's progress has been important for funding sources, it has been equally so for the formulation of agency policy. In particular, to determine how well Project Match's clients are being served by its programs, a study of the matches being made was undertaken. The study was designed to provide information about the nature of the matches being made and the reasons for matches terminating.

THE NATURE OF MATCHES

A number of important issues arise in relation to homesharing such as the types of persons who share housing, the reasons for participation, what types of facilities and services are shared, and the personal relationships that exist among participants. Data analysis on these issues is based on information gathered from a 30-minute structured telephone interview with a random sample of 144 past and continuing participants selected from the project's file of matches arranged between July 1, 1982, and November 1983. In addition, 7 matches were selected from the prior year for qualitative purposes. Since only provider's addresses were maintained in the roster and seekers who were no longer matched seldom left a forwarding address, it was not possible to locate the latter once they left the homesharing project. As a consequence, 74% (107) of the 144 respondents were providers and 26% (37) were seekers.

Characteristics of Sharers

Among those interviewed, 82% of all providers and seekers were women. Other studies (Howe, Robins, and Jaffe, 1984; Pritchard, 1983) have supported this finding that homesharing programs disproportionately attract women. By contrast, the age composition varies significantly among different programs depending on the target population, location, and housing market. The sample studied here ranged in age from 24 to 96, with an average age of 65. Providers tended to be older than seekers: 70% of providers were at least 60 years of age compared with 59% of the seekers. (See Table 10.1.)

The majority of those sampled were Caucasian. As expected, widows and divorcees were more often providers than seekers, and singles showed the reverse tendency. Given the age of the respondents, most were retired: almost 70% of the providers and 51% of the seekers. Many other seekers appeared to be in transitory roles: 19% were unemployed and 5% were students. Nearly 80% of

Table 10.1
Characteristics of Sharers

	Percent of Respondents	Provider	Seeker
	(N=144)	(N=107)	(N=37)
Age			
Under 45	10	9	11
45-59	18	15	27
60-74	49	49	49
75 and old	23	27	13
Ethnicity			
Caucasian	82	82	81
Hispanic	10	9	16
Black	5	6	3
Other	3	3	0
Marital Status			
Widowed, divorced, or separated	83	86	73
Single	10	6	22
Married	7	8	5
Employment Status			
Retired	64	69	51
Working full-time	14	15	11
Working part-time	8	8	8
Unemployed	6	2	19
Other	8	6	11
Fixed income: Yes	78	--	--
No	22	--	--
Monthly income:			
under $300	15	10	26
$300-$600	47	46	48
$601-900	15	14	17
over $900	24	30	9
Health Status			
Nonfrail	33	32	34
Slightly frail	35	32	44
Frail	32	35	22

Table 10.2
Factor Analysis for Determining Frailty Index

ITEM	FACTOR LOADING
Doctor visit	0.589
Hospital days	0.638
Self-reported health	0.685
Health interferes with doing things	0.901
Amulation limitations	0.859

Eigenvalue = 2.77

respondents were living on fixed incomes, and more than half (62%) of the subjects had monthly incomes under $600.

The health status of subjects was defined by a composite score based on (1) the number of doctor visits in the past year, (2) the number of days spent in the hospital in the past year, (3) self-appraised health status (poor to excellent), (4) the extent to which health problems were reported to interfere with "doing things," and (5) number of ambulation limitations including walking, climbing stairs, boarding a bus, and using a walker or wheelchair. These five variables were entered into a factor analysis (see Table 10.2) to test for internal validity and to generate factor scores. The resulting factor revealed a high level of internal validity and therefore supported the use of the five variables.

Factor scores were then generated and the resulting range of scores was divided into thirds to define respondents as either nonfrail, slightly frail, or frail. The respondents falling into the *frail* category exhibited more than three ambulatory problems (55% of the *frail* had four such problems), compared with none to one reported for the *slightly frail*. The *nonfrail* respondents reported no ambulatory problems. As expected, due to the physical requirements of seeking housing, a higher proportion of providers (35%) were frail compared with seekers (22%).

Demographic Characteristics of Matches

With regard to gender and ethnicity, individuals tended to be matched with partners who had characteristics similar to their own. Sixty-one percent of the matches were male–male or female–female. Similarly, 83% of the matches involved individuals of the same ethnic or racial background. In contrast, intergenerational matches, which for purposes of this analysis were defined as one in which the age of the partners differed by more than 10 years, were frequent (60% of the matches could be defined as intergenerational).

Motivations for Sharing

Overall, the primary reasons considered by both providers and seekers in deciding to homeshare were financial need (44%) and companionship (21%) (see Table 10.3). D. C. Pritchard (1983) and S. R. McConnell and C. E. Usher (1980) also identified these two factors as the most common in motivating people to houseshare. Frail subjects were more apt to share because of health-care needs, help in the home, or security, rather than for companionship.

Housing Type and Facilities Shared

One reason that homesharing has recently gained attention is the increased use of available space on which this housing alternative capitalizes. It therefore was anticipated that providers would be more apt to share because they had extra space in their residence—in 64% of the cases, a single-family home. The data, however, revealed that only 20% of the respondents identified their house as "too big." Nevertheless, in 98% of the matches the residence contained at least two bedrooms; bedrooms were seldom a shared space. Communal spaces most often shared included kitchen facilities (95%), entrance (94%), living room (93%), and laundry facilities (92%). Bathrooms were shared in 53% of the matches.

Financial Arrangements

Four types of financial arrangements were established between providers and seekers: (1) seeker pays rent only (61%), (2) seeker pays rent and provides service (11%), (3) seeker provides services only (11%), and (4) seeker receives wages and free rent for services (17%).

Service Provision and Exchange

As would be expected, frail respondents indicated the highest service needs, with more than half needing help with shopping, housework, and getting places and almost all needing help with household chores (see Table 10.4).

The majority of those who needed help with laundry, meals, and housework did receive this assistance, as indicated in Table 10.5. Those tasks that are less a part of the daily household routine, however, such as heavy household chores and getting around in and outside the house, were less apt to be provided.

Arrangement Typology

It was hypothesized that matches might fall into three basic types: (1) *service free*: no services given or provided by either partner, (2) *service exchange*: at least one service given by the respondent to the partner and at least one service

Table 10.3
Motivations for Sharing

PRIMARY REASON	% OF SAMPLE (N=141)	PROVIDER (N=107)	SEEKER (N=37)	FRAIL (N=42)	SLIGHTLY FRAIL (N=42)	NON FRAIL (N=43)
Financial needs	44	42	50	26	52	56
Companionship	21	23	14	12	24	26
Security	6	8	0	12	4	2
Help in the home	10	11	5	19	4	5
Health care	9	11	3	24	4	0
Other	10	5	28	7	11	12

Table 10.4
Percent Indicating Need for Assistance with a Specific Task

SERVICE	TOTAL SAMPLE (N=131)	FRAIL (N=42)	SLIGHTLY FRAIL (N=46)	NON FRAIL (N=43)	CHI SQUARE	p
	%	%	%	%		
Household chores	42	88	28	14	51.49	.000
Shopping	24	59	13	2	41.09	.000
Housework	22	53	15	0	35.38	.000
Help getting places	24	61	13	0	47.55	.000
Meals	15	34	9	2	19.03	.000
Laundry	13	40	0	2	36.56	.000
Help getting around the house	5	15	0	0	13.65	.001

Table 10.5
Number and Percentage of Those Needing Help Who Received Help from Partner*

SERVICE	TOTAL SAMPLE		FRAIL		SLIGHTLY FRAIL		NON FRAIL	
	N	%	N	%	N	%	N	%
Household chores	54	28	35	29	13	38	6	0
Shopping	31	42	24	42	6	50	1	0
Housework	28	71	21	62	7	100	0	0
Help getting places	26	35	20	40	6	17	0	0
Meals	19	84	14	79	4	100	1	100
Laundry	17	59	16	56	0	0	1	100
Help getting around the house	6	33	6	33	0	0	0	0

* Test of significance could not be performed since sample sizes were too small.

Table 10.6
Service Typologies by Degree of Frailty*

	N	SERVICE FREE (%)	SERVICE EXCHANGE (%)	SERVICE DEPENDENT (%)
Nonfrail	43	70	28	2
Slightly frail	46	50	26	24
Frail	42	40	12	48

* (Chi-square = 25.00; $P \leq .001$)

given by the partner to the respondent, and (3) *service dependent*: at least one service with which respondent identified as needing help provided by his or her partner. It was expected that the third type would be more apt to include frail respondents and take on more of an employer-caretaker nature than that of the previously described matches. Within this sample, 54% of all matches were of the service-free type, 20% were service exchange, and 26% were service dependent.

In the majority (72%) of either service-free or service-exchange matches, the seeker "paid rent only." In the service-dependent matches, however, 31% of respondents "paid rent only," and 36% were involved in "wages and free-rent matches." Most respondents (80%) whose primary reason for sharing was financial were involved in service-free (54%) and service-exchange (48%) matches. Furthermore, 85% of the respondents who entered housesharing arrangements because of health-care needs were engaged in service-dependent matches.

As hypothesized, the relationship between the three service-provision typologies and the degree of frailty of the respondent was significant. (See Table 10.6.) As expected, nonfrail residents were most apt to be in service-free matches (74%), and frail respondents were most often in service-dependent matches (48%).

Consistent with Dale Jaffe's (1984) hypothesis, the data revealed a significant positive relationship between service-typology type and levels of friendship. Satisfaction with the match was also significantly related with the service-typology arrangement. Although the level of friendship was a factor in developing the satisfaction index, it was not the strongest determinant variable (see Table 10.7). Hence it does not necessarily follow that satisfaction will exist in all matches in which friendship is significant. Providers who were engaged in matches in which services were not commonly provided or exchanged reported lower levels of friendship and satisfaction than those in relationships in which services were provided.

Table 10.7
Service Typologies by Friendship Scale and Satisfaction Level*

	N	SERVICE FREE (%)	SERVICE EXCHANGE (%)	SERVICE DEPENDENT (%)
Friendship Scale				
Low (value = "0")	65	75	9	15
Medium (value = "1 or 2")	57	40	28	22
High (value = "3")	22	32	32	36

* significant at the .05 level (Chi-square = 24.93 and significance = .000)

	N	SERVICE FREE (%)	SERVICE EXCHANGE (%)	SERVICE DEPENDENT (%)
Satisfaction Level				
Low (lowest quartile)	29	72	14	14
High (highest quartile)	30	23	23	53

* significant at the .05 level (Chi-square = 15.00 and significance = .001)

Emerging Relationships

As noted, companionship was mentioned often as a motivation for housesharing. Even in situations in which companionship is not an initial motivator, it is likely that close proximity of the housesharing environment will foster the growth of friendship. In this sample, 49% of the respondents reported that they had become "friends" or "close friends" with their partners during the match; 41% reported that they could confide in their housemate on personal matters. In addition, 47% of the respondents indicated that they would be willing to care for their partner for at least a week if he or she became ill.

To investigate whether the degree of friendship was related to any identifiable characteristics of the matched pair, a strength of friendship index was developed. A score of "1" was assigned for each of the following conditions: (a) if the respondent perceived the partner as a "close friend" (compared to "acquaintance" or "friend"), (b) whether or not the respondent could confide in the partner, and (c) if the partner would aid the respondent in case of an illness. Thus the scale ranged from a low of zero if no conditions were met, to a high of 3, if all conditions were met.

Characteristics, such as the respondent's frailty status; sameness in ethnic origin, gender, or generation; and the primary reason for sharing did not show a relationship to the level of friendship. The friendship level expressed by respondents differed significantly only for the variable describing whether the respondent was still matched. Sixty-two percent of the respondents who had a score of zero on the friendship scale were no longer matched at the time of the study, compared with 18% of those who scored a 3 on the friendship scale. The data revealed indicative trends for stronger friendship interactions when either fewer problems were reported or when more "somewhat" or "important" needs were met by sharing.

UNDERSTANDING MATCH TERMINATIONS

The agency conducted a special analysis of terminations to understand why matches break up. Project Match uses a standardized terminations form that is completed by a counselor when a match breaks up. The agency learns about terminations in one of two ways: a client calls to tell the staff, which is the most frequent mode, or the breakup is identified through a standardized follow-up procedure. Through this process accurate records of each termination are recorded.

The analysis of breakups is based on data obtained from all termination forms for the 112 matches that ended between July 1, 1986, and June 30, 1987. It is important to note that the date of origin of these matches did not necessarily occur in that period; some matches had been in existence for a much longer time.

Many of the reasons for termination suggest that breakups were unavoidable,

Table 10.8
Reasons for Termination

Reasons for terminations	n=112 Total	100%
Geographic move necessary (usually to another state or county)	23	21%
Incompatibility (could not work out problems)	12	11%
Death	10	9%
Change in family circumstances	10	9%
House no longer available	9	8%
Senior housing (Section 8) or own house became available	7	6%
Seeker did not fulfill services (live-in)	7	6%
Institutionalization or hospitalization	6	5%
Conflicts with housemate's relatives or friends	5	4%
Seeker could not afford rent	4	4%
One partner did not like sharing	4	4%
Match was originally temporary	3	3%
Other (other all 2 or less -- seeker did not pay rent, drinking problem, not enough time to oneself, pet problems, no answer)	12	11%

as Table 10.8 indicates. Terminations occurred in 14% of all matches because one partner died or had to be institutionalized. Another 9% of the matches broke up because of change in family circumstances. In most of these cases an adult child or parent of the client became widowed and the client left the match to live with the relative. In 8% of the cases the house of the provider was no longer available. Most often the house was sold; in two cases the room used by the seeker had to be used for other purposes.

The major reason for breakups was the necessity of a geographic move. This factor accounted for 21% of the breakups. Often the client (usually the seeker) moved to another county or state or even out of the country. Many of these clients were younger persons who were matched with seniors. Perhaps these younger halves of intergenerational matches were "trying out California." In two of these cases, the seekers were students who had completed their schooling and moved back home. In several other cases, the clients moving were seniors whose health had worsened and who were moving away to live with adult children.

In 6% of the cases, senior housing or low-cost housing became available or the senior was able to return to his or her own home, and in 3% of the cases the matches were set up to be temporary. In a few cases (4%), the seekers lost their jobs and could not afford even the low rent being charged.

The above reasons account for 65% of the breakups. None seem to indicate that the match was not successful. For the most part, the comments on the terminations form are extremely positive. What actually occurred was unavoidable, or alternative situations presented themselves to the clients that better met their needs or preferences. It appears that even in matches that dissolved, many of them satisfied the needs for which they were intended.

Some matches involved some interpersonal problems, but they are fewer than might be expected. Twelve matches or 11% broke up because of incompatibility between the sharers; only 4% broke up because of conflicts with friends or relatives of the housemate, and 4% terminated because one partner decided that he or she did not like sharing. Project Match counselors try to give a realistic description of sharing to clients at the time of the intake, and the fact that so few matches break up because persons are not prepared to share may indicate that the counselors are doing a good job. These interpersonal reasons for breakups are important, but they constitute only 19% of the total.

There is another category, although not large, that deserves attention: 6% of the terminated matches involved arrangements in which seekers were providing live-in services to frail elderly providers. Although living and service agreements had been developed by the Project Match staff and the clients, it appeared that these agreements were not holding up. As the health of the providers worsened, their needs grew greater, and the demands upon the seeker were more than originally anticipated in the live-in agreement. Basically, the homeseekers got more than they bargained for and were not equipped or willing to handle such serious situations. This situation is one facing most homesharing programs that serve seniors.

The average length of a match that terminated was 8.9 months, indicating that the breakups do not necessarily occur immediately. This finding is compatible with the data on reasons for terminations, suggesting that even when matches break up, many appear to serve a purpose at least temporarily.

SIGNIFICANCE OF THE FINDINGS

Although it is difficult to generalize from any one case, data from Project Match indicate that overwhelmingly, housesharing participants are female, either widowed, divorced, or separated and on fixed incomes. The age distribution of participants, although dependent on the target group of the specific program under consideration, can be wide—in this case ranging from 24 to 96 years of age. Providers were generally older than seekers, compatible with the greater likelihood that individuals acquire assets (i.e., housing) with increased years. The analysis also suggests that many frail older persons seek to share housing, in this case nearly one-third of the participants.

Many participants received significant assistance from their partners in tasks such as meal preparation, housework, and laundry. Interestingly, although help with heavy household chores was needed by the greatest percentage of the respondents, it was the service least likely to be provided by the housesharing partner. This result may indicate that such tasks are either too much to ask from a partner or are provided by outside resources. Gaps in services that the home-sharing partner is unable or unwilling to provide can result in the early dissolution of matches unless other support programs are in place. This is an especially salient issue for referrals at risk of institutionalization. Counselors need to be aware of the degree of dependency some participants will impose on their partners so that other programs can supplement the homesharing arrangement.

Most participants indicated no problems with their matched partner; however, 25% identified one moderate or serious problem, and 20% had at least two problem areas. Interestingly, privacy was not a central problem. The most common problems were identified as personality incompatibilities. Nevertheless, as indicated by the analysis of termination, breakups were more related to unavoidable problems such as health problems or change in situation than they were to issues of incompatibility. Most sharers appear to learn to live with another person's idiosyncracies. This is confirmed by data from the study indicating that more than 80% of sharers were either moderately or highly satisfied with the arrangement. Not surprisingly, their response was related to whether or not they were still matched.

Other variables that influenced satisfaction included the level of friendship achieved, as measured by the friendship index, and the number of problems identified. When the satisfaction scale was cross-tabulated with the three service arrangement typologies, a significant relationship was identified. Sharers involved in ''service-free'' arrangements reported lower levels of satisfaction compared to respondents who exchanged services or were dependent on their partners for assistance.

Housesharing relationships are often a source of friendship and intimacy. G. F. Streib, W. E. Folts, and M. A. Hilker (1984) raised the issue of whether or not shared living arrangements represent genuine families. Based on a study of group homes, they suggest that such arrangements differ from natural families for a variety of reasons, such as certain kinds of foibles that may not be tolerated and the tendency of sharers to withdraw from the obligation during difficult times such as illness. Previous studies concerning such issues have concluded that older homeowners do not view their matches as a social context conducive to intimacy (McConnell and Usher, 1980). Contrary to this conclusion, almost half of the present sample indicated moderate to strong levels of friendship, and more than 40% reported that they could confide in their partner on personal matters.

Furthermore, half of the respondents said that they would be willing to care for their partners if they became ill for at least a week. This suggests that although homesharing arrangements fall short of family obligation, they nevertheless can develop far beyond the notion of strangers occupying a common living space.

Matches were differentiated on the basis on the type of service arrangements that emerged. A study by Dale Jaffe and Elizabeth Howe (1988) identified three distinct kinds of role relationships—independent, transitional, and dependent care—based on the level of impairment and subsequent degree of dependency of the elderly resident and the sense of control over the household. *Independent matches* characteristically involve residents with no health problems who generally need minimal assistance with heavy chores or home maintenance, with seekers generally paying the rent. *Dependent matches* involve residents with severe health problems and multiple disabilities: seekers are either the primary care provider or one member of a support system, which includes professional nursing care during the day. These residents are dependent and logical candidates for nursing-home care. Preliminary evidence by Jaffe (1989) and Jaffe and Howe (1988) suggests that in dependent matches relationships tended to take the form of familylike models. In *transitional matches*, seekers are expected to provide services like shopping, preparing meals, vacuuming, and doing laundry in exchange for room and board.

The service-exchange typology presented in this research on Project Match offers alternative interpretations to those presented by Jaffe. The analysis here suggests that the above characterization of matches is not straightforward. Although this research found a strong relationship between the type of service provision and exchange and the degree of frailty, it was not a one-to-one relationship. Approximately 40% of the *frail* respondents in this research were living in service-free housesharing arrangements; an additional 12% were living in service-exchange arrangements. This suggests that even an older person who is severely impaired has some valid choices in the housesharing arena and is not limited to a dependent role. Furthermore, those who are in a service-dependent relationship are not necessarily powerless in accepting an unsatisfying living arrangement because of their physical disabilities. In fact, those respondents living in service-dependent relationships were found to be among the most satisfied, had high levels of friendship with their partners, and were involved in matches of longer duration.

BENEFITS OF HOMESHARING

This study suggests that there are a number of benefits to individual sharers as well as to the larger community through programs such as Project Match. It documents that positive relations can develop in terms of friendship formation, thereby potentially alleviating the loneliness and sense of social isolation often felt by many older persons. Sharing can also generate needed service that otherwise might be difficult to organize or too expensive to purchase. For frail older persons, such assistance may dramatically improve the quality of their lives and even, in some instances, help postpone or prevent moves to more institutional settings. Sharing may also provide a sense of protection against crime or a feeling of security if sudden physical illness should strike.

Sharing can also make better use of the existing housing stock by occupying space such as bedrooms that would otherwise be empty and making better use of spaces such as kitchens and living rooms. Given the high cost of housing, sharing a home may be the only housing alternative that is affordable and available for some senior and low-income persons. Although federally subsidized housing, such as the Section 8 program, restricts the amount of rent to 30% of income, the average wait in Santa Clara County is five to seven years compared with the two weeks it often takes to arrange sharing through Project Match.

Housesharing has many benefits, but it should not be seen as a panacea for all housing problems or a solution for everyone. Data on terminations suggest that some matches may, in fact, be somewhat short term or provide transitions for persons at certain points in their lives. Because sharing involves two previous strangers living together, certain stresses are likely to occur. These types of outcomes underscore the importance of providing resources to housesharing agencies so that they can provide adequate counseling and backup, especially for those matches that involve frail older persons.

REFERENCES

Howe, E.; Robins, B; and Jaffe, D. *Evaluation of Independent Living's Homeshare Program.* Madison: Independent Living, 1984.

Jaffe, D. "The Social Relations of Homesharing." Paper presented at the Annual Scientific Meeting of the Gerontological Society of America, November 1984.

———. *Caring Strangers: The Sociology of Intergenerational Homesharing.* Greenwich, Conn.: JAI Press, 1989.

Jaffe, D. and Howe, E. "Agency-Assisted Shared Housing: The Nature of Programs and Matches." *The Gerontologist* 28 (1988):318–24.

McConnell, S. R. and Usher, C. E. *Intergenerational House Sharing.* Los Angeles: Andrus Gerontology Center, University of Southern California 1980.

Pritchard, D. C. "The Art of Matchmaking: A Case Study in Shared Housing." *The Gerontologist* 23 (1983):174–79.

Streib, G. F.; Folts, W. E.; and Hilker, M. A. *Old Homes-New Families: Shared Living for the Elderly.* New York: Columbia University Press, 1984.

11

Habits of Living and Match Success: Shared Housing in Southern California

It is generally recognized that the population of the United States is growing older. Those of age 65 and older will constitute a larger proportion of the overall population in years to come, and within the elderly population itself the fastest growing segment is of those over the age of 84 (U.S. Senate Subcommittee on Aging, 1985). These changes in the profile of our population have two important implications for the housing of older adults in this country. First, elderly persons will account for a continuously increasing proportion of the housing consumers in this nation. Second, the nature of housing consumption will change because multiple health impairments and low income, two of the most serious problems associated with aging, are concentrated in those of at least 85 years of age (Newman, Zais, and Struyk, 1984). A third important factor that affects housing for all adults is the rising cost of housing. In many metropolitan areas the cost of owning or renting a house or apartment has increased at a staggering rate. In Orange County, California,—for example the site of the shared housing programs studied here—the fair-market rental for a one-bedroom apartment rose at a rate three times faster than the consumer price index during the period from 1980 to 1986 (Fair Housing Council of Orange County, 1986). All of the factors cited so far point to a need for more housing units, more housing that is suitable for more dependent individuals, and more housing that is affordable. One form of housing that is both affordable and is capable of providing support for more dependent older adults is shared housing.

Shared housing programs have increased rapidly in the past few years because they address the need for affordable housing and supportive services with a very small commitment of resources. In spite of this, until the publication of this book there were few published studies of shared housing, and relatively little is known about the individuals in agency-assisted shared households.

What we do know about shared housing participants indicates that the providers of shared housing (homeproviders) and those seeking shared housing (home-seekers) differ from each other in several important respects, including age and reasons for sharing. Two studies (Pritchard, 1983; Schreter, 1984, 1986) found that in many matches older individuals were sharing with persons middle-aged or younger. In addition, both Carol Schreter (1986) and David Pritchard (1983) found that seekers were drawn to shared housing for financial reasons whereas providers of shared housing were motivated by needs for companionship and assistance, as well as for financial reasons. With notable differences in age and reason for sharing, it is reasonable to ask in what other ways seekers and providers differ. Another reason for studying shared housing is that most shared housing matches do not last very long. Pritchard (1983), for example, found that 63% of the matches that he studied dissolved within one year. Of those matches that had ended during the year-long period of study, 92% ended within the first three months. Similarly, Schreter (1986) found that 60% of the matches that she examined ended within six months. This high rate of match dissolution, especially in the first several months, raises questions about the factors that cause a match to end, particularly matches that end quickly. Could the differences between seeker and provider be leading to conflict and early dissolution? How important is the similarity of those sharing to the success of the match when match success is measured in terms of match length?

Previous research in social psychology provides some theoretical and empirical guidance in developing hypotheses regarding interpersonal differences within shared housing matches and their relation to match length. Research on relationship development (Altman and Taylor, 1973) indicates that the initial dynamics of a shared housing relationship are likely to involve the mechanics of sharing common space rather than the more complex interactions of two personalities. Research on roommate compatibility in college situations (Lapidus, Green, and Baruh, 1985) suggests that the living habits of roommates may have a greater effect on compatibility than personality differences or differences in background. Finally, research on the territorial behavior of experimentally isolated pairs of men (Altman and Haythorn, 1967; and Altman, Taylor, and Wheeler, 1971) found that early territorial behavior led to the most stable living situations.

The research cited here indicates that habits of daily living are most likely to have the greatest initial impact on the success of a shared housing or similar type of relationship. Given the short length of most matches, the resolution of issues involving living habits appears crucial for a match to endure more than a few months. Characteristics of the match that reflect either similarity of living habits or limited opportunity for conflict over living habits are most likely to influence match length. The basic assumption is that providers and seekers who are more similar on basic demographic characteristics will also have more similar living habits and will be able to establish rules for the use of common space more quickly than providers and seekers who are more dissimilar.

It was hypothesized that (1) match participants of very different ages would have different life-styles and living habits and that this would lead to conflict and result in significantly shorter matches; (2) match participants of different sexes would encounter more conflict and have significantly shorter matches than those in same sex matches; (3) matches in which one or both parties worked would be significantly longer (due to reduced opportunity for conflict); (4) matches in which the seeker provided services for the provider would be significantly longer than other matches (it was thought that these matches would require more rules at the onset of the match and that this would decrease subsequent conflict); and (5) matches that ended for reasons of incompatibility would be significantly shorter in duration than matches that ended for other reasons.

To pursue the above hypotheses, matches from two shared housing programs in Orange County, California, were examined. Since the characteristics of a community may influence the characteristics of the matches themselves, it is important to understand the context in which the match was made. Therefore, before discussing the programs used in the study in greater detail, a short description of the community context will be given.

COMMUNITY CONTEXT

Orange County is a suburban area of 2.2 million people located south of Los Angeles in California. It is a county that is becoming more ethnically diverse as immigrants from Mexico, Latin America, and Southeast Asia continue to settle there. Although the county's population is fairly young due to the recency of its growth, its population of age 65 and older is still estimated to be about 300,000. Its residents, on average, earn incomes well above the national median, but their incomes are offset by housing costs that are among the highest in the country. Once known for its agricultural products, Orange County experienced explosive growth during the years following World War II. This growth was greatest during the 1960s and 1970s, but all of Southern California has continued to grow rapidly as the region becomes more important in domestic and international trade. One consequence of the great growth experienced in Orange County has been a tremendous shortage of affordable housing. The median cost of a home in Orange County is now over $200,000. The tremendous cost of homes has put an additional pressure on the rental market. Vacancy rates for housing in the county were 2.1% in 1985, and the Fair Market Rents (as determined by HUD in establishing Section 8 payment rates) were $647 and $757 per month in 1988 for one- and two-bedroom apartments, respectively (Fair Housing Council of Orange County, 1986). Waiting lists for Section 8 housing and voucher programs range from three to seven years and average five years for Section 202 housing (subsidized housing for seniors and disabled). For those individuals who earn low wages, live on fixed incomes, or have large families, finding affordable housing in Orange County is an extremely difficult task. This makes shared housing an attractive option for many people in the county.

Another incentive for sharing, more specific to older adults, is the need for in-home supportive services. Many of the individuals who moved to Orange County while in their 60s to enjoy its excellent climate are now approaching their 80s and are in need of support if they wish to remain in their homes. The sprawling characteristics of suburban growth in Southern California create difficulties for individuals with mobility impairments, particularly for those no longer able to drive a car. The relative lack of density in its development makes Orange County a difficult area to serve adequately with public transportation. Long walks to bus stops, infrequent service, and lengthy waiting times for "Dial-a-Ride" services are common. With many older residents of the county "house-rich" and "cash-poor" shared housing offers an inexpensive way to receive in-home supportive services by providing an opportunity for services to be given in exchange for rent.

Aside from financial- or service-related needs, many older people desire the companionship and security that a housemate can provide. Many frailer older people fear that they may have a fall or other mishap and go undiscovered for days. Sharing with another may provide additional income while making the older person feel more secure in his or her home.

In Orange county a wide variety of services are available, but few are administered on a countywide basis. Rather, each community tends to provide its own services funded by city revenues and state funds. Because there are more than two dozen cities of varying size in Orange County, services vary from municipality to municipality. In general, the large communities in the northern and central parts of the county offer the best access to services. Information about services can be obtained from local authorities or through the information and referral service at the county's Area Agency on Aging. The strong emphasis on local control of services is reflected in the large number of shared housing programs (15) that operate in the county. The county has so many shared housing programs that a full-time shared housing coordinator position has been created at the Area Agency on Aging, funded by federal funds distributed by the Orange County Housing Authority. The individual in this position is responsible for providing technical assistance, training sessions, a central source of information on shared housing programs, and a central place for reporting and filing information for the various shared housing programs. The vast majority of the shared housing programs in the county are funded for only 20 hours a week. This allows the program to handle telephone calls, conduct intake interviews, and refer potential seekers to one another. At this level of staffing case management is impossible. Two programs in the county, however, have received more funding through grants from the California Department of Housing and Community Development and have been able to fund a full-time staff position. These two programs, San Clemente in South County and Santa Ana in Central County, were the primary focus of this study of shared housing matches conducted in 1986.

City of Santa Ana Senior Shared Housing

The Senior Shared Housing Program is sponsored by the City of Santa Ana through the housing component of Santa Ana's Division of Community Development. Funding comes from a grant from the California Department of Housing and Community Development and matching funds from the city of Santa Ana, Community Development Block Grants (CDBG), and tax increments. There is one full-time shared housing coordinator and a half-time intern position. In the past additional staff assistance has come from senior volunteers, and the program continues to seek volunteer help. In addition, a volunteer from Santa Ana's sizable Vietnamese community translates and assists with matches involving Vietnamese. The shared housing coordinator spends approximately one day every two weeks at the Vietnamese community center conducting intake interviews.

The matching procedure involves conducting an intake interview with potential homeseekers and homeproviders. References are asked for but are not checked. Clients are matched on the basis of compatible needs and living habits. Both housing-oriented and service-oriented matches are made. Once potential matches are identified, based upon the intake interviews, potential seekers and providers are referred to each other. Potential seekers and providers are given a list of items to discuss. The program strongly encourages those entering a shared living arrangement to write down the terms of their living arrangement in a contract. This is very strongly encouraged in any sharing situation in which there is an exchange of services. Also strongly encouraged are trial periods lasting from one week to one month in which either party in the match can terminate the match with relative ease. The matches are followed up (the status of the match is checked with a telephone call) at intervals of one month, three months, six months, and every six months thereafter. Matches are considered successful if they meet the needs of the individuals in the match. Generally, any match that lasts more than one month and does not end for reasons of incompatibility is judged successful.

Clients for the program are recruited through articles in the media, advertisements in local papers, fliers displayed at community centers, congregate lunch sites, and through shared housing mixers. These mixers are monthly events where individuals currently in shared housing matches, and those who would like to share, gather socially to discuss what it is like to share and to provide an opportunity for potential seekers to meet one another.

During the past two years there has been an increase in the case management aspects of the program. Frequently, housing is only one of several needs that individuals contacting the program have. In many instances individuals wait until their needs are urgent before contacting the program. Between 300 and 450 inquiries are received each month. These inquiries involve anything related to housing needs and almost anything related to the needs of those with low incomes. Many of the referrals come from other agencies. There has been a noticeable rise in inquiries from the homeless, single-parent families and the Vietnamese. In 1987 the program matched 255 seniors. The shared housing coordinator has found that more of her time is being devoted to administrative duties, such as grant writing, and another full-time staff person is urgently needed to assist with intakes and to answer telephone inquiries.

The program initially developed out of an internship in which the present shared housing coordinator studied shared housing for the city of Santa Ana. In 1984 the city was encouraged by the Area Agency on Aging to respond to a request for proposals from the state Department of Housing and Community Development. Funding for this program has been steady since the first grant was received in 1984. The program is currently on its third grant from the state and applying for its fourth. The number of applicants for these grants increases each year, and sufficient matching funds from local government are essential if money from the state is to be secured.

South County Senior Shared Housing Program, San Clemente

The South County Senior Shared Housing Program is sponsored by the San Clemente Senior Center and the city of San Clemente. For the period covered in the study, funding came entirely from a grant for a pilot demonstration project from the California Department of Housing and Community Development. This initial two-year grant did not require matching funds and funded one full-time position of which 30 hours were devoted to shared housing coordinator duties and 10 hours to casework management. Currently, the program is receiving a mixture of funds from the city of San Clemente and the Orange County Housing Authority, with the Housing Authority providing most of its support from a reserve fund for local housing programs. The program was denied its request for a grant from the Department of Housing and Community Development in 1987. In addition to the full-time shared housing coordinator, a senior volunteer puts in considerable hours assisting in intake interviews, reference checking, and follow-up calls. The program also has an individual from the Senior Training Employment Program who provides 20 hours of office staffing a week.

All matches involve at least one person over age 65. Both housing and service-oriented matches are arranged. Each potential seeker has an intake interview and potential homeproviders also have visits in their home from the shared housing coordinator. References are checked and, as in the Santa Ana program, potential seekers and providers are matched on the basis of the complementarity of their needs and living habits. Potential seekers and providers, once they are referred to each other, are strongly encouraged to develop a written shared living agreement. Providers and seekers are also strongly encouraged to try sharing on a trial basis for one week during which either party may terminate the arrangement easily.

Program clients are recruited through presentations at senior centers, senior clubs, American Association of Retired Persons (AARP) meetings, churches, health fairs, and mobile-home owners meetings (a sizeable portion of mobile-home owners are over age 65). In addition, hospital social workers and social security offices are given fliers advertising the program. The current shared housing coordinator made a video about shared housing with money received from a grant from the California Community Foundation for Cable Vision. This video is shown frequently on the local cable channel. Finally, there are two social mixers a month for current and potential seekers. Calling current seekers to remind them about the mixers also provides the program with an opportunity for follow-up of ongoing matches.

Shared housing has a relatively long history in the southern part of Orange County. Starting in the early 1970s as a volunteer-coordinated effort to respond to senior's need for companionship, the program grew and was eventually supported by the San Clemente Senior Center. In 1985 the Area Agency on Aging asked the program to apply to the California Department of Housing and Community Development for a pilot demonstration project grant, which it received. One intent of the grant was to provide funds for an outreach worker. The program was not chosen for funding when it reapplied in 1985 and has survived through 1987 with a patchwork of local funding. A key element in obtaining funding from the state has been the amount of support available from the local community. Because San Clemente has one-tenth the population of Santa Ana, the city has fewer resources to devote to the program. Without sufficient matchup funding, the program's chances for renewal were considerably diminished. Currently, the program is reapplying to Housing and Community Development for funding.

The program has seen an increase in its casework management functions during 1985–1987. As in Santa Ana, the program receives inquiries that are related to all kinds of housing problems, not just shared housing. Between 400 and 700 inquiries are made each month and come from potential clients, other agencies, and drop-ins. There has been an increase in inquiries from single-parent families but the program has found that older people do not generally like matches involving children. Aside from more staffing, the program would like funding for more advertising in local papers, as is done in Santa Ana. In 1987 the program matched 111 seniors.

A STUDY OF MATCH CHARACTERISTICS AND MATCH LENGTH

To determine if the characteristics of individuals in shared housing matches affected match length, a study was conducted that used intake interviews and program case records from matches that ended during a one-year period. The primary data were derived from shared housing program intake interviews and program case records on 38 matches (19 from each program) that ended during the one-year period. Only records for matches listed as terminated were used because the outcomes of other matches were not known to program staff, who relied upon shared housing participants to contact the program when a match ended. Because these data were not originally collected for this study, the analyses reported represent secondary analyses. These archival data have not previously been analyzed in other studies. A second source of data consists of 13 telephone and 2 in-person interviews conducted with consenting participants who lived in a shared housing arrangement at the time of the interview.

The use of archival data is always restricted by the conditions of collection (Webb et al., 1966), and the current data are no exception. Many intake interviews conducted by the agencies were not fully completed. This was particularly true of intake interviews with homeproviders. The use of matches that have terminated, although useful in providing data on match length and reasons for dissolution, is apt to afford insights only about matches that were less successful or were problematic. Both of the agencies that provided the data lacked sufficient resources at the time the data was collected for adequate follow-up of matches. Without follow-up, only failed matches that reported problems or matches in which one party wanted to be matched again were likely to be listed as dissolved by the agency. In addition, matches involving Asians (specifically Vietnamese) were kept in separate files and were not reviewed when the files were being examined for terminations in the year-long period used in the study.

The participants were 23 males and 48 females who ranged in age from 19 to 99, with a mean age of 63.25. Each had participated in a shared housing living arrangement that had terminated. The participants were involved in 38 matches that ended sometime during the period from July 1985 to July 1986. Five of the participants were in more than one match that terminated during the period sampled. Matches involving these participants did not differ significantly in match length from the other matches. All matches that were listed as terminated during this one-year period were used in the study.

The two sites used in this study were chosen because they represented two economically and ethnically different parts of the county. By using sites that served different populations, it was thought that a more representative sample of the county would be obtained. Site 1 (Santa Ana) was in an area characterized as more urban, with a large proportion of lower-income and Hispanic residents. Site 2 (San Clemente) was located in a more rural part of the county, with residents who were characteristically Caucasian and had higher incomes than residents of other parts of the county. An additional reason for using the two sites was the similarity of the intake forms used. This allowed data from the two sites to be more easily pooled.

Data for this study were obtained from intake information sheets filled out by the shared housing coordinators during an interview with the prospective seeker or sharer. The information recorded included the age, sex, marital status, current or former occupation, education, income and source of income, medical disabilities (e.g., hearing and visual problems), and self-rated health. In addition, information about the individual's personal habits and preferences was recorded (such as rising and bed times, smoking or drinking practices, interests and hobbies, pet ownership and attitudes toward visitors). Another section of the intake form indicated whether the individual was willing to share or needed help in different household activities such as vacuuming and cooking. Whether individuals could drive a car or climb stairs was also recorded. Homeproviders indicated dwelling type and their desire for in-home supportive services. Potential seekers were asked to provide references and the name and address of their nearest friend or relative.

The records of two shared housing programs were examined by the investigator for shared housing matches that had terminated. Terminated matches were identified with the assistance of the shared housing coordinator and an examination of the counselor's notes that were kept on each match. Reasons for match termination were determined from the counselor's notes. When the notes were ambiguous, the investigator questioned the shared housing counselor as to his or her recollection of the match history.

Once terminated matches were identified, the intake records for each participant in the match were examined and a copy of each file was made to insure accurate recording of data. Case notes made by the shared housing program staff were also copied to provide additional information on the reason for match dissolution. The primary unit of analysis was the shared housing match itself.

Study Findings

Providers were significantly older than seekers (70.26 years compared with 56.24 years) and a greater percentage of providers were women (71.1%) than were seekers (63.2%). Seekers were more likely to have lower incomes than providers (81.0% of seekers had annual incomes of $10,000 or less compared with 40.0% of the providers). Most providers were retired (81.1%) whereas 53.6% of the seekers worked full or part time. An additional 14.3% of the seekers were unemployed, and 21.4% were retired. The average match length was 14.34 weeks. A frequency distribution revealed one match (length = 89 weeks) that was more than three standard deviations from the mean. If this match was eliminated from analysis, match length would be reduced to 12.3 weeks. In 29.0% of all matches both seeker and provider were 60 years of age or older, and in 35.0% of all matches either the seeker or provider had been in an agency-assisted match before. There was an exchange of services in 50.0% of the matches, and in 44.7% of all matches the seeker and provider were of opposite sex.

A comparison between the Santa Ana and South County programs revealed some interesting differences in the two program's participants. Compared to providers in South County, those in Santa Ana were younger (66.17 versus 74.37 years), and seekers were older (60.31 versus 52.15 years). Seekers in Santa Ana were poorer (all reported incomes below $15,000) than those in South County (where 26.7% of seekers had incomes above $15,000). More matches in South

County involved the provision of supportive services (63.2%) than in Santa Ana (42.1%). Overall, matches in South County involved more older providers who required more assistance than those in matches in Santa Ana. This suggests that shared housing matches in Santa Ana were more oriented to seekers looking for inexpensive housing and providers who wanted to supplement their incomes whereas matches in South County were more likely to be a response to a need for supportive services. There was no significant difference between the programs in match length.

Providers were more likely to report poor (5%) or fair health (30%) than were seekers who generally reported good health (92.3%). Individuals were considered at risk for mobility impairment if they had no access to or could not drive a car, had impaired vision, or could not climb stairs. A large proportion of providers (70.8%) were at risk for mobility impairment. Although 44.0% of the seekers were at risk for mobility impairment, mobility impairment for seekers was mainly determined by lack of access to or inability to drive a car.

An analysis of variance revealed no significant differences in match length for same- versus opposite-sex housemates, for matches in which one or both parties worked full or part time, or for matches in which a service was provided in exchange for rent. No significant correlation was found between the age difference of members in a match and the length of the match. The mean difference in age between provider and seeker in a match was 19.68 years. Matches with one or both parties working showed a nonsignificant trend in the direction of the hypotheses (12.94 weeks) compared with matches in which no one worked (8.5 weeks).

Of the hypotheses, only the relationship between match length and reason for termination was supported. When reason for termination was collapsed into two categories, incompatibility (mutual incompatibility, behavior of seeker, and behavior of provider) and other (all others, including disputes over provision of services) and compared with long and short matches (determined by a median split) in a cross-tabular analysis, a significantly higher proportion of short matches ended for reasons of incompatibility compared to long matches (X^2 (1, N = 38) = 4.54, $p < 0.04$). A distribution of reasons for termination and their corresponding match lengths is shown in Table 11.1.

Discussion

One of the hypotheses in this study was supported by the data. A significantly greater proportion of shorter matches ended for reasons of incompatibility than did longer matches. Differences in age, sex, and work status among participants in shared households did not predict match length. Nor was there any difference in match length between matches involving the exchange of services and those not involving an exchange. The only hypothesis that showed any trend in the data involved work status.

The assumption underlying these hypotheses was that a failure to state clearly

Table 11.1
Match Termination and Match Length

Reason for Termination	% (n)	Match Length (in weeks)
Incompatibility (mutual)	23.7% (9)	8.67
Behavior, Provider	2.6% (1)	89.0
Behavior, Seeker	28.9% (11)	12.0
Time Limited at Onset	5.3% (2)	15.0
Health, Provider	10.5% (4)	15.75
Dispute over Provision of Service	10.5% (4)	12.25
Other	18.4% (7)	14.86
	100.0% (38)	14.34

match expectations and rules for living together leads to incompatibility and match failure. Unfortunately, the nature of the data required that this general hypothesis be tested through use of surrogate measures (individual differences were assumed to reflect differences in living habits). The failure of these surrogate measures to predict match length may reflect the inadequacy of the measures rather than the inadequacy of the theoretical framework behind them. Confirmation of the relationship between match length and reason for dissolution does indicate a pattern for match dissolution. Matches that tended to last longer were also more likely to end for reasons other than incompatibility.

The failure to find a significant relationship between differences in a match's participants and match length is an interesting finding in itself. The large average age difference in matches and the large percentage of opposite sex matches seem to indicate that very different individuals are willing to live in a match. Some of these matches were fairly successful. Matches in which there would have been an obvious source of conflict, however, were avoided whenever possible by the two programs studies (e.g., smoker with a nonsmoker). A second interpretation of the study's findings may be that individual differences did reflect differences in living habits but these differences did not predictably lead to conflict or early match dissolution. It is conceivable that individuals with very different living habits could share common space as long as they were able to come to some sort of agreement on rules for the use of common space and could respect each other's privacy. The findings from the studies of college roommates may have been misleading because college roommates, unlike people in shared housing arrangements, almost always share a single room and thus all of their living space is "common." In shared housing arrangements, individuals may have one set of living habits for common areas and another set of living habits for their own rooms. This ability to separate between "private" and "public" living habits could allow individuals with very different living habits to coexist successfully. Future research in shared housing should examine the extent to which providers and seekers define public and private space and how this relates to the success of the match. Future research in shared housing should also concentrate on the manner in which conflicts are resolved in the match rather than the role of similarities or differences between the individuals in match success.

Although the findings of this study are limited, they do suggest that individual differences may not be good predictors of match success. Of greater importance may be the procedures used by different programs in attempting to create successful matches. All shared housing programs have severe limitations on staff time. Only 2 of 14 programs in Orange County, for example, had a full-time staff devoted to shared housing. Examining program differences and their relation to match success would appear to be more practical at this time than advocating more complicated intake and assessment procedures.

Differences in intake forms and intake procedures, reference checking, the manner in which seeker and provider are referred to each other, and the presence or absence of regular follow-up by program staff could have a great impact on the success of a match. Seekers who provided references, for example, were in longer matches than those who did not. Of particular importance is the need to study the methods by which different programs prepare the seeker and provider for this new living arrangement. How are disputes over living habits to be resolved? How are the details of daily living laid out before the start of the match? How is honesty encouraged in the interview process? Do contracts or living-together agreements contribute to the success of a match? How is it determined that an individual may be inappropriate for shared housing? These are the questions that future researchers of shared housing must pursue.

The impact of funding level and funding source on differences in shared housing programs is another important area for future research. A program funded at 10 staff hours a week can do little more than answer the telephone and conduct intake interviews. Program effectiveness is often evaluated by the number of matches that the program makes in a given period. This type of evaluation fails to measure the length of matches or their quality. Another consideration is the amount of commitment that the staff has to shared housing. Agency staff are likely to resent the additional time demands of a shared housing program, especially if it is one of a number of required activities. Few resources and poor match success may lead to a cycle of failure and apathy within a program.

In this study match success was measured by match length. Match length is an outcome measure that can be clearly defined and measured and is convenient for conventional data analyses. Match length, however, is not necessarily a measure of the quality or success of a match. Many matches, particularly those that last longer than several months, are successful in that they have met the needs of the individuals involved in these matches. The information gathered from interviews revealed little association between satisfaction with the living arrangement and the length of the ongoing match. This may indicate that match length measures only one aspect of match quality.

Shared housing matches do not last very long. The rate of dissolution within the first three months in this study (58%) corresponds almost exactly to the rate of dissolution found by Pritchard (1983). The average length of terminated matches in this study, slightly over 3.0 months, was close to the average of 3.8 months for terminated matches reported by the Department of Housing and Community Development for all shared housing programs in California.[1] Few matches last longer than one year.

The temporary and transitional nature of shared housing living arrangements is the result of several factors. Seekers thought that financial reasons and the need for temporary housing were the most important reasons for sharing. Neither of these reasons reflects a desire for a long-term living arrangement. Schreter (1984) found that 56% of individuals in shared housing had lost a housemate in the six months preceding their entry into a shared living arrangement. In this same six-month period, 43% suffered a major loss of income and 30% suffered an acute health problem. Many of the individuals who seek shared housing may be going through a period of transition in their lives. Shared housing provides temporary, stable, and affordable housing for individuals during this time of transition.

Another concern raised by the short length of most matches is their effect on very old homeproviders who depend on the assistance of the seeker for some of their daily needs. Abrupt and unpredictable changes in the provision of these services may present a source of stress that negates the benefits derived from the assistance given.

One way of redefining match success may be to emphasize the smoothness or ease with which individuals enter and leave shared living arrangements. Match success may be better measured by indicators of satisfaction with the arrangement when it is ongoing and the level of disruption when it ends rather than by sheer length. Two of the most successful matches in this study were time limited at their onset. A planned dissolution allows both provider and seeker to plan ahead for the next living arrangement.

CONCLUSION

This study of agency-assisted shared housing has been exploratory. Although limited by many factors, this research indicated that differences between provider and seeker were not predictive of match success. Rather than directing future research toward more detailed studies of living habits and personality differences, a more fruitful approach would be the investigation of how shared housing programs with different matching strategies vary in their rate of success. Priority should be given to the study of the impact of funding level on the effectiveness of shared housing programs because this could directly affect the formation of policy guiding the funding of shared housing programs. A related issue is the need to redefine match success by moving away from match length as the sole criterion of success. Finally, it is important to recognize that housing issues, like many others, are intergenerational problems that require intergenerational solutions. Shared housing offers the opportunity to match the needs of one generation with the resources of another.

NOTE

1. Personal communication. Susan Kessler, California Department of Housing and Community Development, December 1986.

REFERENCES

Altman, Irwin, and Haythorn, W. W. "The Ecology of Isolated Groups." *Behavior Science* 12 (1967):169–82.

Altman, Irwin, and Taylor, D. A. *Social Penetration: The Development of Interpersonal Relationships*. New York: Holt, Reinhart, and Winston, 1973.

Altman, Irwin; Taylor, D. A.; and Wheeler, L. "Ecological Aspects of Group Behavior in Social Isolation." *Journal of Applied Social Psychology* 1 (1971):76–100.

Dobkin, Leah. *Shared Housing for Older People: A Planning Manual for Match-up Programs*. Philadelphia: National Shared Housing Resource Center, 1983.

Fair Housing Council of Orange County. "Housing Costs in Orange County." Unpublished report, 1986.

Lapidus, J.; Green, S. K.; and Baruh, E. "Factors Related to Roommate Compatibility in the Residence Hall—A Review." *Journal of College Student Personnel* 26 (1985):420–34.

Newman, Sandra J.; Zais, J.; and Struyk, R. "Housing Older America." In *Elderly People and the Environment*, edited by Irwin Altman, Joachim Wohlwill, and M. Powell Lawton. New York: Plenum, 1984.

Pritchard, David C. "The Art of Matchmaking: A Case Study of Shared Housing." *The Gerontologist* 23 (1983):174–79.

Schreter, Carol A. "Residents of Shared Housing." *Social Thought*, Winter 1984, pp. 30–38.

Schreter, Carol A. "Advantages and Disadvantages of Shared Housing." *Journal of Housing for the Elderly* 3 (1986):121–38.

U.S. Senate Special Committee on Aging. *Aging America: Trends and Projections*. Washington, D.C.: U.S. Department of Health and Human Services, 1985.

Webb, Eugene J.; Campbell, Donald T.; Schwartz, Richard D.; and Sechrist, Lee. *Unobtrusive Measures: Non-reactive Research in the Social Sciences*. New York: Rand McNally, 1966.

12

Share-A-Home of Wichita

Janet B. Underwood and Connie Wulf

In the Midwest, community is defined by caring. It is not coincidence that a weekly magazine supplement to the local newspaper is entitled "Neighbors." People in this region of the country place value on relationships, family, and rootedness. It is within this context that Share-A-Home of Wichita was able to personify highly esteemed community values.

Share-A-Home of Wichita is located in a metropolitan area with a population of 393,470. The community is predominantly comprised of blue-collar workers with manufacturing of aircraft as its primary industry. Of the 393,470 residents, 39,983 persons are 65 years of age and older. Seniors from the ages of 65 through 74 represent 60.4%; 30.1% are between the ages of 75 and 84; and those 85 and older make up 9.5% of this senior population. Of particular concern from the perspective of housing policy is the fact that the group that appears to be growing the fastest over time (female owners) and the group that increases substantially over the life cycle (female renters) also have the highest concentration of the lowest income, elderly-head households (Newman, 1985). In Wichita the senior population has increased 42.0% since 1970, compared with a 4.5% increase for the total population of the city. Demographers project an increase of 11.5% in the elder population by 1990.

Currently, Wichita has 15 retirement and life-care communities, including a new life-care community completed in the fall of 1988. Public or subsidized housing in the area has waiting lists ranging from 18 months to two years. Although the community is service rich in residential facilities, a senior center, and recreational opportunities, it is not service rich in the areas of in-home services (i.e., home health aides/personal care, homemaker/chore service, or respite), general support (i.e., transportation, adult day care or outreach), physical environment (i.e., home maintenance, repair service or renovations) or congregate residential facilities. These services do exist in the Wichita area, but they are not readily available because demand exceeds capacity.

THE DEVELOPMENT OF SHARE-A-HOME

The Share-A-Home program of Wichita arranges for people to share housing. It is one component of the Kansas Elks Training Center for the Handicapped, a private, nonprofit agency providing services to the handicapped and to the elderly. The concept of shared housing and the subsequent establishment of the Share-A-Home program in June 1982 developed from planning meetings between the Kansas Elks Training Center for the Handicapped, the Social Rehabilitation Services, and the Sedgwick County Department on Aging. This group of concerned service providers were seeking to determine the housing needs of the elderly in the Greater Wichita/Sedgwick County area.

The program began with one graduate intern student on a part-time basis, funded by the Kansas Elks Training Center for the Handicapped in cooperation with the Area Agency on Aging and Social and Rehabilitation Services for a period of six months. Then, in 1983, a one-year grant was approved through the County Aging Mill Levy funds. The County Aging Mill Levy funds are a specific portion of the tax base designated for aging projects. This grant was consequently approved for five consecutive years resulting in increased funding and staff in incremental levels. Not until 1987 was funding approved to operate Share-A-Home on a full-time basis. In 1988 Share-A-Home secured funding for two paid staff members: one full-time director and one part-time administrative assistant. Volunteers are used on an as-needed basis.

The umbrella agency was very supportive since federal funding for housing programs for the handicapped was tied to funding for senior housing. The case in point was HUD Section 8–202 housing funds. The host agency wanted to broaden its impact in the community and supported its development both philosophically and financially. The host agency also saw this as a chance to gain credibility in the community via the positive media attention that would be generated by Share-A-Home. The local county agencies supported the development of Share-A-Home philosophically but not financially since they had other priorities. Additionally, the Kansas secretary of aging was not supportive either verbally or financially of the Share-A-Home concept. As the program gained considerable support and success during the next two years the state secretary of aging reversed her philosophical position toward the program. As federal monies became increasingly tighter, the local Area Agency on Aging became more demanding and controlling of the program. Therefore, the program has been allowed to expand only in ways that would benefit agency goals and in ways that would not create competition for funding.

Due to the service gaps within the in-home supportive services network and lack of housing alternatives, Share-A-Home was able to fill a need in the community. Still, much of the continuing success of the program has to do with

Wichita's combined university population of 17,709 students, the initial support of an umbrella agency, and the interest of a media reporter.

There are several lessons to be learned from these kinds of cooperative relationships. One lesson involves the role of the university. Share-A-Home of Wichita works particularly well with an intergenerational university population to draw from. In the six years of the program's existence students, faculty, and staff from local colleges have participated in matched living arrangements. In this way the university not only provides academic credibility and campus visibility by example but also advances the idea of an educational and relational bridge between generations. Another positive by-product of this partnership is the student intern. Share-A-Home of Wichita offers students an opportunity to test academic theories of aging by practical application. In turn, student interns provide much-needed supplemental staffing.

The Kansas Elks Training Center for the Handicapped played a crucial role in shaping the success of the program. The agency provided all of the initial support to surround the fledgling program with security and stability. Without the aid of an umbrella agency it would have taken much longer for the program to become established, and the program would have had to struggle to find an appropriate niche in the community. As the program became solid and procured primary funding, however, the host agency would not allow Share-A-Home to compete for other sources of funding. The host agency, being dependent on financial subsidization itself, did not want the Share-A-Home program competing for the same shrinking dollars. This factor alone has inhibited the program from growing and expanding in more significant ways throughout the years. The lesson here pertains to the dependent nature of programs of this kind versus the political context in which they find themselves. Share-A-Home of Wichita is still housed within the framework of the Kansas Elks Training Center for the Handicapped. Share-A-Home is tied to the host agency, which will never let it go elsewhere. Although Share-A-Home maintains a level of success, it remains controlled and limited by the host agency. Thus security has come at a price of limited growth.

Both the media and local social service providers have contributed to the ongoing vitality of Share-A-Home. The newspaper and television both were unusually cooperative by extending to Share-A-Home a high degree of visibility. In March 1982 a local television news reporter saw a tape profiling a few social service pilot projects that had been successful in other communities around the country and that seemed indigenous to Wichita. Shared housing was one of these programs. He succeeded in convincing the Area Agency on Aging, Social and Rehabilitation Services, and Kansas Elks Training Center for the Handicapped to take it on as a cooperative venture. Because of his investment in the pilot project he was able and eager to insure coverage by his station. The end result of his interest became a nine-minute tape that he made, which went to the President's Council of Private Sector Initiatives and Volunteerism. Share-A-Home of Wichita won national recognition by this highly esteemed and influential council.

There is no question that the media are necessary allies in shaping the image of a program like Share-A-Home. They are able to communicate the ideological concepts efficiently and effectively to reach the target audience the program wants to attract. The relationship provides valuable instruction about how to maximize a very low budget and become a household word very quickly. It is hard to imagine Share-A-Home of Wichita without the headlines, cover stories, and live interviews that have become such an integral part of its identity.

THE HOMESHARING PROCESS

Recruitment

Homeowners and homeseekers are recruited by using public-service announcements via television, radio, and newspaper; presentations at local clubs, organizations, and churches; flyers, brochures, and posters distributed and mailed throughout the community; referrals from family, friends, and other homesharing participants; and university newspapers, class schedules of courses, and advertising and articles in *Active Aging*, a monthly, 20-page newspaper provided by the Gerontology Center of the Wichita State University and mailed free of charge to every household with someone of age 60 or older in a Tri-County area (estimated circulation 30,000). These sources are used in creating a pool of applicants as well as maintaining ongoing visibility. Recruitment must be a continuous process. It must be understood that although the influence of the media is critical to community acceptance of the program, people seem to inform themselves or think about such programs only when they need them, not necessarily before. A program of continuous advertising, presentations to likely groups, and regular contacts with human-service providers are all necessary to maintain a large enough pool of qualified applicants. As events occur in peoples' lives that change their needs, the homesharing solution then has a greater chance of being considered.

The matching process begins with an in-depth interview of both the homeowner and potential homeseekers. Seniors are interviewed in their home, and potential homeseekers are interviewed in the Share-A-Home office. The interview survey is an instrument used to assess and clarify homesharing needs and expectations. Home interviews conducted in the senior's home provide the staff with an opportunity to assess the client's home and determine suitability for homesharing. At the same time, homeowners and potential homeseekers have the opportunity to ask additional questions regarding the program and matching process. Both homeprovider and potential homeseeker also receive interview guidelines for the purpose of addressing issues that may apply to their particular situation or household. The interview guideline is used during the initial meeting between homeprovider and homeseeker.

Potential homeseekers are required to submit three letters of reference or names of references of individuals that they have known for one year or longer. References are checked and each potential homeseeker's name is checked through the Kansas Bureau of Investigation for criminal-history information. This was initiated in 1985 and adds another key element to the screening process. The end result is enhanced credibility for the program.

Once a client is deemed appropriate for homesharing, the staff refers potential seekers to appropriate homeproviders for an acquaintance interview. If needed, the staff will participate during this meeting. At this time expectations and needs are articulated. If the senior and the individual agree to share, the staff will then facilitate the negotiation of homesharing agreements. The agreement clarifies in writing the responsibilities and expectations of each person in the shared living arrangement. If responsibilities should change during the match, the staff will once again assist in the renegotiation of homesharing agreements. If either party fails to abide by the written agreement or is unable to renegotiate an agreement, a 20-day written notice of intent to terminate is recommended. Should a match terminate and participants want another match, the match process is repeated.

The program staff monitor the matches at regular intervals. The first check is made by telephone two weeks after the match is made and then in three months; a follow-up questionnaire is mailed to both parties at the end of the sixth month. Checks are made thereafter by telephone when necessary. It is crucial to the success of any shared housing matchup program to provide ongoing follow-up service to its clients with an emphasis on continuous counseling. Conflicts often occur during the initial stages of the relationship. Early follow-up can help increase the longevity of the matches.

The Matches

The first "match" for Share-A-Home of Wichita was made in August 1982. Since that time there have been 235 matches made between persons from diverse socioeconomic classes and religious and ethnic backgrounds. Students and other young people initially come to Share-A-Home looking for inexpensive housing, whereas elderly homeowners come to it looking for assistance. It is important to understand that beyond the initial incentive of inexpensive housing, live-in homeseekers in the Wichita program report that they chose this arrangement because they (1) want to help someone, (2) have an ideological commitment to helping the elderly remain independent, and (3) think their experience will be useful in their career training. These reasons are not mutually exclusive and usually some combination of reasons is given.

There are three styles of matches that are prevalent in the Share-A-Home program of Wichita: independent matches, dependent matches, and transitional matches (Jaffe and Howe, 1988).

Independent Matches. With homeproviders who have no health problems seekers are actually roomers. They pay rent. This gives the homeowner the power to define what kind of relationship they would have, but at the same time it gives homeseekers greater independence as well. Generally, the only help these homeowners want is the security of having someone in the house at night or some minimal assistance with outdoor chores or home maintenance and companionship. Fifty-two percent of the ongoing matches fall into this category.

Dependent Matches. This type includes homeproviders who have severe health problems—stroke, multiple disabilities, or extreme frailty—and who need a lot of assistance. Services performed in the arrangement include managing the household, meal preparation, shopping and errands, laundry, yard work, housekeeping, and, at times, personal care. Additionally, these extremely dedicated homeseekers give warmth and companionship to homeowners who could not otherwise manage on their own. Dependent matches constitute 24% of the shared living arrangements.

Transitional Matches. In between the "independent" and the "dependent" relationships are matches in which the homeowner is somewhat impaired and the seeker is expected to provide some services in return for room and board. These services include shopping, meal preparation, vacuuming, and errands. Twenty-four percent of the matches are grouped into the transitional category.

The essential difference between the Wichita program and many other shared housing programs is its original intergenerational nature. Although many programs eventually evolve into intergenerational programs the Wichita Share-A-Home program has always attracted primarily young people. The average age for homeseekers was 25 years of age until 1987. After this period the average age increased to 32 years of age. This can be explained by an increase in the number of older international students entering into the program. Potential seekers participating in the program are mostly young females. The homeowners, on the other hand, are overwhelmingly older females with an average age of 79. More than three-quarters of all live-in homeseekers are students, and most others are young people who are unemployed or who are working at low-paying jobs. The length of the matches has varied from 16 days to more than four years.

CONCLUSION

Universally, shared housing matchup programs appear to be in a constant struggle for survival. Frequently, homesharing programs are compared to each other despite differences in services offered, size, duration, target populations, and community exposure to and acceptance of the homesharing concept. This is often an unfair methodology and one that has not plagued Share-A-Home of Wichita. Demonstrating cost-effectiveness, however, is an issue for the program whenever funding comes up for review. The central issue lies in placing a dollar value upon companionship and security. Knowing what constitutes success and how to measure it is the ultimate challenge for matchup programs (Dobkin, 1985).

In assessing the success or effectiveness of matches, the emphasis must be placed on the participants themselves. The agency performs the primary functions of handling recruitment, facilitating referrals, negotiating contracts, and doing follow-up evaluations. How the informal relationships develop between both parties and how they resolve unstated expectations are key factors in the definition of success. The agency's perspective of success, however, involves three criteria: (1) longevity of the match, (2) whether the stated needs were met, and (3) whether the relationship is mutually satisfactory.

Finally, factors that add to the program's organizational stability also can make stability problematic. Community support, consistency of staffing, follow-up services, the personalized nature of the program, and support of an umbrella agency all contribute to a successful program. The same support of an umbrella agency, however, can present obstacles to growth. This is due to the competitive nature of funding for private nonprofit agencies. In the case of Share-A-Home of Wichita, funding and related political restriction by a nonprofit umbrella agency have clearly hindered growth. On the other hand, programs that are constantly threatened with inadequate funding often become extinct.

The future of shared housing is a political enigma. Although various state governments and federal organizations have given verbal and legislative sanction to shared housing, they have not been willing to insure a place for shared housing in the continuum of long-term care. This implies that either shared housing will continue to be a small stop-gap measure without sustained support or it will eventually become absorbed into other social service programs. Regardless, gerontologists and seniors themselves must decide that housing is a priority issue. Shared housing represents the essence of community, and if young people are to understand the other side of age 65 accurately, they must have the opportunity to live with, as well as work with, seniors.

REFERENCES

Dobkin, L. "Homesharing Programs: Are They Cost-effective?" *Generations* 9 (1985):50–52.

Jaffe, D., and Howe, E. "Agency-Assisted Shared Housing: The Nature of Programs and Matches." *The Gerontologist* 28 (1988):318–24.

Newman, S. "Housing and Long-Term Care: The Suitability of the Elderly's Housing to the Provision of In-Home Services." *The Gerontologist* 25 (1985):34–40.

13

The Nature of Problematic Homesharing Matches: The Case of Share-A-Home of Milwaukee

Dale J. Jaffe and Christopher Wellin

What makes for a successful homesharing match? This is a question that readers and writers of the chapters in this volume have posed and, based on their own research or experience, have attempted to answer. An evaluation of a new component of a homesharing program in Milwaukee, Wisconsin, offered us an opportunity to pose this question as well, and in this chapter, we examine some of the results of a survey of homesharing participants that bear most directly on this question. Before considering that data, however, we describe the community and programmatic context of these homesharing experiences, the methodology employed for the survey, and the characteristics of the individuals and matches that comprise the sample.

THE SETTING

Located 90 miles north of Chicago on the shores of Lake Michigan, Milwaukee is among those "rustbelt" cities in which the loss of heavy industry has created major economic dislocations. The basically blue-collar character of the city is enriched by strong ethnic enclaves. In keeping with the politically progressive tradition of Wisconsin, Milwaukee is generous in its provision of government and social services. This is reflected in the high tax climate of the city, and the latter is implicated in the slow but steady loss of population during the past two decades. The changing age composition of the city mirrors the national pattern: the elderly population is increasing both in absolute numbers and as a proportion of the total. Of the approximately 1 million Milwaukee County residents in 1985, 127,000 or 13.6% were age 65 or over. The growth is especially marked among those over age 75, who, although numbering 11,000 in 1980, will total over 50,000 by 1990, according to recent estimates. As for the pool of younger homeseekers, Milwaukee is home to Marquette University, the University of Wisconsin–Milwaukee, and several small, private colleges.

A major organizational actor in the provision of services to older adults is the Interfaith Program for the Elderly, a nonprofit, nondenominational social service agency dedicated to promoting independent living for the elderly. Interfaith follows a "cluster" approach in which neighborhood religious groups sponsor, either through dollars or in-kind services, a neighborhood coordinator. The agency is thus able to offer clients a broad range of program options and centrally compiled information while drawing on the strengths of neighborhood outreach. Since its inception in 1973, Interfaith has grown from three staff persons to almost 100, about half of which are older adults. Funding is provided by the state and county offices on aging, the Board of Vocational and Technical Education, and private donations.

Among Interfaith's programs is the Older Adult Living Alternatives Program, of which Share-A-Home is a part. Share-A-Home was begun in 1981 in response to client's needs for additional noninstitutional housing options. The lone original coordinator has now been joined by a 75%-time staff person, and support for Share-A-Home has come from United Way and The Faye McBeath Foundation, a local private foundation dedicated to aging issues. Until the time of this study, Share-A-Home had functioned primarily as a housing program. Recent additional funding had opened up the possibility of expanding its target group to include elders who need assistance to remain in their homes, and it is the most recent group of matches in which explicit bartering plays a major role that is the focus of this research.

METHODOLOGY

The criteria for inclusion in the survey were (1) that one must have been involved in a barter match that was constituted during the calendar year 1986 through Interfaith's Share-A-Home Program and (2) that the match must have been constituted at least one month before the beginning of the data collection process. (This would insure that at least some patterns would have emerged before the interviewing of the participants.) A *barter match* is defined as a relationship in which the homeseeker receives some form of assistance, usually reduced rent or room and board, in exchange for providing some assistance to the older homeprovider, usually in the form of help with personal care, help around the house, or shopping and errand chores. The sample also consists of persons in both current and dissolved matches. Thus the sample includes all 42 persons and 22 matches that meet the specifications described above as of September 22, 1986, the day that the sample was drawn.

The instrument developed for this survey was an eight-page questionnaire designed to be administered over the telephone in 10 to 15 minutes. The content included questions about how the respondent heard about the Share-A-Home Program, what other sorts of living arrangements were being considered, why homesharing was ultimately chosen, and what the major reasons were for considering the homesharing arrangement. Many questions dealt with the nature of the homesharing relationship, and it is the analysis of these responses that is most relevant to the issue of understanding the nature of problematic matches. Here, respondents were asked to identify any problems with their housemates that may have occurred; to characterize their relationships as familylike, businesslike, or friendship; and to assess the equity of the norms of give-and-take that emerged over time. Also included were questions regarding the extent to which expectations about one's housemate were met.

For homeproviders and homeseekers who were still involved in matches at the time of the interview, the final section of the questionnaire was designed to get a sense of the expected future trajectory of the match. For those no longer homesharing, questions focused on the perceived reasons for dyad dissolution and whether or not homesharing was still considered to be a viable alternative.

The data-collection phase of the survey involved contacting by telephone the 42 persons deemed eligible for inclusion in the sample. The survey was administered during the one-week period of October 1–7, 1986. The average interview length was 20 minutes; the shortest was completed in 15 minutes, and the longest lasted approximately 45 minutes. Respondent cooperation was promoted by an introductory letter that we composed and that was signed by the Share-A-Home program director. The letter explained the purpose and procedures of the survey and emphasized the desire to elicit clients' suggestions for program improvement. Also stressed was the confidentiality of all information given during the interview.

Interviews were completed with 31 of the 42 individuals in the sample for a response rate of 74%. This group of 31 consisted of 17 elderly homeproviders and 14 live-in homeseekers. The 3 homeproviders who could not participate included 2 with serious hearing loss and 1 with profound memory loss. The 6 homeseekers in the sample that were not interviewed were no longer in matches and could not be located despite our most resourceful attempts to find them. Thus no one who could be located and was physically able to communicate over the telephone refused our request for an interview.

Once the interviews were completed, responses to closed-ended questions were tabulated in terms of the frequency with which certain responses were given. Responses to more open-ended questions were recorded in abbreviated form and analyzed in terms of patterns and salient points.

DEMOGRAPHIC CHARACTERISTICS OF THE SAMPLE

The demographic profile presented here includes the 17 homeprovider units and 14 homeseeker units who participated in the survey as well as the 20 matches that were described by these 31 individuals. We use the term *units* because in a few cases, it is a married couple that functions as homeprovider or homeseeker.

The 17 homeproviders are overwhelmingly white females. Ninety-four percent are white and 76% are female. Another 12% are male and an additional 12%

of this group are two married couples living together. Forty-seven percent are widowed, by far the most common marital status of this group. Eighteen percent are single, 12% divorced, 12% living alone but married (spouse in institution), and 12% living together as married couples. Thus almost one-quarter of the homeproviders are still married, a pattern that should not be overlooked when attempting to recruit new homeproviders into a program. Only one homeprovider (6%) is under the age of 50. Twelve percent are between the ages of 51 and 65, 41% are between 66 and 75 (the largest group), 29% are between 76 and 85, and 12% are 86 or older. This program does seem to be serving individuals who fall into the middle-old and old-old age categories. This conclusion is bolstered by the fact that our 3 homeprovider nonrespondents were from the two oldest age categories listed above. Clearly, the dominant profile here of the Share-A-Home homeprovider is that of the older white female who is living alone.

The 14 homeseeker units are also predominantly white. Seventy-nine percent are white, 7% are black, and 14% asian. They, too, are likely to be female, but this group is not as overwhelmingly female as the homeprovider group. Sixty-four percent are female, 29% are male, and a married couple constitutes 7% of this group. Homeseekers tend to be single (43%) or, if not single, legally or functionally separated (29%). Only 7% are widowed (one person), 14% are divorced, and 7% are living together as a married couple. The age distribution reflects a relatively wide range. One percent is aged 18 to 22. Twenty-one percent fall into the category of 23 to 27. Twenty-one percent also have an age between 28 and 32, and 21% are between 33 and 42. Seven percent fall into the age group of 43 to 52, and another 21% are 53 or older. Thus although this range and the data on the distribution of homeprovider ages suggest that barter matches are almost always intergenerational, these data also suggest that there are no set generations from which homeseekers are consistently drawn. Thus the typical homeseeker in this program is an unmarried white female under 50 years of age.

Additional insights are revealed when we consider the demographic characteristics of the 20 matches. Forty percent of the 20 matches consist of homeproviders over the age of 65 living with homeseekers of age 30 or younger. Forty-five percent of the matches consist of homeproviders over the age of 65 living with homeseekers over the age of 30. The remaining 15% of matches are those in which the homeprovider is under the age of 65 and the difference in the age of the individuals is less than 10 years. Thus, these matches are overwhelmingly intergenerational, and it is almost equally likely for the seekers to be over age 30 as it is for them to be under age 30.

The dominant pattern with regard to the sex composition of matches is for females to be matched with females (50%). In 15% of the matches, a male homeseeker is matched with a female homeprovider. Ten percent of the matches portray the reverse situation with a male homeprovider living with a female homeseeker. Ten percent are males matched with males and another 15% include married couples as the homeprovider, homeseeker, or as both. Thus 60% of the matches are sex homogeneous, 25% are sex heterogeneous, and 15% are heterogeneous due to the marital status of the individuals involved. As these figures suggest, the majority of matches involve individuals who have never been or are no longer married, but it must be emphasized that a significant proportion of all individuals involved in the Share-A-Home barter homesharing program in 1986 were married. This suggests that targeting and recruitment should not be limited solely to unmarried people.

Of the 20 matches in this study, 50% were still intact at the time of data collection and 50% had dissolved. Three-quarters of the matches had lasted three months or less and only 25% had lasted more than three months. This is due to the fact that the sample was drawn in September and the majority of the barter matches had not begun until the summer months. What is important to glean from this data is that the responses to our questionnaire were often based on homesharing experiences that at the point of discussion had not been particularly long lasting.

DEFINING PROBLEMATIC AND NONPROBLEMATIC MATCHES

The success of a homesharing program is often seen in terms of the success of the matches that are created by the program staff. It is assumed that a well-organized and well-run program will produce matches that are successful and that a program that is poorly structured will produce a large number of unsuccessful or failed matches. Given this assumption, it is not surprising that many program evaluations of homeshare programs begin with the question of what makes for a successful match. These evaluations then proceed to design methodologies for categorizing the existing matches as successes and failures and then, on the basis of the relative proportion of each, make a determination as to the relative success or failure of the program as a whole.

It is tempting to conceive of match success in terms of longevity and stability. It makes intuitive sense to suggest that successful matches last longer than failures and that they exhibit more social stability and harmony in the relationships that develop between homeproviders and homeseekers. Thus an agency that is able to match individuals who then live together for a relatively long time and who speak fondly of one another is "doing a good job" and one whose matches dissolve quickly amid all sorts of interpersonal conflict is not.

Our previous research suggests, however, that this conception reflects somewhat of a misunderstanding of the nature of homesharing (Jaffe, 1989). For one thing, individuals who present themselves as candidates for barter homesharing are in transition. Their lives are in some way up in the air. For an older adult, this may mean widowhood or the onset or worsening of a chronic and debilitating disease. For a young adult, being in transition may mean being newly divorced, being in between jobs, or being in school with limited financial resources. In general, living with a stranger is not one's preference, but if the alternative for the older adult is institutionalization or dependency on one's adult offspring, it is the best of a few undesirable possibilities. Similarly for the young adults, if the alternatives are living with parents and expensive apartment living, home-sharing may be viewed as the least undesirable option. The importance of these situational factors in structuring the decision to get involved in homesharing is clearly evident in this sample as well. These two factors—the fact that home-sharing is not the first choice of either party and the fact that the individuals are usually in some sort of transition (implying temporariness)—suggest that there are significant limits to the longevity of barter matches. As the unstable aspects of life become more stable, other living-arrangement options may become more viable and the attractiveness of homesharing may then decline. These changes may occur within two months of the beginning of the homesharing match or not until after two years of cohabitation. The key point is that this is a "natural" progression, and as such, the match that ends relatively soon after its constitution is not necessarily less successful than one that lasts several years.

The element of interpersonal harmony is also problematic as an indicator of match success. To suggest that a relationship without any conflict is better than one with conflict is to promote a simplistic and unrealistic conception of what makes for a successful relationship. In fact, one could argue (as have several sociologists and psychologists) that conflict can actually strengthen rather than weaken a relationship. In situations in which norms are ambiguous to begin with, as is the case with homesharing, it seems somewhat "natural" that at least some conflict occur as homeproviders and homeseekers attempt to arrive at a common definition of their respective roles.

Since an objective of most barter homesharing programs is to help older adults maintain their independence in their own homes, it seems reasonable to suggest that any match is almost by definition a success as long as it functions to delay (for however long or short of a period) a move out of one's home.

On the other hand, there are qualitative differences between homesharing matches that relate to the degree to which participants are satisfied or dissatisfied with their arrangements. Rather than speak about these differences as indicators of success or failure, however, we prefer to think of them as reflecting generally problematic or nonproblematic relationships. Since match duration and internal conflict do not necessarily correlate with the qualitative differences between matches, we must proceed inductively and leave it up to our respondents to give us a clue as to how to conceptualize the difference between a generally prob-lematic and a generally nonproblematic homesharing arrangement.

To accomplish this task, we looked first at the responses to the question of whether or not the homeprovider/homeseeker had experienced any problems or difficulties getting along with the housemate. If the individual responded affirm-atively, the question was followed up with probing to get at the nature of the problem and to get the respondent to speculate as to its causes. Since we expected that the majority of problematic matches would have dissolved by the time we interviewed their participants, we also looked at a question that was asked of all individuals who were no longer in homesharing arrangements ("What was the major reason that you stopped homesharing?'') On the basis of responses to these questions, we were able to divide the 20 matches into two groups. One group contained individuals who identified "breach of agreement" as a major problem in their matches. This perceived breach was operationalized in one of two ways by the respondents. One way was to indicate that there had been unmet expectations and the other was to state that the problem was incompatibility between the two parties. Our assumption is that in these cases there was an initial ambiguous or unrealistic assessment of needs. As the relationship evolved, and needs were not being met (usually a perception of the homeprovider), the individuals involved concluded that either one could not meet the expectations of the other or that the two were simply incompatible as housemates. Nine of the 20 matches (45%) fell into this category of problematic arrangements.

The other group consisted of those who indicated that no problems had developed or gave us reason to believe that to the extent that if problems did emerge, they were relatively minor or easily overcome. In any case, the responses of the individuals in this group gave no indication of a problematic or ambiguous initial assessment of needs. Some of these matches were dissolved, but the dissolutions were due to the sort of "natural" progression toward more stable roles described above. Eleven of the 20 matches (55%) fell into this category of nonproblematic matches.

In the following section, we search for correlates of problematic and nonproblematic matches. Clearly, the discovery of any differences between the two groups would be helpful in terms of furthering our understanding of why individuals in some matches are more likely to perceive a breech of agreement than individuals in other matches.

CORRELATES OF PROBLEMATIC MATCHES

The Exchange Agreements

Three general categories of exchange agreements were developed according to responses to our questions. The first category involved an exchange of personal-care services for the homeprovider for room and board for the homeseeker. This category involves the most extensive exchange of the three, and 20% of the matches in this study were in this group (4 of 20). The second category involved an exchange of household tasks and errands for the homeprovider and, again, room and board or simply reduced rent for the homeseeker. This was the most common type of exchange agreement negotiated, accounting for 70% of all matches (14 of 20). The final category involved the least amount of exchange between housemates. Here, the homeprovider received additional income by renting out a room and the homeseeker was able to rent the room at a price that was substantially less than what would be required in other sorts of private housing living arrangements. Two matches or 10% of the total were in this category. Thus matches involving personal care or simply monetary exchange are not common among this group of homesharing matches.

Interesting differences between the problematic and nonproblematic matches do appear here, although one must be cautious in interpreting these differences due to the relatively small numbers involved. Roughly equal proportions of both groups fell into the household chores/room and board category (72% of the nonproblematic matches and 67% of the problematic matches). However, 22% of the problematic matches involved only monetary exchange compared with none of the nonproblematic matches, and 28% of the nonproblematic matches involved personal-care assistance compared with only 11% of the problematic matches. Thus the more involved exchange agreements seem to be associated with the nonproblematic group, and the matches with the least amount of exchange (money only) appear to be associated with the problematic matches.

Patterns of Everyday Life

Many of the questionnaire items were designed to provide a sense of the everyday life in these barter matches. The first asked the respondents to characterize the equity of exchange in their relationships. Seventy-four percent of all respondents felt that things were fairly equal in the give and take of everyday life. Twenty-three percent said that they give more than they get, and only 3% believed that they get more than they give. Homeproviders are more likely than homeseekers to feel that there is an inequity in the exchange—29% of the homeproviders thought that they give more than they get compared with 14% of the homeseekers. Homeseekers are more likely than homeproviders to feel that the exchange is equitable (86% compared with 65%). Not surprisingly, members of problematic matches are also more likely to perceive an imbalance. Fifty percent of the individuals in problematic matches perceive an imbalance in their housemate's favor compared with only 5% of the individuals in nonproblematic matches.

Respondents were also asked to characterize the nature of the social relationship that they had with their housemates. The majority of those answering (45%) labeled their relationships as friendships. Thirty-two percent thought that their relationships were businesslike, and only 23% said they were familylike. Thus the very intimate relationship is the least common in these matches. Homeproviders and homeseekers differ on this question. Forty-seven percent of the homeproviders used the businesslike label compared with only 14% of the homeseekers. This relationship conception was most common for the homeproviders and the least common for the homeseekers. The largest group of homeseekers (50%) used the label of friendship as did 41% of the homeproviders. The familylike label was the least common for the homeproviders (12%) but not unusual for the homeseekers (36%). In general, the homeproviders see these relationships as either friendships or business relationships, and the homeseekers see them as either friendships or familylike relationships.

Interestingly, 73% of members of problematic matches defined their relationships as businesslike compared with only 10% of those in nonproblematic matches. Individuals in nonproblematic matches were most likely to view their relationships as friendships (60%). The data clearly suggest that friendship and familylike relationships are associated with nonproblematic matches and the businesslike conception with the problematic matches.

From there, specific questions were directed at the respective homeprovider and homeseeker groups. Homeproviders were asked if they believed that their homeseekers were more willing to assist them than expected, less willing than expected, or about as willing as expected. The largest group (47%) thought that their homeseekers were less willing to help than expected. Twenty-nine percent said that their homeseekers helped them more than they expected. The final 24% thought that the level of assistance was about as expected. Thus most home-provider's expectations are violated; some are pleasantly surprised, but more are disappointed. Major differences are apparent between problematic and nonprob-lematic matches. Eighty-eight percent of the homeproviders in problematic matches thought that their homeseekers were providing less than they expected compared with only 11% of the homeproviders in nonproblematic matches. Conversely, 56% of the homeproviders in nonproblematic matches said that they were receiving more than they expected, and no homeproviders from the prob-lematic group felt this way. Finally, one-third of the nonproblematic match homeproviders said that they were getting about what they expected compared with 12% of the homeproviders in the problematic group. Thus viewing what one is receiving as expected or more than expected is associated with a non-problematic match, whereas the response that one is receiving less than expected is associated with a problematic match.

Homeproviders were also asked if their homeseekers had ever violated their trust. Most responded negatively (76%), and, as expected, this is also related to whether or not one is in a problematic or nonproblematic match. Only 11% of the homeproviders in nonproblematic matches thought that their trust had been violated compared with 38% of the homeproviders in problematic matches.

Homeseekers were asked about whether or not their expectations about the functional status of their homeproviders were met. Most (60%) believed that the physical and mental abilities of their homeproviders were about what they ex-pected. One-third stated that their abilities were greater than expected, and only 7% thought that the homeprovider was more impaired than he or she expected. The perception of greater than expected impairment does not appear to make a difference in terms of a problematic or nonproblematic match. In fact, 40% of the homeseekers in nonproblematic matches indicated that their homeproviders were more impaired than expected compared with only 20% of the homeseekers in problematic matches.

Differences between the two types of matches do show up in homeseeker perceptions of being pressured to devote more time to their homeproviders. Although one-half of all homeseekers felt such pressure, those in problematic matches were much more likely to acknowledge this pressure (75%) than those in nonproblematic matches (40%).

Finally, all respondents were asked if they believed that their obligations had interfered with other aspects of their lives. An overwhelming 87% responded negatively. Those who felt otherwise did not tend to be in any particular subgroup of the sample (i.e., homeprovider versus homeseeker; problematic match versus nonproblematic match).

Overall, then, the majority of these individuals believe their exchanges are equitable, see their housemates as friends, do not find their expectations about their housemates to be violated in any major ways, and do not see their involvement in homesharing as interfering with other aspects of their lives. Significant differences do appear, however, between members of problematic and nonproblematic matches. What is important to emphasize here is that we do not know if the patterns observed in the problematic groups are causes or effects of the perception of a broken agreement. It may be, for example, that individuals who define each other as business partners are more likely to create a pattern of everyday life that leads one or both parties to later perceive a breach of the initial agreement. Alternatively, it may be that individuals who violate the expectations set forth in the exchange agreement create a situation in which social distance is maintained and both members of the match define their relationship in businesslike terms. Thus the patterns described here must be seen as associated with particular sorts of matches and not necessarily as the cause of a problematic or nonproblematic match.

DISCUSSION

Data on who is involved in these 1986 barter matches and how they came to become involved in the Share-A-Home program suggest patterns that are not significantly different from other homesharing programs across the United States. On the other hand, two surprising findings do stand out among these data. First, a significant portion of these participants are married, and that is generally not the case in most programs. We usually think about the pressures that lead people into homesharing as not applicable to most married couples. After all, married older adults have each other as companions and to help each other out with everyday tasks, and young married adults often have the earning capacity of two individuals. Yet the prevalence of married couples in this sample, both as homeproviders and homeseekers, suggests that it may indeed be a mistake to think about eligibility and recruitment for homesharing simply in terms of unmarried adults. We have no data here to assess the pros and cons of married couples playing these roles and suggest that staff persons in various programs monitor the differences between matches with singles and couples as participants in the future. It is possible that married couples adapt to the homesharing situation better and are easier to recruit. If that is the case, it may be reasonable to target programs more directly to couples in the future.

Second, the frequency with which the homeproviders in this sample mention companionship as a reason for homesharing is high. Although not inherently problematic, this sort of felt need poses an especially challenging task for the staff whose goal it is to insure an equitable exchange. Providing companionship is not easily broken down into service units and hours, nor does one's felt need for it remain constant over time (as would be the case for many personal care tasks). Thus it is often the case that those who homeshare for the companionship it offers find their expectations violated. It appears that bartering is more difficult when companionship is one of the commodities to be exchanged than when money or meal preparation or house cleaning comprise the content of the exchange.

Given our definition of problematic and nonproblematic matches, it is important to note that the majority of these 1986 barter matches are nonproblematic. Yet a significant proportion *are* problematic and here we attempt to understand the reasons for this perception. Earlier, we defined a *problematic match* as one in which respondents indicated that there had been either a perceived breach of the agreement or an incompatibility of personalities. From other items in the questionnaire and impressionistic data as well, both complaints seem to have a common source—that there was an unrealistic or ambiguous assessment of needs to begin with. The central question that this reasoning raises, then, is whether this ambiguity in needs assessment is due to certain individuals simply having more ambiguous needs than others or whether it is due to the process of determining needs that the staff employ. In other words, is the needs assessment and agreement negotiation process faulty, or do some individuals who desire homesharing simply have needs that are difficult to assess and operationalize for purposes of barter? We suspect that there is some validity to both of these hypotheses.

The frequent complaint among members (especially homeproviders) of problematic matches that their matches were unsatisfactory because of a basic incompatibility between themselves and their housemates, we believe, is to some extent a result of agency practices and personnel. In these instances, the homeprovider would suggest that more data on the "maturity" of the homeseeker would have been useful. The question raised by this pattern is really one of whether the staff collect enough of the right kind of information from prospective clients or whether they collect enough but do not communicate it well enough to the prospective housemates. We do not have the sort of data that would permit us to answer this question with a great degree of certainty; however, we do have a hunch. It does not appear that the intake form upon which all sorts of biographical and behavioral data are recorded has any serious flaws or gaps. Consequently, we are persuaded that the problem may lie in whether and how much of this information is communicated to a prospective housemate. A perusal of the program's guidelines and procedures for assessment and matching also reveals no major gaps or inadequacies, so it does not appear that the source of this problem is with any formal aspect of program structure. The only remaining possibility, then, is that the established procedures regarding communication to one prospective housemate about the other have been violated, and there is evidence from other sources to support this claim. In fact, before the implementation of this survey, the program director realized that a staff person had been overzealous in "creating matches at any cost." Although it is unfortunate for both the homeproviders and homeseekers who find themselves to be incompatible in some significant way and the present staff who must deal with the "fallout" from these sorts of situations, it does suggest an important lesson: Minimal work up front creates maximum work later ("haste makes waste").

The data reported here support, perhaps even more strongly, the other hypothesis that the ambiguous assessment of needs is unavoidable because many of the homeproviders in this program simply have somewhat ambiguous or uncertain needs. The main evidential support for this contention is that the problematic matches are more likely to be based on monetary exchange or companionship only whereas the nonproblematic matches are much more likely to include the personal-care dimension. It is probably much easier to translate personal-care activities into quantitative indicators such as number of times per day or week. Furthermore, for those homeproviders who require personal care, they are likely to be more frail and be most concerned with getting those needs taken care of. Anything that comes to them beyond that is considered a bonus. For those whose perceived needs are mainly social, it is not only more difficult to quantify them for purposes of an exchange agreement, it is likely that the need itself changes from day to day. Some days, one may want as much company and visiting as possible and on others prefer solitude. In addition, we should note that there are strong norms in our society against expressing a need for companionship (that is, admitting one's loneliness). It is for some combination of these reasons, we believe, that the homeproviders in problematic matches complain about unfulfilled expectations.

One obvious implication is that social needs should be considered a legitimate and important part of the needs assessment process when individuals are initially interviewed by the staff. At the same time, we must recognize, and it should be emphasized to participants that these needs are not easily translatable into a set number of hours or times per day or week. The problem is inherent in the nature of sociability as an exchange commodity. Flexibility is important in establishing expectations about companionship as a service since one's need or desire for it does not remain constant. That same flexibility, however, is also a major source of strain in matches in which companionship is the key element of exchange for the homeprovider. Our sense is that complaints about unfulfilled expectations are going to be more common in homesharing programs (like Share-A-Home) whose clients are relatively healthy and view homesharing as a means to meet social needs than in programs that serve a much more frail group of older adults whose needs are much more health- and personal-care oriented.

Both lines of argument—the notion of a faulty process and the prevalence of individuals whose needs are relatively ambiguous, uncertain, and fluctuating— have led us to consider the degree of structure that is built into the needs-assessment and agreement-negotiation processes. Although we have suggested that there are limits on just how structured this process can be, beyond a certain point, formalization and quantification may not be desirable. Part of the appeal of this sort of program is its informality and lack of legalistic overtones. To promote tighter structure may, in fact, compromise these appealing qualities and create additional problems later.

Finally, involvement in a problematic match does not seem to turn people against the homesharing concept in general or to the Share-A-Home program in particular. Of all of the individuals who were no longer in matches at the time of the interview (n = 11), and most of them were individuals who were in problematic matches, 82% said that they would consider homesharing again in the future. A similar proportion of individuals still in matches at the time of the interview (89%) indicated that they would also consider homesharing again if their present arrangement were to end. Ninety-three percent of all individuals in this sample said that they would recommend homesharing to a friend. Thus even people who are disappointed with their matches do not attribute their problems to either the agency or anything intrinsic to homesharing.

NOTE

We wish to thank Mimi Chernov for her support of this research and the Faye McBeath Foundation for its funding of the research project.

REFERENCE

Jaffe, Dale J. *Caring Strangers: The Sociology of Intergenerational Homesharing*. Greenwich, Conn.: JAI Press, 1989.

Selected Bibliography

Dobkin, Leah. *Shared Housing for Older People: A Planning Manual for Match-Up Programs*. Philadelphia: National Shared Housing Resource Center, 1983.
————. "Homesharing Programs: Are They Cost-Effective?" *Generations*, Spring 1985, pp. 50–51.
Fenger, Alfred, and Danigelis, Nicholas. *The Shared Home: Evaluation of a Concept and Its Implementation*. Final Report to Andrus Foundation, 1984.
Howe, Elizabeth. "Homesharing for the Elderly." *Journal of Planning Education and Research* 4 (1985):185–94.
Howe, Elizabeth; Robins, Barbara; and Jaffe, Dale. *Evaluation of Independent Living's Homeshare Program*. Madison: Independent Living, 1984.
Jaffe, Dale. *Caring Strangers: The Sociology of Intergenerational Homesharing*. Greenwich, Conn.: JAI Press, 1989.
Jaffe, Dale, and Howe, Elizabeth. "Agency-Assisted Shared Housing: The Nature of Programs and Matches." *The Gerontologist* 28 (1988):318–24.
————. "Case Management for Homesharing." *Journal of Gerontological Social Work*, in press.
Levenson, Marjorie. "Intergenerational Housemate Matching: An Analysis of the Operation Match Program." Paper presented at the Gerontological Society of America Annual Meeting, Boston, 1982.
McConnell, Stephen R., and Usher, Carolyn E. *Intergenerational House Sharing*. Los Angeles: Andrus Gerontology Center, University of Southern California, 1980.
Modell, John, and Hareven, Tamara. "Urbanization and the Malleable Household: An Examination of Boarding and Lodging in American Families." *Journal of Marriage and the Family*, August 1973, pp. 467–79.
National Shared Housing Resource Center. *National Directory of Shared Housing Programs for Older Persons*. Philadelphia, 1988.
Peace, Sheila, and Nusberg, Charlotte. *Shared Living: A Viable Alternative for the Elderly?* Washington, D.C.: International Federation on Aging, 1984.

Pritchard, David. "The Art of Matchmaking: A Case Study in Shared Housing." *The Gerontologist* 23 (1983):174–79.

Robinson, Timothy; Martin, Richard; and Shafto, Martin. *Share-A-Home: Final Report.* Minneapolis: The McKnight Foundation, 1983.

Schreter, Carol. "Residents of Shared Housing." *Social Thought*, Winter 1984, pp. 30–38.

———. "Advantages and Disadvantages of Shared Housing." *Journal of Housing for the Elderly* 3 (1986):121–38.

Schreter, Carol, and Turner, Lloyd. "Shared and Subdividing Private Market Housing." *The Gerontologist* 26 (1986):181–86.

Streib, Gordon F.; Folts, W. Edward; and Hilker, Mary Anne. *Old Homes—New Families: Shared Living for the Elderly.* New York: Columbia University Press, 1984.

Index

About the Editor and Contributors

NICHOLAS L. DANIGELIS is an associate professor of sociology at the University of Vermont. Along with his coauthor, Alfred Fengler, Danigelis has published articles on the importance of family structure and rural residence for elders. Since they began their study of Project HOME, they have presented half a dozen papers at national and international meetings on their evaluation of the program and its clients. They have just completed a book on Project HOME. Danigelis's other research interests include a cohort analysis of the effects of aging on social and political attitudes (with Stephen Cutler) and the development of a theory of social integration dealing with life-cycle changes. His Ph.D. is in sociology from Indiana University.

ALFRED P. FENGLER is an associate professor of sociology at the University of Vermont. In addition to his work with Nicholas Danigelis on Project HOME, he is interested in the relationship between aging and religion, with a particular emphasis on parapsychological phenomena. Fengler has a Ph.D. in sociology from the University of Wisconsin–Madison.

MARY GILDEA is the director of the Delaware Valley Shared Housing Services, a project of the National Shared Housing Resource Center's local division. She is a graduate of Temple University's School of Social Service Administration with a specialization in social planning. A former homesharer, Gildea has been providing shared housing training and technical assistance since 1983.

MARY HART is assistant professor of gerontology at California University of Pennsylvania and the director of the California Senior Center. She was recently chosen by the Heinz Foundation to join an Alzheimer's study group in London. She has a masters degree in career studies from Duquesne University.

KAREN HORNUNG is a professor of gerontology and chairperson of the Gerontology Department at California University of Pennsylvania. She received her doctorate in Gerontology/Community and Human Resources from the University of Nebraska–Lincoln. In addition to shared housing, her research interests are in aging in rural society and aging in Third World nations. In pursuit of the latter interest, she spent a summer studying aging in India as part of the Fullbright Summer Studies Abroad Program.

ELIZABETH HOWE is associate professor of urban and regional planning at the University of Wisconsin–Madison where she teaches social planning. In addition to doing substantial work on homesharing, she has been involved in research on the service needs of older women. She has a doctorate in city and regional planning from the University of California–Berkeley.

MELANIE HWALEK is owner and president of Social Programs Evaluators and Consultants, the firm that was contracted by the Michigan Office of Services to the Aging to conduct a comprehensive evaluation of the state-supported homeshare programs. She holds a Ph.D. in social psychology and has a specialist certificate in gerontology from Wayne State University. She is an adjunct assistant professor of psychology at Wayne State University and adjunct associate professor in the Department of Family Medicine at Michigan State University.

DALE J. JAFFE is assistant professor of sociology at the University of Wisconsin–Milwaukee. He holds a Ph.D. in sociology from the University of Chicago and has interests in the sociology of aging and medical sociology. Jaffe has published articles on homesharing in *The Gerontologist* and the *Journal of Gerontological Social Work* and has written a monograph on homesharing entitled *Caring Strangers: The Sociology of Intergenerational Homesharing*. In addition to being interested in homesharing, he is currently involved in a qualitative study of a group home for victims of Alzheimer's Disease funded by a grant from ADRDA.

ARLYNE JUNE has been executive director of Project Match since July of 1983. She received her bachelors degree in sociology from Douglass College in New Brunswick, New Jersey, and her masters degree in sociology from Rutgers University. Most of her professional experience has been in the area of social planning.

ELIZABETH A. LONGLEY has been under contract with the state of Michigan's Office of Services to the Aging as the Shared Housing Manager since January 1986. Her primary responsibility was to monitor and provide technical assistance to the existing shared housing sites and to agencies in Michigan wishing to establish new shared housing programs. Before assuming this position, she was a private development consultant in Southeast Michigan. She has a bachelors degree in political science/urban studies from Marygrove College.

NORMA MAATTA is emeritus professor of English at California University of Pennsylvania and taught courses in the Gerontology Department before her retirement. She is currently a research assistant for the University of Pittsburgh in the Mon Valley Development Elder Survey, part of the National Alzheimer's Disease Patient Registry, funded by the National Institute on Aging. Maatta has a masters degree in arts and English from West Virginia University.

JOYCE MANTELL is the executive director of the National Shared Housing Resource Center, a nonprofit corporation founded in 1981 to promote shared housing options across the country. She was appointed director in 1986 after serving as operations manager and program planner for the center. She is a graduate of Antioch University with a masters degree in human services administration with a specialization in adult development and aging.

JOELLE PERKOCHA has a masters degree in human services with a specialization in gerontology from San Jose State University. She is director of Home-sharing Help and Information Program sponsored by the Human Investment Project in San Mateo, California. She coauthored the original proposal to establish a homesharing program in San Mateo.

KAREN PRIMM has a bachelors degree in gerontology from California University of Pennsylvania and serves as project coordinator and counselor for the SHARE program in California, Pennsylvania. She has conducted workshops in Pennsylvania on shared housing and is also interested in adult day-care programs.

DAVID C. PRITCHARD has a masters degree in social work from San Diego State University and a Ph.D. in higher and postsecondary education from the University of Southern California. He is associate professor of social work at San Diego State University and teaches courses related to the aging population. He has conducted research and presented papers on homesharing since 1981.

JON PYNOOS is director of the Program in Policy and Services Research, a division of the Andrus Gerontology Center, at the University of Southern California. He holds a joint appointment with the School of Urban and Regional Planning and the Leonard Davis School of Gerontology where he is the United Parcel Service Foundation associate professor of gerontology, public policy, and urban planning. He is a fellow of the John Simon Guggenheim Memorial Foundation and the Fulbright Council for International Exchange of Scholars. He is the author of several books on elderly housing policy and is considered one of

America's foremost scholars in this field. His Ph.D. is in urban planning from Harvard University.

BARBARA ROBINS is director of marketing for the architecture, planning, and engineering firm of Barrientos and Associates in Madison, Wisconsin. She was formerly on the faculty of the Department of Urban and Regional Planning at the University of Wisconsin–Madison where she taught courses in social planning. Robins has a doctorate in city and regional planning from Cornell University.

DAVID H. SPENCE is a policy and program development officer with the Ontario Ministry of Housing. During the past five years he has worked on a variety of innovative housing alternatives for senior citizens including shared housing, ECHO housing, and retirement communities. Before this he worked for a number of provincial and municipal government agencies in the Province of Ontario. He has a masters degree in urban and regional planning from the University of Waterloo.

PAUL D. THURAS is a doctoral student in the Program in Social Ecology at the University of California–Irvine. He is currently a research fellow at the Clinical Research Center of the Philadelphia Geriatric Center, where he is involved in conducting a longitudinal study of depression and aging funded by the National Institute of Mental Health. His research interests include social support and family interaction in later life and the influence of the built environment on the health and well being of older people.

JANET B. UNDERWOOD was the founder and director of Kansas Alternatives for Senior Housing, the Share-A-Home program of Wichita. She now lives in Redlands, California, and is the administrator of Villa Linda, a congregate living retirement complex in Loma Linda, California. She is also the cofounder and clinical coordinator of the Multidisciplinary Geriatric Council of Loma Linda University Medical Center. She received a masters degree in Gerontology from Wichita State University.

CHRISTOPHER WELLIN is a research assistant in the Department of Sociology at the University of Wisconsin–Milwaukee. His interests are in the sociology of aging, gender, and qualitative methods. He intends to pursue a Ph.D. in sociology at Northwestern University in the next several years.

CONNIE WULF was the director of Wichita's Share-A-Home Program from 1985 to 1988. In addition to her work on Share-A-Home, she has developed and administered an elderly group home residence and consulted on the design of Section 202 housing units in Wichita, Kansas. She holds a bachelors degree in gerontology from Wichita State University and is currently pursuing a masters degree in social welfare from the University of Kansas.